MW00398254

Be Transformed

Discovering Biblical Solutions to Life's Problems

A Discovery Group Study Series presented by Scope Ministries International

Copyright © 1998, 2001, 2005, 2007 by Scope Ministries International, Inc.
Oklahoma City, Oklahoma

ALL RIGHTS RESERVED

All rights reserved. No part of this publication may be reproduced, stored in a retrieval system, or transmitted in any form or by any means - electronic, mechanical, photocopy, recording, or any other - except for prior, written permission of the Publisher's Media Department.

International Standard Book Number
ISBN
0-9766939-4-1
Library of Congress Catalogue Number
LCCN 98-61073

Scriptural quotations are from the following versions of the Bible indicated as follows:

Amplified Bible Expanded Edition	(Amplified)
The Living Bible	(LB)
New American Standard Bible	(NAS)
New International Version of the Bible	(NIV)
New Testament in Modern English by J.B. Phillips	(Phillips)

Any reference to Bibical Personal Guidance Ministry, or One-on-One Ministry are one in the same.

About The Cover

The theme of the cover is based on the word pictures given by the prophet Jeremiah and Jesus in the following passages:

Blessed is the man who trusts in the Lord and whose trust is the Lord. For he will be like a tree planted by the water, that extends its roots by a stream and will not fear when the heat comes; but its leaves will be green, and it will not be anxious in a year of drought nor cease to yield fruit. Jeremiah 17:7-8 NAS

"If any man is thirsty, let him come to Me and drink. He who believes in Me, as the Scripture said, '*From his innermost being shall flow rivers of living water.'*" John 7:37b-38

Scope uses the tree to represent man's three-part nature: spirit, soul, and body.

- The roots of the tree represent the *spirit* of man, which is the means of knowing and worshipping God.
- The trunk represents man's *soul*, the means of expressing the mind, will, and emotions.
- The leaves represent the *body*, the most noticeable and changing aspect of man and the means of doing.
- The sky depicts the wind of God's Spirit at work in the world.
- The river of living water is the Holy Spirit indwelling the believer's spirit (roots), filling the soul (trunk) and producing fruit in the body (leaves).
- The roots of the tree are rooted in God's love and are one with Christ's Spirit.
- The believer is drinking from the river of life and being filled with the Holy Spirit.
- The leaves of the tree pointed upward are depicting a life of worship and praise.
- Jesus is visible in the tree, reproducing His life in the soul (trunk) and expressing Himself through the body (leaves).

© COPYRIGHT 1998, 2001, 2005, 2007 SCOPE MINISTRIES INTERNATIONAL INC.

Table of Contents

© COPYRIGHT 1998, 2001, 2005, 2007 SCOPE MINISTRIES INTERNATIONAL INC.

Preface

This workbook was originally written to be a personal aid to those seeking spiritual help for life's problems through attending a Scope Discovery Group. A discovery group is a small group that investigates God's Word and how it applies to emotional, spiritual, and relational needs. There are two segments to the discovery group: the lesson presentation and small group interaction. Its purpose is to help people overcome life's challenges.

These lessons will introduce you to a new way of thinking about your problems, whether they be personal, emotional, or relational. For each lesson there are five daily assignments that are intended to help you interact with God in such a way that you receive understanding of underlying causes and direction in dealing with them.

Be Transformed lays a Biblical foundation of truth that opens the door to an experiential relationship with God. Whether you choose to use this individually or in a small group, it is our prayer that the Holy Spirit will be your counselor and will use this material to draw you into a more intimate relationship with your Heavenly Father, resulting in a transformed life.

The *Be Transformed* lessons are available on video, along with *Be Transformed* leaders' guides. To find out how to start a *Be Transformed* discovery group or to order materials, contact:

Scope Ministries International
700 NE 63rd Street
Oklahoma City, OK 73105-6410
USA
405.843.7778

resources@scopeministries.org
Website: www.scopeministries.org

This workbook does not attempt to address the many different types of problems we encounter; however, **it does attempt to lay a proper Biblical foundation for a healthy relationship with God and to demonstrate how God's Word applies to the entire scope of life.**

© COPYRIGHT 1998, 2001, 2005, 2007 SCOPE MINISTRIES INTERNATIONAL INC.

Acknowledgements

This workbook was compiled over the course of three years. What began as a simple outline with personal assignments evolved into what you hold today. Originally it was written to enable our ministry to meet the needs of an increasing number of people seeking help in relating to God in the midst of their problems. As God used the material to heal broken lives and marriages, more and more people requested copies of the workbook. To our great delight, many have used this material in their personal lives, their churches, and their ministries.

The principles in this workbook are based on the Biblical personal guidance model used at Scope Ministries International, a model developed by Scope's President Emeritus and founder, Jim Craddock. I am grateful for his faithfulness to God's call and for his dedication to the sufficiency of Christ and His Word. I thank Jim for placing confidence in me to venture off in the direction of developing discovery group materials.

Over the course of the development of this workbook, many have contributed to this final form. My thanks to the Scope staff who have persevered through my constant changes and rewrites with great patience. Their critiques and suggestions have been invaluable to the fine-tuning of this work. Rene George, my faithful assistant and friend, supported and covered for me, freeing me to focus on this project. She spent many hours brainstorming with me and giving me her honest input throughout the writing of this material.

Scope Ministries extends its gratitude to the following people for their part in making this workbook a reality: Jody Humber and Tom Hill for financially investing in this project; Thomas Hill and Phyllis Mantik for their expertise in developing the format and graphics; Claude Baker, Cyndee Bardwell, Julie Duncan, Teresa Flater, Melissa Hawley, and Rich Johnson for their proofreading and editing help; Judi Boyer, Jim Craddock, Donna Edwards, Kaylon Plugge, and Kathy Young for their assistance in developing this material; and Rev. Roc Bottomly and Rev. Derek Duncan for taking the time to review the material and to give me valuable critique and input.

We gratefully recognize New Life Bible Church of Norman, Oklahoma, for being the first church to use this material and develop their own Discovery Group ministry. As they field tested this material, they helped us to see the wonderful possibilities of God using this material within the local church to bring healing and hope to broken lives.

We deeply appreciate those who have shared their stories with us of how God has changed their lives as they have worked through the daily assignments. Thank you for being transparent and letting us see the marvelous work God is doing in your hearts. May there be many, many more like you in the future.

Many others, too numerous to mention, have helped make this book a reality. Many have prayed, given financially and encouraged this into existence. This project is a beautiful picture of team effort and the necessity of diversity in the Body of Christ. May it build up Christ's Bride and prepare her for His return.

Renée Roberts

Scope Ministries International

© COPYRIGHT 1998, 2001, 2005, 2007 SCOPE MINISTRIES INTERNATIONAL INC.

Introduction

Dear Reader,

You are about to embark upon a thrilling adventure of Christian living. Since 1973, Scope Ministries International (Scope) has been taking life-changing truths from the Bible and developing them into practical solutions that transform lives.

From its inception, Scope has sought to deal with solutions rather than symptoms, and with people's potential rather than their problems. The workbook, *Be Transformed*, is the result of many years of observation and research. Designed not simply to impart information but to bring transformation, it has been instrumental in seeing thousands of lives changed.

Be Transformed brings several crucial distinctives into play. First, it is centered around Christ. Second, it is based upon the authority and sufficiency of Scripture. Third, it brings individuals into a practical, life-changing experience through the renewing of their belief systems.

The dynamic behind the success of this workbook is its adherence to the Word of God. Biblical truth has been turned into therapeutic tools, which, in turn, have been developed into transferable concepts. This allows the power of God to be the vital force in the life-changing process presented in *Be Transformed*.

The Bible teaches that God did not send His Son to die simply to get man to Heaven, but rather to get God out of Heaven into man! In other words *Be Transformed* stands upon God's ability to reproduce Himself within us.

Three great doctrines of the Bible support this truth. First, there is the doctrine of the deity of Christ. In short, we accept the fact that Jesus Christ is God. Second, there is the doctrine of authority. This means that the Bible is, indeed, the words of God. Third, there is the doctrine of sufficiency. This means that the Bible is wholly adequate to provide the solutions to the problems we face.

Jesus Christ claimed to be God. The life Jesus lived, the words He spoke, the miracles He performed, the lives He changed, and the truths He presented, all prove Him to be God incarnate. Either what He says about Himself as God is true, or He is, at best, a liar, or a lunatic, or at worst, a devil.

2000 years have come and gone, and no one has yet proven Jesus false, His Word untrue, or that His resurrection did not happen. While the great men of history have passed into oblivion, Jesus Christ remains the centerpiece of human experience. If He had not lived, the world would be entirely different and our Western civilization non-existent.

Of the 11 great religions of the world, only one, Christianity, deals with man's basic problem—sin. Of all the great religions of the world, only in Christianity do we find God seeking man. Of all the founders of the religions of the world, only Christ claimed to be God. Of all the founders of the great religions, only Jesus lived a sinless life. Of all the religions of the world, only Jesus was raised from the dead. While the other founders of the great religions are admired, only Jesus is either cursed or revered. While all the others offer a religion, only Jesus offers a relationship. He alone can change the human heart.

Be Transformed is based on the fact of the Deity of Jesus Christ.

Just because a person believes something to be true doesn't make it true. Some people still hold to the idea of a flat earth!

© COPYRIGHT 1998, 2001, 2005, 2007 SCOPE MINISTRIES INTERNATIONAL INC.

It is only what is really true that makes one's faith true. It isn't because someone believes Jesus to be God that makes Him God, rather it is because He *is* God that validates a person's belief in Him.

The Bible claims to be the Word of God! It says that God supernaturally inspired men to write down what He told them. Throughout human history, men of God wrote the Word of God and compiled it into one book—the Bible. This is God's way of revealing Himself to men.

The Word of God is true whether anyone believes it to be true or not. It is true because *God* is true. Because the Bible is the Word of God, it is set apart from all other books. The Greek word *logos,* which means "word," is used first of Jesus, Who is the Living Word, and second, of the Bible which is the Written Word.

Because God has chosen to express and reveal Himself through the Living and Written Word, there is tremendous power and authority inherent within the Word. As one theologian wrote, "The Word of God is a living and active power, a timeless moment at which, in our own time and space, we can meet the living God. God expresses Himself in His revealed Word and continues to act through it."[1]

Whenever the Bible is read, it is as though God were speaking. Also, whenever the truths of Scripture are applied personally to one's life, a transformation takes place. All the authority of God is expressed in and through His Word. Because the Bible is reliable and relevant, it is the authority that transforms. Because it is God's final word to man, it is man's final and supreme authority in all things that pertain to faith and life.

Be Transformed is based on the authority of the Word of God.

Whatever God creates, He creates with all the characteristics necessary for its proper function. For example, when God created man, He created man with a nature necessary to his God-given function. So it is with the Word of God. The Bible has all the attributes necessary for its natural function. We call this sufficiency.

The Written Word is simply an extension of the Living Word, and as such, takes on the same character as the One Who spoke it. Consequently, the Bible is sufficient to address every human problem and need, because Christ is sufficient.

To understand what sufficiency means, let us look at five key words that explain the nature of sufficiency. First, the Bible is sufficient because it is *alive*! This means that the very vitality of Jesus exists in the truths the Bible reveals. This life is a transforming life, and God's Word received and acted upon will bring dramatic changes in a person's life.

Second, the Bible is sufficient because it is *powerful*! This means that the Bible deals with solutions—not with symptoms. It has within itself the power to bring about change. The Word of God becomes the catalyst that the Holy Spirit uses to bring about change.

Third, the Bible is sufficient because it is *relevant*! Neither time nor culture affect the impact of the truths of God's Word on the human heart. No other book addresses the issues of our time as does the Bible.

Fourth, the Bible is sufficient because it is *reliable*! The Written Word is simply an extension of the Living Word—Christ.

---

[1]   Richards, Lawrence O. *Expository Dictionary of Bible Words.* Grand Rapids: Regency Reference Library, Zondervan Publishing House, 1985, p. 635.

© COPYRIGHT 1998, 2001, 2005, 2007 SCOPE MINISTRIES INTERNATIONAL INC.

Therefore, because Christ is true, His words are true. Because Christ is trustworthy, we can trust His promises.

Fifth, the Bible is sufficient because it is *relational*! Of all that God is, He is love. His love is the key to every relationship. The intensity of that love is revealed in the fact that God has chosen to take up His residency within us.

Be Transformed is based upon the sufficiency of Scripture.

Because the Bible is sufficient, it addresses every need, every problem, every hurt that we ever face. In the lessons that follow, the sufficiency of Christ and His Word is demonstrated practically—resulting in transformed lives.

Because the Bible draws its sufficiency from the total sufficiency of Jesus Christ, it addresses every need, every problem, every hurt that a person will ever face. During the next few weeks, as you learn and absorb the truths presented, you will discover personally the transforming power of Christ and His Word. Remember, God never fails—you will be transformed!

Jim Craddock
Founder and President
Scope Ministries International

© COPYRIGHT 1998, 2001, 2005, 2007 SCOPE MINISTRIES INTERNATIONAL INC.

Be Transformed

Part One

Discovering God's Perspective

Discovering the Root of Our Problems

And do not be conformed to this world, but be transformed by the renewing of your mind, that you may prove what the will of God is, that which is good and acceptable and perfect.

Romans 12:2 NAS

Lesson 1

A Life Transformed

Towards the end of my college years, I realized that I had two possible directions: run to God or run away from God. It all depended upon what I believed about everything.

My parents separated when I was 6 years old, and I was raised in a non-Christian home by my mother. I felt like I was a burden to her because she had to begin working to support us when she and my dad divorced. I saw my dad inconsistently, and I always felt as if he visited me from obligation, not because he truly wanted to see me.

I always felt that something was wrong with me, and I struggled for acceptance as long as I can remember, trying everything, both good and bad, to get it. I tried to act like an adult rather than a child so I wouldn't bother my mom. I tried to be a perfect and proper person — a polite daughter, a good student, and a skilled athlete. I excelled at school, and I tried not to cause trouble, but I also drank, smoked and partied with the wild kids. I looked everywhere to everyone for the acceptance I craved.

As a college student, I even became very religious, and I worked at religion the same way I worked at being a daughter - doing the right thing so that God would be pleased with me. I was still dissatisfied and empty. My beliefs about God were directly related to my life experiences, so I was unable to have a relationship with Him.

I believed that I was just as much an inconvenience to God as I had been to my mother. I believed that God was just like my dad — not involved in my life except for the occasional appearance motivated by obligation rather than by love. I also felt that God had failed me. I had done all the right things, but I wasn't rewarded. When I really needed His help, I felt as if He had abandoned me. I began to question His goodness.

I felt like a failure, and I became depressed to the point of suicide.

to be continued...

© COPYRIGHT 1998, 2001, 2005, 2007 SCOPE MINISTRIES INTERNATIONAL INC.

Discovering the Root Of Our Problems - Lesson One

We all face problems every day, and we all struggle from time to time in our Christian lives. Jesus assured us that we would have trouble in this world, but He also promised that He would be with us and would make us overcomers. Only Jesus has the power and authority to overcome the problems of this world, and only Jesus can overcome the personal, internal problems we struggle with each day. Our Creator understands us better than we understand ourselves. He came that we might have and enjoy life.

> I came that they might have *and* enjoy life, and have it in abundance (to the full, till it overflows). John 10:10b Amplified

Why then, are we experiencing so little victory and joy in our lives? Why are so many Christians plagued with personal problems? Why are we not experiencing the abundant life that Jesus promised? Whether we are struggling with emotional, relational, behavioral, or spiritual problems, Jesus is the answer and has revealed the solution in His Word. The Bible contains everything we need to know to live a successful and abundant life. Through the lessons and daily assignments, you will discover just how relevant God's Word is to the needs and problems you face every day. The assignments are designed to help you interact with God and receive from Him the wisdom and strength to overcome life's challenges.

Where do you turn for help in the midst of life's problems? Where do you look for solutions? To whom do you turn for wisdom? Do you try to resolve your problems in your own strength and with man's wisdom? Do you become so focused on the problems that you fail to apply the supernatural resources available to you in Christ? Are you focused on the symptoms instead of the solution? Do you turn to God as a last resort? In the midst of your confusion, do you find it difficult to know where to turn in His Word for answers?

Regardless of our problems or confusion, God's Word is Truth, and Jesus is the Answer. May this workbook be a catalyst to your knowing experientially Jesus as the Answer to your every need.

God's Word Reveals the Root of Our Problems

The solution to the problems we struggle with can be discovered by addressing the root of our problems as revealed in God's Word. Romans 1:25 identifies man's basic root problem.

> For they exchanged the truth of God for a lie, and worshipped and served the creature rather than the Creator.
>
> Romans 1:25 NAS

© COPYRIGHT 1998, 2001, 2005, 2007 SCOPE MINISTRIES INTERNATIONAL INC.

The root of our problems began in the Garden, when Eve believed the serpent, and being deceived, chose to disregard God's warning. Adam chose to join Eve rather than obey God. They both decided to determine for themselves what is true and what is good. They chose to live life independent of God and rely on their own reason rather than God's Word (see Genesis 3:1-7).

The consequences of their choice were passed on to us all. We have all tried to live life independent of God, by relying on our own reason. The root problems we need to address are the lies we have believed about God, ourselves, life, and others. The Bible addresses more than just our behavior. It exposes the lies we have believed and reveals the truth. It shows us how God created us to live in relationship with Him.

Scripture gives us God's viewpoint of life; therefore, we need to:

- learn to address life's problems and issues from God's Word

  > The whole Bible was given to us by inspiration from God and is useful to teach us what is true and to make us realize what is wrong in our lives; it straightens us out and helps us do what is right.   2 Timothy 3:16 LB

- recognize that the Bible addresses not only our behaviors, but also our thoughts and beliefs
- from Scripture, develop correct beliefs about God, self, life, and others
- learn to think as God thinks

  > If you abide in My word, *then* you are truly disciples of Mine; and you shall know the truth, and the truth shall make you free.
  > John 8:31b-32 NAS

If truth is what sets us free, then it must be a lie that produces bondage in our lives. Jesus desires to speak truth to our hearts and set us free from whatever bondage we are in. The purpose of these lessons is to help you recognize the lies that are hindering you from experiencing the abundant life that is yours in Christ.

A Key Principle

"A lie believed as truth will affect your life as if it were true—even though it is a lie."

A Belief That...

Money provides security and happiness

To be happy I must be married

I am the way I am; I can't change

Failure deserves to be punished

The more I do for God, the more He will love and bless me

My worth is determined by what I do and what others think of me

© COPYRIGHT 1998, 2001, 2005, 2007 SCOPE MINISTRIES INTERNATIONAL INC.

Our Beliefs Influence and Control Our Lives

God addresses us as believing beings.

Because God created us as believing beings, Scripture speaks to us concerning our beliefs about God, ourselves, life, and others. A "belief" is an assumption we hold to be true: a presupposition or conviction. We do not usually question it and are often not even consciously aware of it. We have beliefs about everything. We do not live by animal instincts, but by beliefs that have been developed and reinforced throughout our lives. Just as our eyes recognize color but fail to perceive x-rays or radio waves, so our beliefs cause us to process certain information and block other information. *Like a filter, our beliefs cause us to accept or reject new data.*

A glaring example is racial prejudice. Based only upon long-held assumptions, many people judge others by their race or skin color without valuing the other attributes they may possess.

As we grow up, we develop beliefs about everything.

Our experiences with our parents, environment, family, school, and peers have all influenced what we believe. We have developed basic life beliefs about:

- who we are;
- whom we can trust;
- what is good or bad;
- what we are worth;
- what our purpose in life is; and
- what God is like

May Result In...

workaholism, materialism, greed, dishonesty, stealing, etc.

unrealistic expectations of spouse, unhappiness being single, discontentment with spouse, divorce if unhappy

feelings of shame, guilt, hopelessness, inferiority, passivity, loss of creativity

criticalness, judgementalism, self-destructive behavior, fear of failure, procrastination, unwillingness to take risks, fear of punishment

legalistic religious activity, serving God to earn His acceptance, spiritual burnout; feeling unacceptable to God, self-righteousness, spiritual pride

driven to succeed, competitive high achiever, comparing self with others, pride—feeling unworthy

For as he thinks within himself, so he is.

Proverbs 23:7a
NAS

© COPYRIGHT 1998, 2001, 2005, 2007 SCOPE MINISTRIES INTERNATIONAL INC.

Our belief system
is like a lens
which
colors our
perception of
reality.

What we believe directly affects the quality of our lives.

All of our beliefs combine to form a belief system.

Our belief system becomes the lens through which we see everything around us. It is just like wearing a pair of sunglasses that colors the landscape around us. We accept or reject new information based on our basic life beliefs. These beliefs color the way we interpret all of life.

If a woman grows up believing (for whatever reason) that she is not pretty, she will more than likely have a hard time accepting compliments about her appearance. She will reject any praise in her thoughts, and those thoughts will determine her response.

Our beliefs control how we respond to life.

We live out what we believe to be true about ourselves. What we believe affects our actions, motives, thoughts, words, emotions and relationships. We make choices based upon our beliefs. As others respond to our behavior, their reactions tend to reinforce our belief system. Our perception of reality is based on the beliefs we hold.

If a person is told frequently as a young child that he is clumsy, he is likely to grow up believing that he is clumsy. He may then behave in a clumsy manner, or he will be overly aware of his movements and try to compensate for how clumsy he thinks he is. This self-consciousness is likely to cause him to act in a clumsy way, unfortunately reinforcing his belief that he is a clumsy person.

Our Belief System Is Corrupted

Most of our beliefs were formed before we had any "spiritual" awareness of God.

Because we had no conscious understanding of God or "truth" as He defines it, we formed our own belief system apart from His truth. We have grown up living independently of God and relying on our own understanding—which has corrupted our belief system. Our corrupted beliefs seem more true than God's Word. They may even seem more rational.

> There is a way which *seems* right to man, but its end is the way of death.   Proverbs 14:12 NAS

Our belief system is further corrupted by sin, the world's influence, and Satan.

Satan uses sinful men and the influence of this world to harm us and to influence our thinking. Satan's greatest strategy is to deceive us with as many lies as possible so he can keep us in bondage to sin and destroy our lives. Satan tempts us to act on wrong thoughts and beliefs, thus reinforcing the wrong beliefs we already have.

> For the god of this world has blinded the unbelievers' minds [that they should not discern the truth], preventing them from seeing the illuminating light of the Gospel [good news] of the glory of Christ (the Messiah), Who is the Image *and* Likeness of God.
> 2 Corinthians 4:4 Amplified

© COPYRIGHT 1998, 2001, 2005, 2007 SCOPE MINISTRIES INTERNATIONAL INC.

> The thief [Satan] comes only to steal, kill, and destroy . . .
> John 10:10a NAS

> He [the devil] was a murderer from the beginning, and does not stand in the truth, because there is no truth in him. Whenever he speaks a lie, he speaks from his own *nature*; for he is a liar, and the father of lies.
> John 8:44b NAS

The root of our problems is our corrupted belief system; however, we don't have to continue believing these lies.

God Transforms Us by Renewing Our Minds

We can learn to recognize and replace our corrupted beliefs with God's Truth.

God has provided a way to free us from our old corrupted belief system. God tells us to no longer walk or live by the same futile way of thinking. He has given us His Word, so we can change our beliefs and experience healing and change in our lives. This change takes place as we allow God to renew our minds (beliefs).

We must reject these false beliefs or lies before the truth can change our lives. The more we believe what God says, the more we can experience a life of joy and peace. Believing and acting on the truth sets us free from sin's destructive power.

> And do not be conformed to this world, but be transformed [changed] by the renewing of your mind . . .
> Romans 12:2a NAS

Notice that God does not tell us to renew our behavior or our emotions, but our *minds*. The problem lies with our belief system. What we truly believe is revealed by how we live, not by what we know. It is not enough to simply be knowledgeable of the truth, we must come to truly believe it. This is possible only as we acknowledge to ourselves and to God the lie we have been believing and make the conscious choice to replace it with God's truth.

Remember: The process of renewing our minds is not a matter of deep introspection nor is it a matter of just replacing our negative thoughts with positive ones. This renewing **process** involves our **relating** to God and **depending** on Him to reveal the lies and teach us what is true. This renewal is possible through the work of the Holy Spirit. We will talk about the work of the Holy Spirit in more detail in future lessons.

> But the Helper, the Holy Spirit, whom the Father will send in My name, He will teach you all things . . . John 14:26a NAS

> But when He, the Spirit of truth comes, He will guide you into all the truth . . . John 16:13a NAS

Renewing our minds consists of:

- Recognizing the lies we've believed;
- Renouncing and rejecting the lies;
- Replacing the lies with God's truth;and
- Redirecting our thoughts to reflect our new beliefs

What we believe is revealed by how we live, not by what we know.

© COPYRIGHT 1998, 2001, 2005, 2007 SCOPE MINISTRIES INTERNATIONAL INC.

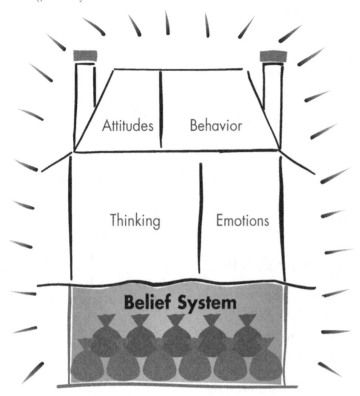

A couple built a new house in a neighborhood where no garbage service was available. They stored their garbage in their basement so it would be out of sight and out of their way until they could haul it to the dump. While they spent their time and energy furnishing their new home and landscaping their yard, the trash began to pile up. The day finally arrived when they invited all their friends and family over to see their new home. Even though the couple's home was exceptionally clean and was filled with beautiful furnishings, their guests were not impressed. The odor from the basement had permeated every room. Cleaning would do little good until they got rid of the garbage in the basement. This illustrates how our corrupted belief system affects all areas of our life. It first affects our thinking and emotions, then our attitudes and behavior. Until we consciously recognize and reject the lies we have believed, the truth will have little impact on our lives.

A Renewed Mind Brings Joy and Peace

The result of a renewed mind is joy and peace. Allowing Jesus to change our thoughts and beliefs will bring healing to our emotions, freedom from destructive behavior, and power to love God and others.

It is our wrong beliefs that produce negative thinking, which gives rise to painful emotions and destructive behavior. Once we correct our beliefs about God, self, life, others and Scripture, our thinking can line up with our new beliefs. This will empower us to make Godly choices, which will produce more positive emotions and a transformed life.

Changing our thoughts and beliefs will eventually result in greater joy.

The more we believe what God says, the more we can experience a life of joy and peace. Problems are inevitable, but joy and peace are optional. We have all been hurt and wounded by others and life's circumstances. Even if these people and circumstances never change, we can still learn to have joy and peace in the midst of all situations. Allowing the truth of God's Word to change our belief system does not alter our past, but it will transform our lives and give us hope and wisdom for the future.

> Behold, Thou dost desire truth in the innermost being, and in the
> hidden part Thou wilt make me know wisdom. Psalm 51:6 NAS

© COPYRIGHT 1998, 2001, 2005, 2007 SCOPE MINISTRIES INTERNATIONAL INC.

Remember, God is always present, full of compassion and grace, and willing to heal our broken hearts and lives. He desires more than we do to fill our lives with His hope, joy, and peace.

> May the God of hope fill you with all joy and peace in your faith [beliefs], that by the power of the Holy Spirit, your whole life and outlook may be radiant with hope.   Romans 15:13 Phillips

The daily assignments that follow are designed to lead you to discover some of the false beliefs that are robbing you of the quality of life that Jesus promised. As you do each assignment, invite God, the Holy Spirit, to be your teacher and counselor. There is no need to be deeply introspective. God desires to reveal to you the lies that need to be rejected and the truth that needs to be received and believed.

> Trust in the Lord with all your heart, and do not lean on your own understanding. In all your ways acknowledge Him, and He will make your paths straight.   Proverbs 3:5-6, NAS

As you begin this journey, make this your prayer:

> Search me O God, and know my heart; try me and know my anxious thoughts; and see if there be any hurtful way in me, and lead me in the everlasting way.   Psalm 139:23-24 NAS

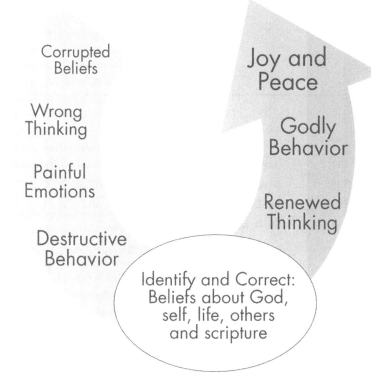

Corrupted Beliefs

Wrong Thinking

Painful Emotions

Destructive Behavior

Joy and Peace

Godly Behavior

Renewed Thinking

Identify and Correct: Beliefs about God, self, life, others and scripture

© COPYRIGHT 1998, 2001, 2005, 2007 SCOPE MINISTRIES INTERNATIONAL INC.

SUMMARY:

1. We are believing beings, and all of our beliefs combine to form a belief system.

2. Most of our problems stem from our corrupted belief system.

3. Our beliefs affect our thinking, emotions, attitudes, and behavior.

4. We can be transformed and experience joy through the renewing of our minds with God's truth.

A Life Transformed, con't.

When I was at my lowest point, God showed me that the key to changing my life was not trying to change the outside but changing what I believed. God helped me to identify the lies that I had believed and to replace them with the truth. I began to believe that God accepts me and that I am pleasing to Him because He is in me. I began to enjoy just being with Him and talking with Him. I now enjoy life because I know He is always with me. I truly feel free to be me. As I changed my beliefs, my behavior changed. My beliefs; feelings, and passions are from God, so I don't have to worry about pleasing others and they don't have to please me. I can give freedom to those around me because they are pleasing to God and He wants me to love them as He loves me.

Choosing to reject the lie and to believe the truth that God loves and accepts me changed my life because I can and I want to have a relationship with God like that. Now my direction in life is running to God instead of away from Him.

Katrina - Teacher

© COPYRIGHT 1998, 2001, 2005, 2007 SCOPE MINISTRIES INTERNATIONAL INC.

Discovering the Root of Our Problems - Day One

Goal: To identify the problem from your perspective and to ask God to reveal His perspective of the problem.

All of us experience problems. Life is full of problems. Success is not the absence of problems but knowing how to respond and resolve the problems. God has not left us alone to try to overcome our problems in our own strength and wisdom. He has given us the Holy Spirit and His Word to empower and teach us.

> Every Scripture is God-breathed (given by His inspiration) and profitable for instruction, for reproof *and* conviction of sin, for correction of error *and* discipline in obedience, [and] for training in righteousness (in holy living, in conformity to God's will in thought, purpose, and action), so that the man of God may be complete *and* proficient, well-fitted *and* thoroughly equipped for every good work.   II Timothy 3:16-17 Amplified

These verses tell us that God's Word is sufficient and profitable to make us adequate and equipped. In other words, God's Word shows us the way or path to abundant living (teaching). God's Word shows us when we get off the path (reproof). God's Word shows us how to get back on the path (correction) and how to stay on the path (training in righteousness). This path is not merely a set of correct behaviors we are to perform. God is committed to showing us when we leave the path of correct beliefs and thoughts as well as correcting our behavior.

1. What problem(s) do you want God to change or address in your life? (conflict in relationship, emotional struggle, habit, or behavior)

2. How is this problem affecting you emotionally?

3. What behaviors or habits in your life are contributing to this problem?

© COPYRIGHT 1998, 2001, 2005, 2007 SCOPE MINISTRIES INTERNATIONAL INC.

4. How is your behavior affecting your relationships with others?

5. What are some prevailing thoughts that run through your mind when you think about your unique problem?

6. How do you see your problem affecting your relationship with God?

In time, as you seek God's perspective, you will be able to recognize the beliefs that are contributing to these problems and replace those beliefs with the truth as revealed in God's Word.

7. Write your prayer, asking God to begin showing you His perspective of your problem(s) and any beliefs that are contributing to it.

© COPYRIGHT 1998, 2001, 2005, 2007 SCOPE MINISTRIES INTERNATIONAL INC.

Discovering the Root of Our Problems - Day Two

Goal: To see from Scripture the effect our beliefs have on our lives.

Part One: Because we are believing beings, we each create a belief system that controls our lives. Our beliefs are corrupted because they were formed while we were spiritually separated from God and because we were born into a world corrupted by sin.

Read the account of the fall in Genesis 2:8-9, 16-17; 3:1-7.

1. What did God tell Adam in Genesis 2:16-17?

2. What did Satan imply by his question in Genesis 3:1?

3. What subtle lie did Satan use to tempt Eve to doubt what is true? (see Genesis 3:4)

4. Whom did Eve believe?

5. How did her belief affect her behavior? What were the consequences?

6. What do you think is Satan's role in forming people's beliefs today?

7. How has the fall of man affected you personally?

© COPYRIGHT 1998, 2001, 2005, 2007 SCOPE MINISTRIES INTERNATIONAL INC.

Part Two:

8. The purpose of this short Bible study is to reveal how our beliefs affect our emotions and behavior. Read each passage and write out the resulting emotion and behavior:

Person(s)	Belief	Emotion	Behavior
The Ten Spies Numbers 13:1-2, 17, 20, 23-33	believed they were small and weak	Fear and inadequacy	gave bad report; unwilling to enter the Promised Land; wanted to stone Joshua, Caleb
Joshua and Caleb Numbers 13:1-2, 17, 20, 23-33	believed God had given them the land and would give them the ability to take possession		
Moses Exodus 4:10-15	believed he was inadequate		
Disciples Mark 4:35-41	believed they were perishing		
Jesus	believed His heavenly Father was in control		

9. What conclusions can you draw from these examples?

   On what was each behavior based?

10. How do your beliefs compare with those in the examples above?

11. Write out a prayer asking God to reveal to you the truth from His Word.

© COPYRIGHT 1998, 2001, 2005, 2007 SCOPE MINISTRIES INTERNATIONAL INC.

Discovering the Root of Our Problems - Day Three

Goal: To begin uncovering some of your basic life beliefs.

Part One:

1. Complete the following sentences with the first answer that comes to your mind:

   I would be more successful if...

   I would be happier if...

   I could never be happy if...

   I would feel more secure if...

   I would be more peaceful if...

2. What beliefs are revealed by your answers?

© COPYRIGHT 1998, 2001, 2005, 2007 SCOPE MINISTRIES INTERNATIONAL INC.

Part Two:

3. Choose one of your beliefs revealed in question 2 and write out your corresponding thoughts, emotions, and behaviors. See the examples below:

> EXAMPLE #1:
> Belief: Making a lot of money means I am successful.
> Thoughts: Consumed with getting ahead, bigger house, better car, etc.
> Emotions: Feel anxious about job; angry at co-workers who seem to block goals;
>   envious of co-workers' success; guilt
> Behavior: Workaholic, drink to relieve stress from job, not spending time with
>   family, critical of others
>
> EXAMPLE #2:
> Belief: If my spouse would change, I'd be happy.
> Thoughts: "If only he/she would . . ."
>   "Why can't he/she be more like _____'s spouse?"
>   "I'm stuck for life. This marriage is hopeless."
>   "I could never be happy married to this person."
> Emotions: Anger, hurt, rejection, resentment, revenge
> Behavior: Manipulating, nagging, withdrawing, withholding affection, demanding

Belief:

Thoughts:

Emotions:

Behavior:

© COPYRIGHT 1998, 2001, 2005, 2007 SCOPE MINISTRIES INTERNATIONAL INC.

Discovering the Root of Our Problems - Day Four

Goal: To see from God's Word how corrupted our minds were when our beliefs were formed.

1. According to the following verse, how does Paul describe the thinking of an unbeliever?

> You walk no longer just as the Gentiles [unbelievers] also walk, in the futility of their mind [foolish and vain thinking], being darkened in their understanding [distorted reasoning], excluded [alienated] from the life of God, because of the ignorance that is in them...
> Ephesians 4:17b-18a NAS

2. What knowledge did man feel it was unnecessary to retain?

> And so, since they did not see fit to acknowledge God *or* approve of Him *or* consider Him worth the knowing, God gave them over to a base [depraved] *and* condemned mind to do things not proper *or* decent *but* loathsome, until they were filled (permeated and saturated) with every kind of unrighteousness . . . Romans 1:28-29a Amplified

3. What kind of thinking did God allow to control man?

4. What knowledge do unbelievers now have?

> For the god of this world has blinded the unbelievers' minds [that they should not discern the truth], preventing them from seeing the illuminating light of the Gospel of the glory of Christ (the Messiah), Who is the Image *and* Likeness of God.
> II Corinthians 4:4 Amplified

© COPYRIGHT 1998, 2001, 2005, 2007 SCOPE MINISTRIES INTERNATIONAL INC.

5. On what do their minds focus?

> . . . whose end is destruction (eternal misery), whose god is *their* appetite, and *whose* glory is in their shame, who set their minds on earthly things.   Philippians 3:19b NAS

6. What can you conclude about the thoughts of the unsaved mind?

Note: This does not mean that every thought of man is totally disgusting, vulgar, and repulsive; however, the end result of wrong thoughts is corruption and the exclusion of God.

> Search me, O God, and know my heart; try me and know my anxious thoughts; and see if there be any hurtful way in me, and lead me in the everlasting way.
> Psalm 139:23-24 NAS

7. Take a moment to reflect on the above verse and to ask God to show you any anxious or hurtful thoughts that need to be rejected and replaced with God's truth. Write down any thoughts He shows you.

8. Write Romans 12:2 on a 3x5 card or a post-it note and place it in a prominent place where you will see it often. Each time you see this verse, personalize it as a prayer.

Sample prayer:

Father, I no longer want to be conformed to the thinking of this world. I desire to be transformed by the renewing of my mind. Make me more aware of what I am thinking and show me the lies that I have been believing. I want to live out Your will, which is good, acceptable, and perfect.

© COPYRIGHT 1998, 2001, 2005, 2007 SCOPE MINISTRIES INTERNATIONAL INC.

Discovering the Root of Our Problems - Day Five

Goal: To continue to identify some of your unique personal beliefs.

Part One: Review

Our beliefs are shaped by our perceptions which are based on our experiences with our parents, family, school, peers, etc.

Scripture clearly states that all are born captive to sin and ignorant of Truth.

> For the wrath of God is revealed from heaven against all ungodliness and unrighteousness of men, who suppress the truth in unrighteousness. Romans 1:18 NAS

> There is none righteous, not even one; There is none who understands, There is none who seeks for God.   Romans 3:10b-11 NAS

> For all have sinned and fall short of the glory of God.   Romans 3:23 NAS

Growing up in a fallen world, we learn about life from our environment, experiences, and what others teach us. We learn:

- Who we are;
- Whom we can trust;
- What is good or bad;
- What we are worth;
- What our purpose is in life; and
- What God is like.

What we learn becomes our belief system by which we evaluate all new information. We accept or reject new information based on our basic life beliefs. These beliefs are like a lens through which we see life and which control our behavior.

Because our perceptions are distorted and the way we process information is distorted, many of our patterns of behaving and relating to others are also distorted. As others respond to our behavior, their reactions tend to reinforce what we believe to be true.

Part Two: Application

1. Name one significant negative life experience that has shaped what you believe about yourself.

© COPYRIGHT 1998, 2001, 2005, 2007 SCOPE MINISTRIES INTERNATIONAL INC.

2. List the beliefs formed from that life experience:

    Who am I?

    Whom can I trust?

    What is good or bad?

    What am I worth?

    What is my purpose in life?

3. How have these beliefs been reinforced over the years?

    > Example: Growing up I was poor at math and my dad called me stupid. Kids at school would make fun of me. I hated math all through school and flunked Algebra. I chose not to go to college. I feel like such a failure but I'm afraid to try anything else. Everyone else in my family has a college degree. My dad has never indicated that he is proud of me. Now I find myself being hard on my children when they don't make A's.

4. How are these beliefs still manifested in your thoughts, emotions, behaviors, and relationships? (In other words, how do these beliefs control you? In what areas do you feel held back because of these beliefs?)

    > And I (Jesus) will ask the Father, and He will give you another Helper, that He may be with you forever; *that is* the Spirit of truth whom the world cannot receive, because it does not behold Him or know Him, *but* you know Him because He abides with you, and will be in you . . . But when He, the Spirit of truth, comes, He will guide you into all the truth.   John 14:16-17 NAS

5. Write out a prayer, asking the Holy Spirit to reveal the truth to you concerning these beliefs.

© COPYRIGHT 1998, 2001, 2005, 2007 SCOPE MINISTRIES INTERNATIONAL INC.

Discovering the Root of Our Problems - Lesson One

Name _____Date _____

Answer the following questions. To turn in page to small group leader, use identical perforated page in back of book.

1. Briefly describe from DAY ONE the problem with which you are presently struggling.

2. What are some of your "beliefs" that relate to your area of struggle?

3. How are these beliefs affecting you (emotionally, relationally, behaviorally)?

4. What is God showing you from this week's lesson?

5. How often do you turn to God's Word for answers to your problems?
   ___never   ___seldom   ___often   ___ very often   ___ always

6. What questions do you have concerning this week's assignment?

7. Mark the graph to indicate how much of this week's assignment you completed.

None	50%	100%

© COPYRIGHT 1998, 2001, 2005, 2007 SCOPE MINISTRIES INTERNATIONAL INC.

Record Your Prayer Requests:

_____

_____

_____

_____

_____

_____

_____

_____

_____

_____

_____

_____

_____

_____

_____

_____

_____

_____

_____

_____

© COPYRIGHT 1998, 2001, 2005, 2007 SCOPE MINISTRIES INTERNATIONAL INC.

Understanding the Good News

You were dead in sins, and your sinful desires were not yet cut away. Then He gave you a share in the very life of Christ, for He forgave all your sins, and blotted out the charges proved against you, the list of His commandments which you had not obeyed. He took this list of sins and destroyed it by nailing it to Christ's cross.

Colossians 2:13-14 LB

Lesson 2

A Life Transformed

My life was in constant turmoil. I was overwhelmed with fear and depression and plagued by thoughts of suicide. I was scared to do anything because it would inevitably be the wrong choice.

I used drugs and alcohol to escape my pain but they just made my misery worse. I tried to fill the hole in my life with sexual relationships that just became an additional problem.

I looked everywhere for help — the occult, eastern philosophies and practices — but I just became more confused. I tried doctors, counselors, healers, psychics, Alcoholics Anonymous, and Narcotics Anonymous. Each attempt brought temporary relief, but then I would feel even worse because of a worse emotional bombardment and the terrible sense of impending doom.

I was so desperate to be free of my misery that I was pointing a gun to my head, ready to commit suicide, but I asked God for help instead. When a friend got me into a treatment program the very next day, I knew God had answered my prayer.

Even after I had been clean and sober for several years, I was still more miserable and depressed than ever. The problem wasn't the drugs and alcohol. The problem wasn't the world around me. The problem wasn't the relationships. The problem was the conflict in me.

I had to lose a lot before I was finally desperate enough to accept God's solution to my problem.

I've always been aware of God's influence in my life. I knew that He was guiding me when my conscience told me that I was making bad choices, especially when I experienced the consequences. Even as a child, I knew that I wasn't here just to wander around aimlessly. I've always had an inner sense that God had a purpose for me, but I avoided it because I've always avoided responsibility.

I always knew that I eventually would turn to God, and, throughout my life, people have pointed me to a relationship with Christ. This time, when a friend started telling me about the changes Christ had made in her life, I finally listened. As she talked, I felt as if I was finally finding true hope, but I was also scared. I was scared of having to admit my faults, and I was afraid of the consequences when I actually faced what I had done and who I had become. I was afraid of change. I knew that I had to turn to God for help, but I was wavering between fear and hope.

My past had almost destroyed me, but now my future scared me. I was afraid of the new responsibilities, and I wasn't sure I could live the Christian life. Because of my old beliefs, I was still feeling the inner turmoil I had experienced all my life. I still believed that God could not accept me or love me because I was unacceptable, unlovable, and unworthy.

to be continued...

© COPYRIGHT 1998, 2001, 2005, 2007 SCOPE MINISTRIES INTERNATIONAL INC.

In our previous lesson we discovered that we are believing beings. The first belief we need to examine carefully is our understanding of the Gospel. The word "Gospel" means "good news." Specifically, it is the good news concerning the relationship with God that is possible through the life, death, and resurrection of Jesus Christ. This "good news" allows us to be forgiven of all our sins and live a meaningful life of joy and peace. However, many people who have received this "good news" still live miserable and defeated lives. How is this possible?

We often still live miserable and defeated lives as a result of our corrupted belief system which still controls the way we live (think, feel, and choose). In order to correct our belief system, we need to begin with correcting any distorted beliefs concerning the "good news" of our salvation.

Often, people do not understand what really happened to them when they put their trust in Christ. So, in order to better understand the good news, we will start by looking at sin's effect on how we relate to God and the meaning and purpose we give to life. This will enable us to better understand the really good news.

We Were Created to Be a Friend and Companion of God

The book of Genesis tells the story of the creation of the world and the beginning of human life. Here we can gain understanding about why we were created and how we are to function.

We are complete only when we are in relationship with God.

- Man was created to have an intimate love relationship with His Creator. Matt. 22:37; John 15:9, 13

- Man was created in God's image to know and enjoy God. Genesis 1:27; Psalm 16:11

- Man was designed to live dependent upon God. John 15:5

- Man was created to contain the very life of God and to live by that life. John 10:10b

Man was deceived and chose to live life independently of God.

God created man and woman and placed them in a garden paradise to live and enjoy His presence. Every day God would fellowship with Adam and Eve in the Garden, and He provided for their every need. Adam and Eve were free to live and enjoy God's presence. Their only restriction was eating from the Tree of Knowledge, which would bring death to their relationship with Him.

Believing
THE LIE
caused a tragic
separation
in man's
relationship with
God ... but this
didn't stop God
from loving us!

© COPYRIGHT 1998, 2001, 2005, 2007 SCOPE MINISTRIES INTERNATIONAL INC.

Sin = Missing the Mark:

➤➤ failing to love and honor God;

➤➤ failing to believe God's love;

➤➤ living independent of God;

➤➤ seeking fulfillment in things or others; and

➤➤ failing to love others as ourselves.

Satan deceived Eve by questioning God's character, word, and motives. Adam and Eve believed the lie that they could be like God, ate from the Tree of Knowledge, and chose to live independently of God. This sin affected every aspect of their lives and caused a tragic separation in their relationship with God.

Separated from God, we are incapable of being what God intended us to be.

All of us have been born physically alive, but spiritually dead and separated from God. Making our own decisions and depending on our own strength to live life has resulted in our being controlled by fear, being prone to selfishness, and being in bondage to sin. Sin simply means "missing the mark." God wanted us to live in fellowship with Him, but our sin has caused us to fall short of the purpose for which we were created. We have failed to know God, to depend upon Him, and to be what He created us to be.

Our separation from God has further distorted our concept of what God is like. Based on this distorted concept of God, we have formed our own beliefs about God, ourselves, life, and others.

The Good News Provides the Solution to the Problem of Our Separation

God took it upon Himself to restore our relationship!

Because we were spiritually separated (dead) from God, there was nothing we could do to restore our relationship with Him, **But** God, in His love, had a plan to take care of our sin problem and to restore us to a right relationship with Him.

> But God - so rich is He in His mercy! Because of *and* in order to satisfy the great *and* wonderful *and* intense love with which He loved us. Even when we were dead (slain) by [our own] shortcomings *and* trespasses, He made us alive together in fellowship *and* in union with Christ; . . . it is by grace (His favor and mercy which you did not deserve) that you are saved (delivered from judgment and made partakers of Christ's salvation). Ephesians 2:4-5 Amplified

God sent Jesus Christ to earth to reveal God's love to us, and to give His life as payment for the sins of the whole world. Jesus Christ experienced physical death and spiritual separation from His Father while paying the penalty for all our sins on the cross. Jesus experienced death for us, so we could be forgiven and receive eternal life (1 John 4:9; Hebrews 9). His perfect sacrifice satisfied the just and righteous demands of a holy God, so that we could enjoy an intimate love relationship with Him. This is good news!

> It was God [personally present] in Christ, reconciling *and* restoring the world to favor with Himself, not counting up *and* holding against [men] their trespasses [but canceling them], and committing to us the message of reconciliation (of the restoration to favor). 2 Corinthians 5:19 Amplified

© COPYRIGHT 1998, 2001, 2005, 2007 SCOPE MINISTRIES INTERNATIONAL INC.

We have been totally and completely forgiven by God!

God's forgiveness cost Him greatly, and reveals the depth of His mercy and love for us (1 John 4:10). Because of Christ's sacrifice for us, we can enjoy a relationship with God and can live as forgiven people. Understanding God's forgiveness cleanses us, so we can have confidence before God and receive His mercy and grace to help us in our time of need (Hebrews 4:16).

- God's forgiveness is **total** and **complete**.

> And when you were dead in your transgressions and the uncircumcision of your flesh [your sinful, carnal nature], He made you alive together with Him, having forgiven us all our transgressions, having canceled out the certificate of debt consisting of decrees against us *and* which was hostile to us; and He has taken it out of the way, having nailed it to the cross.
> Colossians 2:13-14 NAS

- God's forgiveness is a **free gift** which is received only by believing and trusting in Jesus.

> For God did not send the Son into the world to judge the world, but that the world should be saved through Him. He who believes in Him is not judged; he who does not believe has been judged already, because he has not believed in the name of the only begotten Son of God.
> John 3:17-18 NAS

We are deeply and unconditionally loved by God!

God's character is one of perfect, unconditional love. This means that God loves us because of Who He is, not because of who we are or what we have done. We could never earn or deserve His love, and there is nothing we can do that would cause God to stop loving us.

> But God shows *and* clearly proves His [own] love for us by the fact that while we were still sinners, Christ (the Messiah, the Anointed One) died for us.
> Romans 5:8 Amplified

God's love is demonstrated by His unwavering commitment to give us what we truly need through His Son, Jesus. God's Word also reveals His deep emotional attachment and desire to be in a relationship with us. Understanding God's unconditional love frees us from fearing God's punishment or rejection. We can rest in the truth that we are deeply loved.

> There is no fear in love [dread does not exist], but full-grown (complete, perfect) love turns fear out of doors *and* expels every trace of terror! For fear brings with it the thought of punishment, and [so] he who is afraid has not reached the full maturity of love [is not yet grown into love's complete perfection]. We love *Him*, because He first loved us.
> 1 John 4:18-19 Amplified

> He who does not love has not become acquainted with God, . . . for God is love.
> 1 John 4:8 Amplified

All of our sins (past, present, and future) were nailed to the cross.

© COPYRIGHT 1998, 2001, 2005, 2007 SCOPE MINISTRIES INTERNATIONAL INC.

God totally and completely accepts us!

Not only has God forgiven us but He has made us acceptable. This means He accepts us for who we are, and where we are. God's acceptance does not mean that He approves of the wrong that we do. Acceptance by God means that He receives us to Himself with pleasure and responds to us in kindness.

We have been given Eternal Life!

God gives Eternal Life to all who believe in His Son and receive Him as their personal Savior. Eternal Life is God's divine life given to us now. This means we can experientially know God now, in the midst of whatever problems we may face.

> And this is eternal life, that they may know [to perceive, recognize, become acquainted with, and understand] Thee, the only true God, and Jesus Christ whom Thou hast sent.
> John 17:3 NAS

We can experience an abundant life because the Holy Spirit lives in us.

God's eternal, Holy Spirit indwells us, so we can know and enjoy an intimate relationship with God. Eternal Life is not just living forever, but it is the presence of God in us now. We are now, and will be forever, in the loving presence of God. Abundant life is joy and satisfaction in God, regardless of outward circumstances. We do not earn abundant life by our performance. It is produced in us by the Holy Spirit.

> I have come that they may have life, and have it to the full.
> John 10:10b NI

> "When the Helper comes, whom I will send to you from the Father, that is the Spirit of truth, who proceeds from the Father, He will bear witness of Me.
> John 15:26 NAS

God desires to live through us by His Holy Spirit!

The Holy Spirit reveals God's unconditional love to us. The Holy Spirit reproduces in us the character of God.

> But the fruit of the [Holy] Spirit [the work which His presence within accomplishes] is love, joy (gladness), peace, patience (an even temper, forbearance), kindness, goodness (benevolence), faithfulness, gentleness (meekness, humility), self-control (self-restraint, continence).
> Galatians 5:22-23a Amplified

Any Distortion Of The "Good News" Leads to Problems

Whenever we misunderstand the "good news" of the Gospel, we view our relationship with God and the Christian life in a distorted way. The very essence of the Gospel is not to get man into Heaven, but to get God into man!

The very essence of the Gospel is not to get man into Heaven, but to get God into man!

© COPYRIGHT 1998, 2001, 2005, 2007 SCOPE MINISTRIES INTERNATIONAL INC.

Viewing salvation as merely "fire insurance" or a free ticket to Heaven results in our:

- continuing to live independently of God;
- neglecting the relationship He wants us to enjoy now; and
- looking to life's circumstances and others for our happiness.

Most Christians define the Gospel as God's effort to get man into Heaven. However, salvation is more than forgiveness and going to Heaven someday. If we simply try to get into Heaven, we miss the whole point of knowing God as He lives in us.

Viewing God's forgiveness as incomplete or conditional results in our:

- believing Jesus died only for the sins we committed before we became a Christian;
- believing we have to ask for forgiveness before we are forgiven;
- believing God is angry with us and holding our sins against us;
- viewing ourselves as being on parole instead of fully pardoned;
- feeling emotional guilt and fearing punishment, which create distance in our relationship with God; and
- continually asking God for forgiveness but never experiencing the peace His total forgiveness brings.

Believing we are saved primarily to serve God leads to:

- trying to **do things** for God in order to earn His acceptance;
- living from our own strength and ability rather than depending on the power of the Holy Spirit;
- believing God is more interested in our behavior than in a relationship with us; and
- being spiritually proud based on our performance, abilities, or sacrifice.

Believing the "Good News" Progressively Transforms Our Lives

Our purpose and meaning we give to life will change.

Increasingly, our purpose will be to enjoy a love relationship with God. Rather than always trying to avoid pain, we will begin to see problems as opportunities to know God experientially.

> Yes, furthermore, I count everything as loss compared to the surpassing value of knowing Christ Jesus my Lord and progressively becoming more deeply and intimately acquainted with Him. 　　　　　　　　Philippians 3:8-10 paraphrase

We can continue to feel separated from God if we don't believe we are forgiven, loved, and accepted by God.

© COPYRIGHT 1998, 2001, 2005, 2007 SCOPE MINISTRIES INTERNATIONAL INC.

The way we view God and respond to Him will change.

The Gospel demonstrates the beauty of God's grace and unconditional love for us. The more we believe God's love, the more easily we will trust Him in the midst of life's problems. We will draw near to Him in times of trouble and failure.

> Thou wilt make known to me the path of life; in Thy presence is fullness of joy; in Thy right hand there are pleasures forever.
>
> Psalm 16:11 NAS

> As for the rich in this world, charge them not to be proud *and* arrogant *and* contemptuous of others, nor to set their hopes on uncertain riches, but on God, Who richly *and* ceaselessly provides us with everything for [our] enjoyment.
>
> 1 Timothy 6:17 Amplified

The way we view ourselves and how we relate to others will change.

We will see ourselves as God's dearly loved children, not just forgiven sinners. We will begin to relate to others the way God relates to us. We will forgive, love, and accept others in the same way and to the same degree we believe God has forgiven, loved, and accepted us.

> Wherefore, accept one another, just as Christ also accepted us to the glory of God.　　Romans 15:7 NAS

> And be kind to one another, tender-hearted, forgiving each other, just as God in Christ also has forgiven you.
>
> Ephesians 4:32 NAS

> And so, as those who have been chosen of God, holy and beloved, put on a heart of compassion, kindness, humility, gentleness and patience; bearing with one another, and forgiving each other, whoever has a complaint against anyone; just as the Lord forgave you, so also should you.
>
> Colossians 3:12-13 NAS

Receiving Christ into our life is a one-time decision. However, believing the "good news" is not only a one-time decision but an ongoing one. Daily, we must continue believing and acting on the things that are now true about us. This involves believing that Christ's death on the cross guarantees our total forgiveness and enables us to enjoy an intimate love relationship with God. Also, we must affirm that the Holy Spirit lives within us and desires to live Christ's life through us.

Jesus gave His life for us, so He can give His life to us, so He can live His life through us.

© COPYRIGHT1998, 2001, 2005, 2007 SCOPE MINISTRIES INTERNATIONAL INC.

┌─SUMMARY:────────────────────────────┐

1. We were created to be the friend and companion of God.

2. Sin separated us from God and has distorted our beliefs about God, ourselves, and others.

3. Christ restored our relationship with God, and God desires to live through us by His Holy Spirit.

4. The Good News is that we are totally forgiven and can experience God's quality of life now (eternal life).

└─────────────────────────────────────┘

A Life Transformed, con't.

I started studying the Bible a couple of times a week with a friend, and the truth about God and what He thinks about me helped ease my fears. I realized that God wants a relationship with me, not performance from me. I learned that He wouldn't condemn me or reprimand me. I knew that God changes lives, but I wasn't sure that He would change mine. I decided to give Him a try, and I accepted Christ's forgiveness and invited Him to take control of my life.

As I believed and received the truth of God's unconditional love and forgiveness, the feelings of abandonment and rejection began to diminish. I was freed from the thoughts that tormented me to contemplate suicide and despair. My whole perspective has changed. I've got a lot more than I had, but it's not stuff. I have confidence because I don't have to worry about making the wrong choice. I know I have Someone to guide me though all my problems.

Understanding God's approval is the key to everything. People told me before that I'm worthy and OK, but I didn't believe them. Now I know it's true because I have His words on who I am. Otherwise, I would still be believing the lie that there is something wrong with me. I would still be beating myself up all the time about what I've done. Now I don't consider my past failures because I'm focused on the future God has for me.

I used to seclude myself because I was afraid of rejection, and people around me avoided me because they thought I looked angry all the time. Now I am at ease with myself and that allows me to go out and be a part of this world. I have gained many new friends, and people actually talk to me because I don't scare them anymore.

My attitude towards work has also changed. At my job, now I enjoy accomplishing good work and relating to others to achieve a common goal. Daily chores and necessities are enjoyable because I focus on enjoying the work and not worrying about the results.

Now I have a present life instead of past failures and future fears. I discovered this new life from God's truth, and I desire to live and grow in it. I know that it is a Spirit-led journey and that God in me will make me able to live it.

Jeff - Printing Supervisor

© COPYRIGHT1998, 2001, 2005, 2007 SCOPE MINISTRIES INTERNATIONAL INC.

Understanding the Good News - Day One

Goal: To recognize your present view of God and how this has affected your understanding of the "good news."

1. Until now, what has been your understanding of the Gospel?

2. Read the lesson and then write a definition of the "good news."

3. Think of a recent time when you were really disappointed with your behavior, and with this in mind, complete the following statements:

When God thinks about me, He is . . .

God expects me to . . .

God is angry with me when I . . .

God would be more pleased with me if I . . .

The one thing that frightens me most about God is . . .

© COPYRIGHT 1998, 2001, 2005, 2007 SCOPE MINISTRIES INTERNATIONAL INC.

4. Based on your answers from question 3, write a description of how you think God views you when you fail.

   Example: "When God thinks about me, He gets angry." This might reveal a belief that God has not forgiven you.

5. What misunderstanding of the "good news" is reflected by your answers in questions 3 and 4?

   Example: Believing God is unforgiving reveals a misunderstanding of God's total forgiveness of your sins.

6. Your answers may be an example of how your concept of God has been distorted as a result of being born separated from God. Look back at this lesson and find a Scripture that corrects your distorted view of God and the Gospel. Based on this verse, write a prayer to God expressing thanks for this "good news."

© COPYRIGHT1998, 2001, 2005, 2007 SCOPE MINISTRIES INTERNATIONAL INC.

Understanding the Good News - Day Two

Goal: To understand how God responds to you when you sin.

1. Read John 8:3-11, observing the woman's behavior and Jesus' response.

    a. What was the woman's behavior?

    b. What was Jesus' response to her?

2. Read Luke 15:11-24. The father in this parable represents God, and the two sons represent two types of people.

    a. What was the younger son's behavior?

    b. What was the father's response to the younger son?

    c. What did the son do to get his father's forgiveness?

© COPYRIGHT 1998, 2001, 2005, 2007 SCOPE MINISTRIES INTERNATIONAL INC.

3. Based on the above examples, how does God respond to you when you sin?

4. Besides forgiving, what else is revealed about God's character in the above passages?

5. How would viewing God this way affect the way you relate to Him in your present situation?

6. Write a prayer expressing to God your desire to experience Him in this way.

© COPYRIGHT1998, 2001, 2005, 2007 SCOPE MINISTRIES INTERNATIONAL INC.

Understanding the Good News - Day Three

Goal: To understand more accurately from Scripture the total forgiveness God extends
to you.

Knowing and enjoying God's forgiveness is imperative to a healthy Christian life. What incredible joy it brings when we realize what God has done about our sin. We can now come confidently into His presence with the assurance that our sins are not only forgiven—but forgotten! Based on Hebrews 10, God not only forgives, but forgets our sins and transgressions. What this means is that God will never throw our previous sins back in our faces.

1. What sins have you felt God is still holding against you?

2. Read each verse below and write down what God is communicating to you about His forgiveness, personalizing your answers.

> You were dead in sins, and your sinful desires were not yet cut away. Then He gave you a share in the very life of Christ, for He forgave all your sins, and blotted out the charges proved against you, the list of his commandments which you had not obeyed. He took this list of sins and destroyed it by nailing it to Christ's cross.
>
> Colossians 2:13-14 LB

> The Lord your God is in the midst of you, a Mighty One, a Savior [Who saves]! He will rejoice over you with joy . . . and in His love He will be silent and make no mention [of past sins, or even recall them]; He will exalt over you with singing.
>
> Zephaniah 3:17 Amplified

> As far as the east is from the west, so far has He removed our transgressions from us.
>
> Psalm 103:12 NAS

> I, even I, am He Who blots out and cancels your transgressions, for My own sake, and I will not remember your sins.
>
> Isaiah 43:25 Amplified

> Therefore,[there is] now no condemnation (no adjudging guilty of wrong) for those who are in Christ Jesus. . .
>
> Romans 8:1a Amplified

© COPYRIGHT 1998, 2001, 2005, 2007 SCOPE MINISTRIES INTERNATIONAL INC.

3. Based on these verses, how many of your sins has God forgiven? Remember, Jesus died for all the sins of the whole world. That means He has already paid for all your future sins as well.

4. Write a note to God thanking Him for His complete forgiveness.

© COPYRIGHT1998, 2001, 2005, 2007 SCOPE MINISTRIES INTERNATIONAL INC.

Understanding the Good News - Day Four

Goal: To understand more fully the free gift of eternal life.

1. When you became a Christian, what did you receive?

2. According to the following verse, how does one receive eternal life?

> I assure you, most solemnly I tell you, the person whose ears are open to My words [who listens to My message] and believes *and* trusts in *and* clings to *and* relies on Him Who sent Me has (possesses now) eternal life. And he does not come into judgment [does not incur sentence of judgment, will not come under condemnation], but he has already passed over out of death into life.   John 5:24 Amplified

Often we think of eternal life as merely living forever after death (future) instead of something we receive at salvation and can experience now.

The word "life" is the Greek word *zoe* which refers to the principle of life in the spirit and soul (as opposed to life in the body). *Zoe* represents the highest and best, which Christ is and which He gives to those who believe in Him. It is God's quality of life, which is given to His children. We can better experience *zoe*, God's quality of life, the more we know, perceive, recognize, become acquainted with, and understand God as He really is.

3. Remembering the above definition, read the following verses and write below your observations concerning "eternal life."

> In order that everyone who believes in Him [who cleaves to Him, trusts Him, and relies on Him] may *not perish, but* have eternal life *and* [actually] live forever! For God so greatly loved *and* dearly prized the world, that He [even] gave up His only begotten (unique) Son, so that whoever believes in (trusts in, clings to, relies on) Him shall not perish (come to destruction, be lost) but have eternal (everlasting) life.   John 3:15-16 Amplified

© COPYRIGHT 1998, 2001, 2005, 2007 SCOPE MINISTRIES INTERNATIONAL INC.

> The thief (Satan) comes only in order to steal and kill and destroy. I (Jesus) came that they may have *and* enjoy life, and have it in abundance (to the full, till it overflows).
> John 10:10 Amplified

> For this is My Father's will *and* His purpose, that everyone who sees the Son and believes in *and* cleaves to *and* trusts in *and* relies on Him should have eternal life, and I will raise Him up [from the dead] at the last day. I assure you, most solemnly I tell you, he who believes *in Me* [who adheres to, trusts in, relies on and has faith in Me] has (now possesses) eternal life.
> John 6:40,47 Amplified

> I write this to you who believe in (adhere to, trust in, and rely on) the name of the Son of God [in the peculiar services and blessings conferred by Him on men], so that you may know [with settled and absolute knowledge] that you [already] have life, yes, eternal life.
> I John 5:13 Amplified

4. What new understanding do these verses give you concerning "eternal life"?

5. God is eternal life, the source of all life. Apart from Him there is no real life. He has chosen to give His life to those who will believe, and who receive Jesus' offer of forgiveness and eternal life. If you have never personally received Jesus as your life you may do this now by simply taking Him at His word and accepting the gift of His life.

> But to as many as did receive *and* welcome Him, He gave the authority (power, privilege, right) to become the children of God, that is, to those who believe in (adhere to, trust in, and rely on) His name.
> John 1:12 Amplified

© COPYRIGHT1998, 2001, 2005, 2007 SCOPE MINISTRIES INTERNATIONAL INC.

Understanding the Good News - Day Five

Goal: To learn how the "good news" applies to your daily life.

1. Eternal life is not just longevity of life but God's quality of life that is to be experienced now, in the midst of life's problems. How does this give you hope in your situation?

2. How would believing that God has completely forgiven you, unconditionally loves you, and totally accepts you change the way you relate to God when you sin?

3. Eternal life is experienced through knowing, recognizing, and becoming acquainted with God (John 17:3). We can experience God's quality of life because Christ died so that we can live.

> For if while we were enemies we were reconciled to God through the death of His Son, much more, having been reconciled, we shall be saved by His life (in us).
>
> Romans 5:10 NAS

Our salvation is not merely an event in our past, but it is to be our ongoing daily experience. As we call upon Jesus in the midst of life's problems, we can experience God's power to deliver us from the bondage of sin.

Salvation is the present experience of God's power to deliver from the bondage of sin. In what areas of your life do you need to experience Christ's deliverance from sin? (See definition of "sin" on 2.4.)

© COPYRIGHT 1998, 2001, 2005, 2007 SCOPE MINISTRIES INTERNATIONAL INC.

4. Read the following verses and under each one write, in your own words, God's promise to you in your present situation.

> For I am persuaded beyond doubt (am sure) that neither death nor life, nor angels nor principalities, nor things impending *and* threatening nor things to come, nor powers, nor height nor depth, nor anything else in all creation will be able to separate us from the love of God which is in Christ Jesus our Lord.   Romans 8:38-39 Amplified

Example: There is nothing from my past or in my present or in my future that will cause God to stop loving me.

> For He [God] Himself has said, I will not in any way fail you *nor* give you up *nor* leave you without support. [I will] not, [I will] not, [I will] not in any degree leave you helpless *nor* forsake *nor* let [you] down (relax My hold on you)! [Assuredly not!]
> Hebrews 13:5b Amplified

> Do not fear, for I am with you; do not anxiously look about you, for I am your God. I will strengthen you, surely I will help you, surely I will uphold you with My righteous right hand.   Isaiah 41:10 NAS

> [Not in your own strength] for it is God Who is all the while effectually at work in you [energizing and creating in you the power and desire], both to will and to work for His good pleasure *and* satisfaction *and* delight.   Philippians 2:13 Amplified

> And I am convinced *and* sure of this very thing, that He Who began a good work in you will continue until the day of Jesus Christ [right up to the time of His return], developing [that good work] *and* perfecting *and* bringing it to full completion in you.
> Philippians 1:6 Amplified

5. According to what God has promised, is there any reason for you not to have hope? Why or why not?

6. Spend some time thanking God for His promises to you.

2.20

© COPYRIGHT 1998, 2001, 2005, 2007 SCOPE MINISTRIES INTERNATIONAL INC.

Understanding the Good News - Lesson Two

Name_____Date_____

Answer the following questions. To turn in page to small group leader, use identical perforated page in back of book.

1. What has your understanding of salvation been before this lesson?

2. What new understanding of the "good news" did you gain from this lesson?

3. When did you personally believe the "good news" and receive eternal life?

4. Is there anything you have done that you believe God has not forgiven? If so, what?

5. How confident are you of God's presence in your daily life?

6. What wrong beliefs did you recognize from this week's lesson?

7. Mark the graph to indicate how much of this week's assignment you completed.

None	50%	100%

© COPYRIGHT 1998, 2001, 2005, 2007 SCOPE MINISTRIES INTERNATIONAL INC.

Record Your Prayer Requests:

_____

_____

_____

_____

_____

_____

_____

_____

_____

_____

_____

_____

_____

_____

_____

_____

_____

© COPYRIGHT 1998, 2001, 2005, 2007 SCOPE MINISTRIES INTERNATIONAL INC.

Seeing Ourselves As God Sees Us

When someone becomes a Christian he becomes a brand new person inside. He is not the same any more. A new life has begun!

2 Corinthians 5:17 LB

Lesson 3

A Life Transformed

Much of my life I performed to try to gain the acceptance from people — from my family, from my friends, and especially from God. I believed that to be liked and respected, I had to accomplish something to prove myself worthy of their approval.

Many of my childhood experiences developed this belief. Whenever I showed my report card to my parents they didn't say, "Good job for the A's and B's," but "Why the C's? Can't you do any better than that?" I also noticed that the athletes were always the popular people at school. They were asked to parties. They were recognized for their accomplishments. Everyone wanted to be with them. Because I was never athletic, I felt unaccepted and not worthy of attention from my peers.

I carried this false belief into my relationship with God. Who got the recognition in church? Usually they were the overseas missionary, the one with perfect church attendance for 100 years, and the person who gave a lot of money. My definition of a saint was someone who taught Sunday School for 30 years! I hadn't accomplished these things, so I knew I wasn't important there either.

I believed that I had to work to get God's approval by having a quiet time every morning, memorizing two Bible verses every week, and witnessing to anyone and everyone — especially to anyone sitting next to me on an airplane! But as much as I tried to please God, there was always something more that I should have done.

Maybe I should have joined the church choir.

to be continued...

© COPYRIGHT1998, 2001, 2005, 2007 SCOPE MINISTRIES INTERNATIONAL INC.

Seeing Ourselves As God Sees Us - Lesson Three

For definition of terms as Scope understands and uses them, see Appendix A Page 9.26.

The "good news" of the Gospel has many implications, including what is true about ourselves. These basic life beliefs about ourselves were developed from our experiences in this fallen world, not from God's Word. This lesson will help us recognize our corrupted beliefs about ourselves which contradict who God has made us to be.

We Were Created in the Image of God

The way we were designed by God corresponds to His purpose in creating us. Remember, we were created to be the friend and companion of God, to live by His life within us and to express His character.

> So God created man in His own image, in the image *and* likeness of God He created him; male and female He created them.   Genesis 1:27 Amplified

We Are Made of Three Basic Parts: Body, Soul, and Spirit

Scripture addresses us as whole beings. It uses the terms *body*, *soul*, and *spirit* to teach us how we are to function within that whole.

> Then the Lord God formed man from the dust of the ground [body] and breathed into his nostrils the breath *or* spirit of life [spirit], and the man became a living being [soul].
> Genesis 2:7 Amplified

God formed our bodies from the earth, so we can relate to the physical world. He gave us a human spirit so we can relate to Him. We became a living soul, so we can know and relate to both the visible, physical world, and the invisible, spiritual world.

> And may the God of peace Himself sanctify you through and through; . . .and may your spirit and soul and body be preserved sound *and* complete [and found] blameless at the coming of our Lord Jesus Christ (the Messiah). 1 Thessalonians 5:23 Amplified

The analogy of a tree helps us understand our three-part nature.

Because a tree also has three parts, it helps illustrate how our body, soul, and spirit combine to make us a whole person.

Like the leaves, our body is the most visible and changing aspect of who we are. Our body has physical needs such as nourishment, exercise, and rest. Our body is our means of "doing" and of relating to the world through our five senses. Our body is temporal and visible.

© COPYRIGHT 1998, 2001, 2005, 2007 SCOPE MINISTRIES INTERNATIONAL INC.

Just as the trunk gives the tree its unique form, so the soul gives us our unique personality. Our soul has needs such as to be loved, accepted, and significant. Our soul includes our mind to know God, our emotions to enjoy God, and our will to obey God. Our soul expresses our thoughts, feelings, and choices. It is our means of relating to others.

The roots of a tree are not visible; however, they are the most important aspect of the tree. A tree without roots is no longer a tree. In the same way, a body without a spirit is dead. The spirit gives us life and determines our identity. The spirit was made to receive life from God. The spirit is our means of knowing and responding to God, Who is Spirit. Our human spirit is eternal and invisible.

At Creation

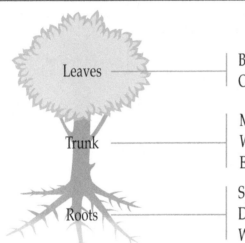

Leaves

Body had capacity for immortality
Obedient to God's ways

Trunk

Mind dependent on spirit for truth
Will in harmony with self and others
Emotions expressed God's character

Roots

Spirit alive and relating to God
Desired to please God
Was God's image bearer

Because of Sin, Man's Spirit is Born Dead to God

Man's choice to live independently of God brought about spiritual death. Spiritual death is the separation of man's spirit from God.

Man's separation from God affected all three parts of his nature.

Being separated from God, the human spirit could no longer receive revelation from God; therefore, man's soul began to determine truth for himself. Void of truth as God defines it, man's mind became darkened, lacking spiritual understanding, believing lies as truth. With his mind deceived, his will became rebellious, and his emotions became controlling. His body began to die and became an instrument of sin.

> For all have sinned and fallen short of the glory of God.
> Romans 3:23 NAS

> For they exchanged the truth of God for a lie, and worshiped and served the creature rather than the Creator, who is blessed forever. Amen. Romans 1:25 NAS

© COPYRIGHT1998, 2001, 2005, 2007 SCOPE MINISTRIES INTERNATIONAL INC.

Believing lies as truth, man lived to gratify himself and to meet his own needs. Having his focus in life on himself, man became selfish and prone to sinful behavior. This is the condition in which we are all born: self-serving and enslaved to sin.

> And just as they did not see fit to acknowledge God any longer, God gave them over to a depraved mind, to do those things which are not proper, being filled with all unrighteousness, . . .and, although they know the ordinance of God, that those who practice such things are worthy of death, they not only do the same, but also give hearty approval to those who practice them.
>
> Romans 1: 28-29a, 32 NAS

At Separation

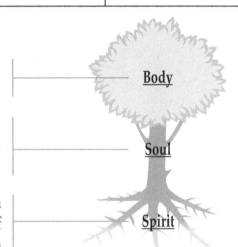

Mortal, weakened and dying
Disobedient to God's ways

— **Body**

Mind darkened, beliefs corrupted
Will enslaved to sin, self-serving
Emotions controlling

— **Soul**

Spirit dead to God, alive to sin
Desired to please self
Child of Satan

— **Spirit**

Jesus Christ Restores God's Image in Us

Christ's death on the cross accomplished more than the forgiveness of our sins. The cross is the instrument of death for our old nature and identity. When Christ died, our old sinful nature died with Him. When Christ was buried, our old identity was buried with Him. When Christ was raised from the dead, we were raised with Him to a brand new life:

- Old sinful nature was crucified with Christ;

> For we know that our old self was crucified with Him so that the body of sin might be done away with, that we should no longer be slaves to sin. Romans 6:6 NIV

- Our spirit is made new and indwelt by Christ's Spirit (Romans 8:9-10);
- Our spirit is now dead to sin and is alive to God (Romans 6:11); and
- We are a new creation with a totally new identity.

> Therefore, if anyone is in Christ, he is a new creation; the old has gone, the new has come! 2 Corinthians 5:17 NIV

© COPYRIGHT 1998, 2001, 2005, 2007 SCOPE MINISTRIES INTERNATIONAL INC.

Christ has given us a brand new identity.

As spirit-born children of God, we have a new nature and identity. God's Word describes how God now sees us. God no longer judges us according to our deeds or performance but according to our spirit. As God's children we are:

- totally and completely forgiven (Ephesians 1:7; Colossians 2:13-14);
- completely acceptable and accepted (Romans 15:7; Ephesians 1:4);
- absolutely righteous (Ephesians 4:24; 2 Corinthians 5:21);
- perfect in Christ (Hebrews 10:14);
- holy and blameless (Colossians 1:22);
- complete, whole, adequate (Colossians 2:10);
- possessing the mind of Christ (1 Corinthians 2:16); and
- loving, joyful, peaceful, patient, kind, etc. (Galatians 5:22-23).

Our spirit is now indwelt by God's Spirit:

- Our spirit has been sealed with the Holy Spirit (Ephesians 1:13);
- We are now one spirit with Christ (1 Corinthians 6:17);
- Our body is the temple of the Holy Spirit (1 Corinthians 3:16); and
- The Holy Spirit desires to live through our soul and body (Galatians 2:20).

At Restoration

Body
Will be made new in the future

Soul
Is being renewed in the present

Spirit
Has been made new in the past

Temple of the Holy Spirit and an instrument of righteousness
Still dying, not yet redeemed
Will be glorified—given a new body

Mind—has capacity of being renewed
Will—can be empowered by Holy Spirit
Emotions—can be God honoring, and express God's heart

Made new and alive to God
Indwelt and sealed with God's Spirit
All of Christ's nature is in me—desires to please God

Now That We Are New Creations, Why Do We Still Sin?

We still have a three-fold enemy.

Our spirit has been made new, and sin no longer indwells or affects our spirit (I John 3:9). However, **indwelling sin** still resides in our body and affects our soul (Romans 7:17, 20-21). Indwelling sin is like a melody that lingers after the song is over. It is the memory of the old way of life, with its beliefs, thoughts, feelings, and habits. But this is **not** who we are!

© COPYRIGHT 1998, 2001, 2005, 2007 SCOPE MINISTRIES INTERNATIONAL INC.

But if I am doing the very thing I do not wish, I am no longer the one doing it, but sin which dwells in me. I find then the principle that evil is present in me, the one who wishes to do good.

Romans 7:20-21 NAS

Satan tempts us by appealing to the memory of the old nature to entice us to walk in our old ways rather than by the Spirit. His strategy is to deceive us into believing that we have not really been changed.

Satan uses the **world system** to deceive us into believing lies as truth. The world tries to conform us into its way of thinking (Romans 12:2) and to appeal to our old desires (1 John 2:16).

We are still prone to walking according to the flesh.

We base most of our beliefs about ourselves on the world system, not on God's Word. Our habit has been to rely on our soul and body, not our spirit. Our soul and body controlled by indwelling sin is called the *flesh*. Our soul continually needs to be renewed with truth and filled with God's Spirit (Romans 12:1-2, Ephesians 5:18).

Why We Still Sin

Indwelling sin still resides in body
Satan tempts us
World system tries to conform us

Mind—is unrenewed
Will—not yielded to the Holy Spirit
Emotions—control behavior

Our soul and body controlled by the outward expression or indwelling sin called the flesh.

Still without sin
Righteous and Holy
New Creation

Satan

Indwelling Sin

World System

Flesh

Soul

Christ in You

But I say, walk by the Spirit, and you will not carry out the desire of the flesh. For the flesh sets its desire against the Spirit, and the Spirit against the flesh; for these are in opposition to one another, so that you may not do the things that you please.

Galatians 5:16-17 NAS

© COPYRIGHT1998, 2001, 2005, 2007 SCOPE MINISTRIES INTERNATIONAL INC.

We Can Experience Our New Identity!

We can progressively become outwardly (in our soul and body) who God has made us in our spirit.

The **GOAL** of experiencing your new identity is to become like Christ (Romans 8:29). This is not accomplished by our own activities and works but by God who works in us (Philippians 2:13). This is **100% God's part** (I Thessalonians 5:24).

The **MEANS** of becoming like Christ has already been given to us by God. The Holy Spirit is a person, not just a divine power (John 14:16-17). The Holy Spirit is the one who enables us to understand and experience who we are in Christ (John 16:12-13). This is also **100% God's part**.

The **METHOD** of experiencing our new identity in Christ is to respond to God **by faith** (Hebrews 11:1, 6; Colossians 2:6, 1 John 5:4-5). We must accept by **faith** the power of the cross (that our old sinful nature was permanently crucified with Christ) and embrace the reality of our new resurrection life (having been raised up with Christ) (Romans 5:10; 6:5-6). This is **100% our part**. We are to recognize and receive the free gift of salvation and live in the conscious reality of that gift (Colossians 2:6; Ephesians 2:8-10).

- Our part is to accept by faith what God says is true about Himself and who we are in our new nature (1 John 4:17; Romans 8:11,16).

> I have been crucified with Christ; and it is no longer I who live, but Christ lives in me; and the *life* which I now live in the flesh I live by faith in the Son of God, who loved me, and delivered Himself up for me. Galatians 2:20 NAS

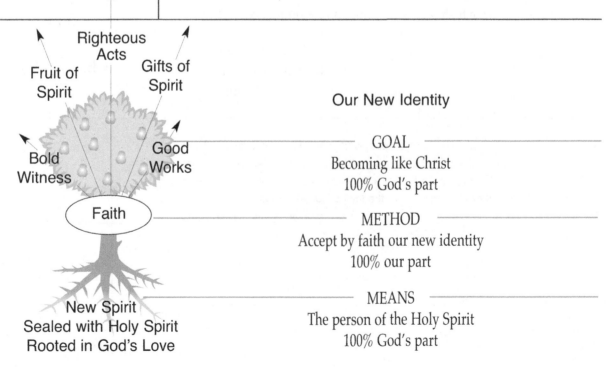

Our New Identity

—— GOAL ——
Becoming like Christ
100% God's part

—— METHOD ——
Accept by faith our new identity
100% our part

—— MEANS ——
The person of the Holy Spirit
100% God's part

Righteous Acts
Fruit of Spirit
Gifts of Spirit
Bold Witness
Good Works
Faith
New Spirit
Sealed with Holy Spirit
Rooted in God's Love

© COPYRIGHT 1998, 2001, 2005, 2007 SCOPE MINISTRIES INTERNATIONAL INC.

This involves a conscious choice to reject the lies we have believed about ourselves and to replace them with the truth of what God says in the Bible. We must make this choice each time we realize we are believing a lie.

The Truest Thing About Us is What God Says!

We must learn to act upon the truth regardless of our feelings, experiences or present circumstances, or others' opinions (Philippians 3:12-14).

This is not passivity or inactivity. True faith is participating in a relationship with Christ, surrendering to the Holy Spirit, and trusting Him to live through us. Experiencing our new identity in Christ involves living by the truth of the Spirit rather than the memory of the old nature.

The truest thing about me is what God says. Not what I think or feel and not what others say or think or do. The truth about me is always what God says!

SUMMARY:

1. We have a three-part nature consisting of our body, soul, and spirit.

2. We were created in the image of God, to display the character of God. The Fall affected all three parts of our nature, and our spirit died to God.

3. Christ's death on the cross is what restores God's image in us and gives us a new spirit and a new identity.

4. We still sin because we have a three-fold enemy: indwelling sin; Satan; and the world system.

5. To become more like Christ, we must accept by faith the fact of our new identity and depend on the person of the Holy Spirit to transform our life.

© COPYRIGHT 1998, 2001, 2005, 2007 SCOPE MINISTRIES INTERNATIONAL INC.

A Life Transformed, con't.

When I began to learn who I am in Christ, I no longer needed to perform to gain acceptance of God and others. He says that I am complete in Christ, that I am adequate, righteous, holy, that I am a joint heir with Christ, and that I share equally in His inheritance. I am a saint, and I never even taught Sunday School! Wow!

My life is different because my beliefs are different.

As a young adult, I was reserved and shy and had a hard time introducing myself to people, individually or in a group. If people didn't introduce themselves to me, I felt as if nobody liked me and that they had rejected me because I wasn't acceptable as Rob. I had to earn their acceptance. Now I know I can go into a group of people and be confident of myself because I am confident about my position in Christ and my attributes in Christ.

When I saw a person who had an asset or strength that I wanted, my standard was to be like that person. Because I was not that person, I never could reach that standard, and I felt unacceptable. Now I don't compare myself with others. For example, I love to listen to the radio commentator Paul Harvey. He's a very eloquent communicator and an excellent storyteller. I would love to be like him, but the truth is that I'm not Paul Harvey. I'm just an ol' country redneck from Oklahoma, but I don't feel unacceptable any more. I understand my strengths, and I no longer have to be like somebody else.

If I'm not in church every time the door is open, I don't feel guilty. My motivation to have a quiet time and memorize Scripture is not to gain approval by God. Now I do these things because He first loved me, and I want to know Him more.

I now know that I don't have to work to be accepted by anybody, including God. John 8:32 says, "You shall know the truth. And the truth will set you free." He has set me free!

Rob - Real Estate Management

© COPYRIGHT 1998, 2001, 2005, 2007 SCOPE MINISTRIES INTERNATIONAL INC.

Seeing Ourselves As God Sees Us - Day One

Goal: To understand what Scripture teaches about the nature of a child of God.

Before we can address our problem from God's perspective, we must first see ourselves from God's perspective.

It is important to realize that the dominant image of man in Scripture is as a whole being. That is, the terms *body, soul,* and *spirit* are frequently used interchangeably to mean "life." For example, Romans 12:1 teaches us to present our bodies to God.

> I urge you therefore, brethren, by the mercies of God, to present your bodies a living and holy sacrifice, acceptable to God, *which is* your spiritual service of worship.
>
> Romans 12:1 NAS

When we present our bodies to God, we present our whole life.

Although Scripture addresses us as whole beings, it uses the terms *body, soul* and *spirit,* also to teach us how we are to function within that whole.

> Now may the God of peace Himself sanctify you entirely; and may your spirit and soul and body be preserved complete, without blame at the coming of our Lord Jesus Christ.
>
> I Thessalonians 5:23 NAS

1. What do the following passages tell you about the human spirit?

> Then shall the dust [out of which God made man's body] return to the earth as it was, and the spirit shall return to God Who gave it.　　Ecclesiastes 12:7 Amplified

> God is a Spirit (a spiritual Being) and those who worship Him must worship *Him* in spirit and in truth (reality).　　John 4:24 Amplified

> The Spirit Himself [thus] testifies together with our own spirit, [assuring us] that we are children of God.　　Romans 8:16 Amplified

© COPYRIGHT 1998, 2001, 2005, 2007 SCOPE MINISTRIES INTERNATIONAL INC.

Remembering that the body is our vehicle of performance or doing, our soul is our thinking, feeling and choosing, and our spirit is our life and identity.

2. List the characteristics of your old identity found in Ephesians 2:1-3; 4:17-22 as they relate to your body, soul, and spirit.

3. List the characteristics of your new identity in Christ found in Ezekiel 36:26-27, Romans 6:11, Romans 8:10, 16, Ephesians 4:24, Colossians 3:10-12, Galatians 5:22-23, and as they relate to your body, soul, and spirit.

Old Identity   New Identity

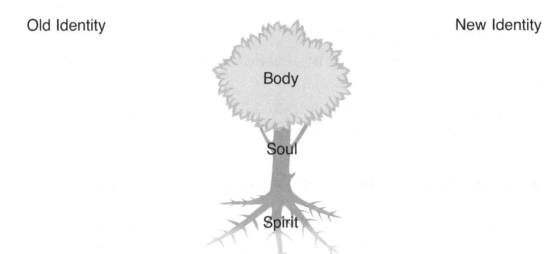

4. Read the article, "What Is Man", on page 3.23.

5. Based on what you have learned, what kind of nature do Christians have?

6. Write a thank-you note to God expressing gratefulness for His giving you a new spirit (nature).

© COPYRIGHT1998, 2001, 2005, 2007 SCOPE MINISTRIES INTERNATIONAL INC.

Seeing Ourselves As God Sees Us - Day Two

Goal: To begin creating a Christian identity.

The following verses reveal that at salvation we were made into new beings. Although this is a reality, the understanding of our new nature must become ingrained into the very fabric of our identity. Remember that your spirit has been changed, but your soul is in the process of being renewed.

> A new heart will I give you and a new spirit will I put within you, and I will take away the stony heart out of your flesh and give you a heart of flesh. And I will put My Spirit within you . . .
> Ezekiel 36:26-27a Amplified

> Therefore, if any man is in Christ, he is a new creature, the old things passed away; behold, new things have come.
> 2 Corinthians 5:17 NAS

Read "Becoming Who You Already Are" on page 3.27.

1. Select five statements from the first column on page 3.28 which reflect how you most often view yourself and write them below.	2. Now write out the corresponding truth from the second column and one of the verses given in the third column.	3. Write any thoughts or feelings you have which contradict this truth.

© COPYRIGHT 1998, 2001, 2005, 2007 SCOPE MINISTRIES INTERNATIONAL INC.

4. How do these negative thoughts affect your daily life?

    your behavior?

    your emotions?

    your relationships?

5. How do your negative thoughts and beliefs about yourself relate to your presenting problem from Week One - Day One?

6. The truest thing about you is what God says! These amazing truths must so permeate your thinking that they define how you see yourself so that you see life in light of who you are in Christ. Spend a few minutes thanking God for your salvation and for giving you a new spirit and a new identity.

© COPYRIGHT 1998, 2001, 2005, 2007 SCOPE MINISTRIES INTERNATIONAL INC.

Seeing Ourselves As God Sees Us - Day Three

Goal: To understand the person and role of the Holy Spirit in our lives.

1. The Holy Spirit is a person, not just a "power." Jesus calls Him, "the Spirit of Truth," "the Comforter," and "the Helper." After each verse below write the role of the Holy Spirit in the Christian's life.

> But the Comforter (Counselor, Helper, Intercessor, Advocate, Strengthener, Standby), the Holy Spirit, Whom the Father will send in My Name [in My place, to represent Me and act on My behalf], He will teach you all things. And He will cause you to recall (will remind you of, bring to your remembrance) everything I have told you.
>
> John 14:26 Amplified

> But when the Comforter (Counselor, Helper, Advocate, Intercessor, Strengthener, Standby) comes, Whom I will send to you from the Father, the Spirit of Truth Who comes (proceeds) from the Father, He [Himself] will testify regarding Me.
>
> John 15:26 Amplified

> But when He, the Spirit of Truth (the Truth-giving Spirit) comes, He will guide you into all the Truth (the whole, full Truth). For He will not speak His own message [on His own authority]; but He will tell whatever He hears [from the Father; He will give the message that has been given to Him], and He will announce *and* declare to you the things that are to come [that will happen in the future].   John 16:13 Amplified

> Such hope never disappoints *or* deludes *or* shames us, for God's love has been poured out in our hearts through the Holy Spirit Who has been given to us.
>
> Romans 5:5 Amplified

© COPYRIGHT 1998, 2001, 2005, 2007 SCOPE MINISTRIES INTERNATIONAL INC.

So too the [Holy] Spirit comes to our aid *and* bears us up in our weakness; for we do not know what prayer to offer *nor* how to offer it worthily as we ought, but the Spirit Himself goes to meet our supplication *and* pleads in our behalf with unspeakable yearnings *and* groanings too deep for utterance.   Romans 8:26 Amplified

Now we have not received the spirit [that belongs to] the world, but the [Holy] Spirit Who is from God, [given to us] that we might realize *and* comprehend *and* appreciate the gifts [of divine favor and blessing so freely and lavishly] bestowed on us by God.
                                                                                1 Corinthians 2:12 Amplified

But the fruit of the [Holy] Spirit [the work which His presence within accomplishes] is love, joy (gladness), peace, patience (an even temper, forbearance), kindness, goodness (benevolence), faithfulness, gentleness (meekness, humility), self-control (self-restraint, continence). Against such things there is no law [that can bring a charge].
                                                                                Galatians 5:22-23 Amplified

2. Review your answers to question 1 and identify the areas for which you have been feeling responsible but which are actually the responsibility of the Holy Spirit.

3. The Holy Spirit is responsible for conforming us to Christ. Express your gratitude to God for the Holy Spirit's presence and ministry in your life. Admit to God the areas in which you have not acknowledged the Holy Spirit or depended on Him for your spiritual development.

© COPYRIGHT1998, 2001, 2005, 2007 SCOPE MINISTRIES INTERNATIONAL INC.

Seeing Ourselves As God Sees Us - Day Four

Goal: To recognize that your part in experiencing your new identity is to live by faith.

The method of experiencing your new identity is to live by faith. Faith is taking God at His Word. Faith is our response to the revelation of Who God is and what He has done for us through Christ. Faith is a gift of God (Ephesians 2:8-9) which can increase over time, much like a muscle that grows stronger with use.

1. What does the following verse tell you regarding how we are saved?

> Because if you acknowledge *and* confess with your lips that Jesus is Lord and in your heart believe (adhere to, trust in, and rely on the truth) that God raised Him from the dead, you will be saved. For with the heart a person believes (adheres to, trusts in, and relies on Christ) and so is justified (declared righteous, acceptable to God), and with the mouth He confesses (declares openly and speaks out freely his faith) *and* confirms [his] salvation. Romans 10:9-10 Amplified

2. What does the following verse say regarding faith?

> So faith *comes* from hearing, and hearing by the Word of Christ. Romans 10:17, NAS

3. What does Colossians 2:6 say about how we are to walk (live moment by moment)?

> As you therefore have received Christ Jesus the Lord, so walk in Him.
> Colossians 2:6 NAS

4. According to Galatians 2:20, how are you to live?

> I have been crucified with Christ [in Him I have shared His crucifixion]; it is no longer I who live, but Christ (the Messiah) lives in me; and the life I now live in the body I live by faith in (by adherence to and reliance on and complete trust in) the Son of God, Who loved me and gave Himself up for me. Galatians 2:20 Amplified

© COPYRIGHT 1998, 2001, 2005, 2007 SCOPE MINISTRIES INTERNATIONAL INC.

5. Faith is not a feeling, nor is it intellectual knowledge. Who is to be the object of our faith, according to Hebrews 12:1-2?

> Therefore, since we have so great a cloud of witnesses surrounding us, let us also lay aside every encumbrance, and the sin which so easily entangles us, and let us run with endurance the race that is set before us, fixing our eyes on Jesus, the author and perfecter of faith, who for the joy set before Him endured the cross, despising the shame, and has sat down at the right hand of the throne of God. Hebrews 12:1-2 NAS

We are not to put faith in our faith. Biblical faith is trust and reliance on the person and character of God. As you confess your new identity with your mouth and believe in your heart what God has said, the Holy Spirit will make it real in your experience (in God's time, not yours).

6. Spend a few minutes thanking God for your new identity (be specific), and express your trust in Him to make it your experience through the power of the Holy Spirit.

© COPYRIGHT 1998, 2001, 2005, 2007 SCOPE MINISTRIES INTERNATIONAL INC.

Seeing Ourselves As God Sees Us - Day Five

Goal: To understand how to experience your new identity, practically, in your daily life.

Experiencing your new identity is more than just a matter of replacing negative thoughts with more positive ones. It is the result of relating to God and believing what He says about who you are in Christ. Daily you choose to put off the old identity and put on your new identity.

1. Read the following passage several times.

> This I say therefore, and affirm together with the Lord, that you walk no longer just as the Gentiles also walk, in the futility of their mind,
>
> being darkened in their understanding, excluded from the life of God, because of the ignorance that is in them, because of the hardness of their heart;
>
> and they, having become callous, have given themselves over to sensuality, for the practice of every kind of impurity with greediness.
>
> But you did not learn Christ in this way, if indeed you have heard Him and have been taught in Him, just as truth is in Jesus,
>
> that, in reference to your former manner of life, you lay aside the old self (identity), which is being corrupted in accordance with the lusts of deceit,
>
> and that you be renewed in the spirit of your mind,
>
> and put on the new self, which in the likeness *of* God has been created in righteousness and holiness of the truth.   Ephesians 4:17-24 NAS

2. Ask the Holy Spirit to bring to your mind one area in your life where you are not presently experiencing your new identity in Christ.

3. Ask the Holy Spirit to show you the lies you are believing in this area of your life and the thoughts that need to be replaced with God's Truth. Write the lie that is to be put off and the truth that is to be put on.

© COPYRIGHT 1998, 2001, 2005, 2007 SCOPE MINISTRIES INTERNATIONAL INC.

4. For each lie you listed, write the truth about your new identity on a 3 x 5 card or post-it note, along with a corresponding verse of Scripture (refer to Day Two's handout, "Becoming Who You Already Are"). Now place these in prominent places (such as the bathroom mirror, refrigerator, dash of car, etc.) so you will be reminded of the truth throughout the day. When reminded of the truth, thank God (out loud if possible) for what is really true about you "in Christ." Continue this daily for the next three weeks.

© COPYRIGHT 1998, 2001, 2005, 2007 SCOPE MINISTRIES INTERNATIONAL INC.

Seeing Ourselves As God Sees Us - Lesson Three

Name _____ Date _____

Answer the following questions. To turn in page to small group leader, use identical perforated page in back of book.

1. According to what you have learned about the nature of man, what changed in you at salvation?

2. How does understanding that you have a new nature give you confidence concerning your salvation and spiritual growth?

3. What wrong beliefs about yourself do you need to put off?

4. How would believing your new identity and relying on the Holy Spirit in your daily life affect the way you respond to your present problems?

5. What questions do you have concerning the nature of man and your new identity?

6. Mark the graph to indicate how much of this week's assignment you completed.

None	50%	100%

© COPYRIGHT 1998, 2001, 2005, 2007 SCOPE MINISTRIES INTERNATIONAL INC.

Record Your Prayer Requests:

© COPYRIGHT1998, 2001, 2005, 2007 SCOPE MINISTRIES INTERNATIONAL INC.

What Is Man?

Supporting Article for "Seeing Ourselves As God Sees Us"
by Jim Craddock

After surveying the wonders and vastness of the universe, David was incredulous that God would even think about and care for man, let alone crown him with glory and honor. To David, man was insignificant when compared with the magnitude of God's created universe. However, to God, the universe was insignificant when compared to what He had created man to be.

When I consider Your heavens, the work of Your fingers, the moon and stars, which You have ordained; what is man that You are mindful of him, the son of man, that You care for him? You have made him a little lower than the heavenly beings, and crowned him with glory and honor. You have made him rule over the works of Your hands; You put everything under his feet.

Psalm 8:3-6 NIV

David's musing made him ask the question that has been asked since time immemorial—"What is man?" Man has always been fascinated with himself. Since the Fall, man has been self-centered and self-focused. Yet, as the centuries have come and gone, man, apart from God, has never been able to answer this basic question— "What am I?"

I have long stated a basic life-principle. It is this: To know man you must know God! It is in our understanding of God that we can understand man. The more a person knows of God, the more he or she will know of themselves. This is basic to a victorious Christian walk.

Consequently, if we want to know the essence of man, and I mean by "essence" his basic nature, then we need to know the nature of God. There are three very basic things that stand out about God in Scripture. The first, stated by Jesus in John's Gospel, is that

God is spirit, and those who worship Him must worship in spirit and truth.

John 4:24 NAS

As God is essentially spirit, so man is essentially spirit. Therefore, the first thing we learn about man is that he is first and foremost a spiritual being.

Second, Jesus made it very clear that God is one God.

Jesus answered, "The first *and* principal *one of all commands* is: Hear, O Israel, The Lord our God is one Lord."   Mark 12:29 Amplified

Jesus was quoting Moses from Deut. 6:4. In other words, God is a whole Person—our God is One. As God is a unified whole, so man is a unified whole. As God is One, so man is one. The second thing we learn about man is that he is a unified being.

The third basic thing we see about God in Scripture is that He revealed Himself as a Triune God: God the Father, God the Son, and God the Holy Spirit. Jesus equated Himself with God when He said,

I and the Father are One.

John 10:30 Amplified

As the manifested essence of God's nature is triune, so is man's. The

Bible says that man is spirit, soul and body (1 Thess. 5:23). The third thing we learn about man is that he has a triune nature—consisting of three parts.

With this simple but basic knowledge, let us carry it a step further. As we see these three fundamental facts about man, the Bible reveals there are three ways to view man: man at creation, man at separation, and man at restoration. These are important because they have a direct bearing on man's nature.

When God created man, He created man with a nature prone to righteousness. Man had one nature, he was one being, and he was created to know and enjoy God while reflecting the image and character of God. Man in the Garden of Eden was both righteous and innocent, enjoying God and ruling over the vast domain that God had entrusted to him. This was man at creation.

However, as we all know from the Bible account, Satan came into the picture and convinced man to believe Satan's lies instead of God's truth. In a cataclysmic moment, man underwent a nature change. Instead of a nature prone to righteousness, man now had a nature prone to sin. Man in his fallen state, did not have a nature that was partly prone to righteousness and partly prone to evil; rather, he was absolutely and totally depraved. His nature was

© COPYRIGHT 1998, 2001, 2005, 2007 SCOPE MINISTRIES INTERNATIONAL INC.

permeated by indwelling Sin. Man was separated from God.

However, God never intended man to exist without His indwelling presence. What makes man *man* is God. Man without God is not man as God intended man to be. Thus, God initiated the whole redemptive process that culminated at the Cross, where God the Son became sin for man. In other words, God provided restoration for man.

God redeemed the human race, and when a person accepts Jesus Christ, that person is regenerated—he has become a new person! (Redemption is the act of God that makes it possible for a person to be regenerated.) What happens when a person receives Christ is a reversal of what happened at the Fall. A sinner receives Christ and undergoes a radical and permanent nature change. At the moment of conversion, man is given a new, righteous nature and is indwelt with the Spirit of God.

I think the Living Bible says it the best; For God took the sinless Christ and poured into Him our sins. Then in exchange, He poured God's goodness into us.   2 Corinthians 5:21 LB

At creation, man had one nature prone to righteousness. At separation man had one nature prone to evil. Now at restoration man has but one nature that is righteous. While having lost our innocence, we have gained Christ's righteousness!

It is at this point that there is a great deal of confusion. After a man is born again, does he have two natures?

Can he be both saint and sinner? (I challenge you to find a single verse in the New Testament that refers to the Christian as a sinner.) Certainly saints sin, but they are not sinners. The Bible simply does not teach that the Christian has a dual nature, one prone to righteousness and one prone to evil.

Now, I realize that red flags will come up for many. The Christian having a sin nature is a long evangelical tradition. Unfortunately, our evangelical traditions have a way of being taught as doctrine when, in truth, they cannot be supported by Scripture. The whole concept of a dual nature came about not through careful study of Scripture, but as a reaction to the holiness doctrine of entire sanctification. Entire sanctification teaches that we can reach a state in this life where it's impossible for us to sin.

To show you how pervasive evangelical traditions are, those of you who own a New American Standard Bible (NASB) will notice that halfway through Romans 7 they headline the topic as, "THE CONFLICT OF TWO NATURES." This is very interesting in that not only have the translators translated the Bible, they translated it for you according to their own interpretation. Remarkable! (By the way, I have used the NASB and enjoyed it since the day it was first introduced.)

As a new Christian, I was steeped in the signature teaching. I fully accepted the fact that there was a part of me that was and always would be opposed to God. I was taught what is called *positional truth*. My position

was in Christ. I was told that Christ didn't die for me, but for the Christ in me. That was my position.

Incredibly, this teaching implies that you have everything in Christ, but you can never experience it here on earth. It is yours, but *not* yours. Why? Because of the so-called "sin nature." It was like being given an assignment that could not be completed. Your position was something you could strive for but could never hope to experience. It was reserved in Heaven.

Slowly but surely, the Spirit of God guided me to what I call *relational truth*. This teaches that because of my relationship with Jesus, what He has promised is mine as my present possession! It is not something I must strive for, but something I have. It is not what I do, but who I am in Him that is most important. Unlike positional teaching that tends to make us a mutation (two-natured), relational teaching makes us partakers of the divine nature now!

The question that immediately comes to mind is, "If I have a nature that is righteous, why do I still do unrighteous things?" Isn't this proof that I have a sin nature? Paul had the same problem with the same question. Here is how he puts it,

For that which I am doing, I do not understand; for I am not practicing what I *would* like to *do*, but I am doing the very thing I hate. But if I do the very thing I do not wish *to do*, I agree with the Law, *confessing* that it is good. So now, no longer am I the one doing it, but sin which indwells me.

Romans 7:15-17 NAS

3.24

© COPYRIGHT1998, 2001, 2005, 2007 SCOPE MINISTRIES INTERNATIONAL INC.

He reiterates this point three times.

You will notice that Paul does not say "sin-nature." He says sin. Paul is not teaching here that man has a sinful nature, but that sin indwells his being. What he is speaking of is a principle of evil, an extremely powerful evil agent that infected man at the Fall, permeating his very being. The problem arises from a misunderstanding or confusion concerning indwelling sin.

Indwelling sin is something foreign to man. Sin was never intended to indwell man, but that is what happened. At the Fall, when man chose to live independent of God, sin ruled his whole being: spirit, soul and body. It is sin operating within a person that causes one to sin.

In non-believers, sin rules as the absolute ruler. Sin has full and free expression in and through the members of that person's body. What a person is, in sin, is what the Bible calls the "old man." What a person is, in Christ, is what the Bible calls the "new man."

Paul makes it very clear in Romans 5:12 - 8:17 that the "old man" was crucified, destroyed with Christ. What I was in Adam (the old man), has been done away with forever. What I am in Christ is guaranteed

forever. Since we are dead to sin and alive to God in Christ Jesus, we are not to let sin reign in our bodies. By faith, we are to consider ourselves dead to sin moment by moment.

It must be understood that my sins are no longer an issue. They died as an issue the moment I received Christ. The issue is Sin, not my sins. Christ dealt with Sin and my sins at the Cross (1 Peter 2:24), and the Holy Spirit effactually deals with the Sin problem as I walk by faith in Christ.

The principle of Sin needs two things to be activated. First, it needs the members of our bodies through which to find expression. Paul tells us to present the members of our body to God, as instruments of righteousness. (Romans 6:13).

Second, the principle of Sin gets its power from the law. Paul makes clear in Romans 7:8-9 that the power of Sin is in the law. God's solution is for us to die to the law and live and walk by the Spirit (Romans 7:6 and 8:4).

This means that I can live a holy life, a Godly walk. No, I am not talking about sinless perfection. I am talking about a victorious Christian life. In Christ I have exchanged my old life for a new one. I can enjoy all the benefits of that new life; they are mine as my present possession.

Therefore if any man is in Christ, *he* is a new creature; the old things passed away; behold, new things have come.

2 Corinthians 5:17 NAS

But all of this is negated if half of me is always prone to sin. The teaching of a dual nature robs me of my blessing in God. For all of what I said becomes a moot point. It can be enjoyed only in Heaven. What rubbish! God intends and made it abundantly possible—not just probable—for each and every one of us to live out our new identity in Christ and experience an abundant life (John 10:10).

It is crucially important that Romans 5:12 - 8:17 be studied as a whole. It is here that Paul deals with three very basic issues:

We are dead to sin

We have died to the law

We are alive to the Spirit

Paul's solution to the whole issue of Sin as a principle is this,
There is therefore now no condemnation for those who are in Christ Jesus. For the law of the Spirit of life in Christ Jesus has set you free from the law of sin and of death.

Romans 8:1-2 NAS

© COPYRIGHT 1998, 2001, 2005, 2007 SCOPE MINISTRIES INTERNATIONAL INC.

© COPYRIGHT1998, 2001, 2005, 2007 SCOPE MINISTRIES INTERNATIONAL INC.

Becoming Who You Already Are

Creating a Christian Identity - Supporting Article for "Seeing Ourselves As God Sees Us"
by Jim Craddock

There exists much confusion in the minds of thousands of Christians because of the contradiction they see between who they are because of their relationship with Christ (their new identity in Christ) and what they experience in their daily lives.

As we experience life, we are programmed by various influences to believe certain things about ourselves, whether they are true or not. As Christians, God has declared certain things to be true about us whether we experience them in our lives or not. Our tendency is to accept our reason, our emotions, our senses, and our circumstances as our absolute and final authority.

The truth of who you are in Christ becomes a reality in your life through a process the Bible calls "renewing the mind" (Romans 12:2). This process is dependent upon, first, the power of God through the working of the Holy Spirit, and secondly, a volitional act of faith on your part. God has given us His Holy Spirit to indwell us and empower us (Ephesians 5:18) and His Word to direct us (2 Timothy 3:16-17). Our part is to choose (an act of our will) to believe what God's Word says about us and to act upon this truth in our lives. As we are in the process of changing our "final authority" and renewing our minds, there will be a time-lag between our recognition of who we really are in Christ and our actual experience of these new truths in our daily lives.

As Christians, we entered into a new relationship with God. This relationship guarantees us a new identity (2 Corinthians 5:17). A new identity results in new experience and lifestyle. It is at this point that for many Christians a dilemma arises. Their experience tends to reflect their old way of life rather than their new identity in Christ. The song (the old life) has ended, but the melody lingers on. Our new identity, through our new relationship with Christ, guarantees a way out of this dilemma. The way out is in the process of renewing our minds. It is also described as "putting off and putting on" in Ephesians 4:22-24.

On the following page, you will find three columns. The first column will reflect the person you may think yourself to be. This old identity comes from your past life, based upon the final authorities of reason, emotions, senses, performance, experiences, and circumstances. The second column reflects what God has declared to be true about you in His Word. The third column offers verses for you to read and even memorize to give you a foundation for your faith.

It is imperative that you count God's Word as truth. This must become the final authority in your life. The time-lag between your beliefs and your experience will diminish as you begin accepting and standing on God's Word rather than your reason, emotions, senses, performance, or experiences. God's Word is true regardless of your experience.

© COPYRIGHT 1998, 2001, 2005, 2007 SCOPE MINISTRIES INTERNATIONAL INC.

Creating a Christian Identity

What I Feel or Think About Myself	What Is True About Me According to the Scripture	Scripture References
I am unworthy/unacceptable.	I am accepted/worthy.	Ps 139; Rom 15:7
I am alone.	I am never alone.	Heb 13:5b; Rom 8:38-39
I feel like a failure/inadequate.	I am adequate.	2 Cor 3:5-6; Phil 4:13
I have no confidence.	I have all the boldness/confidence I need.	Prov 3:26, 14:26, 28:1; Eph 3:12; Heb 10:19;
I feel responsible for my life.	God is responsible/faithful to me.	Ps 138:8; Phil 1:6, 2:13; 2 Thes 3:3
I am confused/think I am going crazy.	I have the mind of Christ.	1 Cor 2:16; 2 Tim 1:7; Eph 1:17
I am depressed/hopeless.	I have all the hope I need.	Ps 27:13, 31:24;Rom 15:13, 5:5; Heb 6:19
I am not good enough/imperfect.	I am perfect in Christ.	Heb 10:14; Col 2:10; Eph 2:10
There is nothing special about me.	I have been chosen/set apart by God.	Ps 139; 1 Cor 1:30, 6:11; 2 Thes 2:13
I don't have enough.	I have no lack.	Psalm 23:1; Phil 4:19
I am a fearful/anxious person.	I am free from fear.	Ps 34:4; 2 Tim 1:7; 1 Pet 5:7; 1 Jn 4:18
I lack faith.	I have all the faith I need.	Rom 10:17; 12:3, Heb 12:2
I am a weak person.	I am strong in Christ.	Dan 11:32; Is 58:11; Phil 4:13
I am defeated.	I am victorious.	Rom 8:37; 2 Cor 2:14; Jn 5:4
I am not very smart.	I have God's wisdom.	Prov 2:6-7; 1 Cor 1:30; Eph 1:17
I am in bondage.	I am free in Christ.	Ps 32:7; 2 Cor 3:17; Jn 8:36
I am miserable.	I have God's comfort.	Jn 16:7; 2 Cor 1:3-4
I have no one to take care of me.	I am protected/safe.	Ps 32:7; Ps 91
I am unloved.	I am very loved.	Jn 15:9; Rom 8:38-39; Eph 2:4, 5:1-2
I am unwanted/I don't belong to anyone.	I have been adopted by God. I am His child.	Rom 8:16-17; Gal 4:5; Eph 1:5; 1 Jn 3:1-2
I feel guilty.	I am totally forgiven/redeemed.	Ps 103:12; Eph 1:7; Col 1:14, 20; Col 2:13-14; Heb 10:10
I am a sinner.	I have been declared holy, righteous and justified. I am a saint.	Rom 3:24; 1 Cor 1:30, 6:11; 2 Cor 5:21
I have no strength.	I have God's power. I am indwelt with the Holy Spirit.	Acts 1:8; Rom 8:9-11; Eph 1:19, 3:16
I can't reach God.	I have direct access to God as a believer-priest.	Eph 2:6; Heb 10:19-20; 1 Pet 2:5,9
I feel condemned.	I am uncondemned/blameless.	Jn 3:18; Rom 8:1; Col 1:22
There is no direction/plan.	God does direct my life/He has a plan for me.	Ps 37:23, 138:8; Jer 29:11; Eph 2:10
I feel like nothing will ever change.	I've been given a brand new life.	2 Cor 5:17; Eph 4:22-24
I am afraid of Satan.	I have authority over Satan.	Col 1:13; 1 Jn 4:4; Rev 12:11
Sin overpowers me.	I am dead to sin.	Rom 6:6,11, 17-18

© COPYRIGHT1998, 2001, 2005, 2007 SCOPE MINISTRIES INTERNATIONAL INC.

Getting to Know Our Heavenly Father

If you had known Me, you would have known My Father also;
from now on you know Him, and have seen Him . . . He who
has seen Me has seen the Father . . .

John 14:7, 9b NAS

Lesson 4

A Life Transformed

Three years ago, I didn't want to live. I was controlled by fear and shame. I couldn't look anyone in the eye.

And I was a Christian. I spoke the "right" words from my mouth about who God is. I talked as if I knew Him and I had a relationship with Him, but, deep inside, the thought of God as my loving Father physically made me sick. I believed that God lurked in the shadows, ready to use me and punish me.

Obviously my view of God was twisted. With both of my parents involved in the occult, I learned from infancy to see God as my enemy. Instead of bonding with my parents, I clung to darkness and the hidden. The rituals of satanic worship consumed me even before I could talk. I thought the sexual abuse was love. Shame was ever-present in my life.

In 1989, I was weary of life, and I gave my life to Jesus because I didn't want to go to hell. But I didn't want to trust Him to love me. Instead I relied on prescription drugs while I filled my head with knowledge about God, but I still didn't know Him. I was trapped in a darkness of lies and deception that my human reason couldn't reveal. I thought that I was such a bad person that I was driven to punish myself through self-mutilation and other destructive behaviors because I felt I deserved to be punished.

I was withdrawn and depressed. I couldn't live this life anymore. I planned a quiet death, but God intervened. I began a journey that I thought was about me and was going nowhere, but this journey was really about God and journeying from my darkness towards His light.

to be continued...

© COPYRIGHT 1998, 2001, 2005, 2007 SCOPE MINISTRIES INTERNATIONAL INC.

In the last three lessons we have looked at our beliefs in general, our beliefs about the "good news," and our beliefs about ourselves. We have seen how corrupted beliefs in these areas have adversely affected us. In this lesson we will discover how our beliefs about God affect us.

The French physicist and philosopher, Pascal, once wrote, "There is a God-shaped vacuum in the heart of every man that cannot be satisfied by anything created, but only by the Creator made known through Jesus Christ." However, our distorted view of God will not only not satisfy us, it will also cause some of our greatest difficulties.

Our Perception of God Affects the Quality of Our Lives

How we see God affects every area of our lives.

Our corrupted beliefs about God hinder us from enjoying an intimate relationship with Him. Our distorted perception of God affects:

- the purpose and meaning we give to life (Philippians 3:8)
- the degree to which we love and obey God (Psalm 16:11; 1 Timothy 6:17)
- how we see ourselves (Numbers 13:33)
- how we relate to others (1 John 4:8)

> Grace and peace be multiplied to you in the knowledge of God and of Jesus our Lord; seeing that His divine power has granted to us everything pertaining to life and godliness, through the true knowledge of Him who called us by His own glory and excellence. For by these He has granted to us His precious and magnificent promises, in order that by them you might become partakers of *the* divine nature, having escaped the corruption that is in the world by lust.   2 Peter 1:2-4 NAS

Our perception of God was distorted by the Fall.

Satan deceived Eve by challenging God's Word and planting doubt in her mind concerning God's character. Doubting God's character and His intentions toward them, Eve and Adam declared their independence from God by eating from the Tree of Knowledge. Since that time, man has determined for himself what is true or false, good or evil, right or wrong, based on his senses, reason, and emotions.

© COPYRIGHT 1998, 2001, 2005, 2007 SCOPE MINISTRIES INTERNATIONAL INC.

Because man's spirit died to the things of God, he could no longer know and communicate with God as his Father. Just as a child has his parents' genes and traits, so we became like our "father" Adam: "spiritual orphans," without an ability to know and relate to God.

Man lost the unique father-child relationship he had with God.

Our experience as "spiritual orphans" distorts our perception of God as a perfect Heavenly Father. We may know a lot about God, yet still not have a personal and intimate relationship with Him as our Father.

Christ has restored us to a permanent father-child relationship with God.

As people who have trusted in Christ, we are now God's children (1 John 3:1-3). We are no longer sinful children of Adam, but righteous children of God. We have a new human spirit, the Holy Spirit indwelling us, and a permanent father-child relationship with God the Father.

Experiences with our earthly fathers have influenced our perception of our Heavenly Father.

Even though our relationship with God has changed, the experience of being a "spiritual orphan" has affected our belief system about our Heavenly Father. Much of our view of God is incorrect because it was developed while we were orphans. Even now, our ideas about God come more from our earthly relationships and experiences with authority figures. Generally, the most significant relationship which influences our perception of God is our relationship with our earthly father. Often, the more negative or painful the relationship is or was, the more distorted our view of God is. For example:

The **Authoritarian** Father

is more concerned with compliance than relationship. He insists on things being done his way. He's not interested in his children's opinions, desires, or goals. He desires no real intimacy with his children—only obedience. Having this view of God usually motivates people to rebel instead of obey.

The **Abusive** Father

deliberately inflicts pain on his children, hurting them emotionally, mentally, physically, and/or sexually. This type of relationship destroys his children's sense of worth and robs them of their natural ability to trust. They see themselves as someone to be used rather than valued in relationships. This view usually destroys people's ability to trust God and relate emotionally to Him.

The **Distant/Passive** Father

expresses little affection. He may be a good provider but interacts very little with his children. He rarely shows emotion or says "I love you." He doesn't share in his children's joy or pain. This kind of father can cause people to view God as distant and uninvolved in their daily lives.

© COPYRIGHT 1998, 2001, 2005, 2007 SCOPE MINISTRIES INTERNATIONAL INC.

The **Accusing** Father

is critical and judges every failure. He thinks this will motivate his children to do better and to try harder. He rarely gives encouragement or affirms them. This kind of father can cause people to view their heavenly Father as an angry judge who is never satisfied with them.

The **Absent** Father

is one who is absent because of death, divorce, work, or disinterest. Unlike the passive father who is there but never communicates, the absent father is just not there. His children feel abandoned and neglected not only by their earthly father but by God as well.

Some possible consequences of an emotionally or physically absent father:

Consequences in a Woman:

- Rejects appearance and femininity
- Craves attention and affection, especially from men, or resents men so much that she wants no male attention
- Perceives rejection in everything; needs constant reassurance of love
- Attracted to older men; she may marry an older man and then experience sexual dysfunction because she has difficulty "sleeping with dad"
- Primarily, she has difficulty trusting God

Consequences in a Man:

- Lack of male role model causes him to seek other sources of information. He may look to his mother, which may result in some effeminate traits. He may look to the world, which may result in a "macho" form of masculinity
- Craves male attention and affection, which may lead to a "tough guy" personality or which may be eroticized and lead to homosexuality
- Attracted to dominant women; may marry a dominant woman and establish a passive role in this relationship
- May be especially sensitive to rejection from male authority figures
- Feels threatened by other men; compares himself to others and feels that he does not measure up
- Primarily, he has difficulty trusting God

Our view of God as Father is often derived from:

- Our personal experiences with our earthly father (or other significant authority figures)
- Unmet needs from our relationship with our earthly father
- The world's information about earthly fathers
- False or incomplete information about God

© COPYRIGHT 1998, 2001, 2005, 2007 SCOPE MINISTRIES INTERNATIONAL INC.

Key Principles:
"We become like God in the same proportion as we see Him as He is."

"The more we know God as He really is, the more we love Him. The more we love Him, the more we become like Him. The more we become like Him, the more we desire to know Him."

"But we all, with unveiled face, beholding as in a mirror the glory of the Lord, are being transformed into the same image from glory to glory, just as from the Lord, the Spirit."
2 Corinthians 3:18

> If you then being evil, know how to give good gifts to your children, how much more shall *your* heavenly Father give the Holy Spirit to those who ask Him?　　　Luke 11:13 NAS

As "spiritual orphans" we envisioned in our minds an image of God as Father based upon our experiences with our earthly father. Some of us had very good and very involved fathers, so the effects of emotional and physical absence are not as drastic in our lives as in the lives of others. However, even if we have outstanding earthly fathers, they are still imperfect and will never give us a complete and accurate view of who God is as Father. We all still need to know God as the perfect Father.

We Need to Know Our Heavenly Father for Who He Really Is

We are worshipping beings and become like the one we worship.

Psalm 115:1-8 reveals that we become like that which we worship. In fact, the essence of Eternal Life is to know God the Father intimately through Jesus Christ (John 17:3). The more we know Him, the more we are like Christ. The more we are like Him, the more we desire to know Him and be in relationship with Him.

However, without a proper view of God, we will create a false or incomplete view of God and worship this image (Romans 1:18-32). This is Satan's objective! Although, he can't take away our salvation, he desires to limit our relationship with God by distorting our view of God. He knows that if we do not worship God as He really is, we will not become like Him.

Our real beliefs about God are revealed by our lives. How we respond to God during difficult times and the way we treat and relate to others reveal a lot about how we see God.

> In this you greatly rejoice, even though now for a little while, if necessary, you have been distressed by various trials, that the proof of your faith, being more precious than gold which is perishable, even though tested by fire, may be found to result in praise and glory and honor at the revelation of Jesus Christ; and though you have not seen Him, you love Him, and though you do not see Him now, but believe in Him, you greatly rejoice with joy inexpressible and full of glory.　　　1 Peter 1:6-8 NAS

The more we know God as He really is, the more we love Him. The more we love Him, the more we become like Him. The more we become like Him, the more we desire to know Him.

© COPYRIGHT 1998, 2001, 2005, 2007 SCOPE MINISTRIES INTERNATIONAL INC.

Beloved, let us love one another, for love is from God; and everyone who loves is born of God and knows God. The one who does not love does not know God, for God is love.
1 John 4:7-8 NAS

Jesus revealed Who our Heavenly Father really is.

He is the visible expression of our Heavenly Father. Through Jesus we can come to know the character and heart of our heavenly Father.

And the Word became flesh, and dwelt among us, and we beheld His glory, glory as of the only begotten from the Father, full of grace and truth.
John 1:14 NAS

If you had known Me, you would have known My Father also; from now on you know Him, and have seen Him . . . He who has seen Me has seen the Father.
John 14:7,9b NAS

We may know a lot about God but still not relate to Him as Jesus revealed Him or as Scripture teaches about Him. If we know God as He truly is, we can regain a true father-child relationship with Him, and then we can "image" or express His likeness.

God's Word reveals Who our Father really is.

We must approach Scripture for what it says, rather than reading our experience into it. If we read Scripture without exploring what wrong perceptions we have about God, we may read into God's Word the passivity, disinterest, or meanness that we have assumed to be true of God. We need to ask ourselves if we have attributed to God any feelings we have about our own earthly father.

With this in mind, we need to read God's Word, depending on the Holy Spirit to reveal God's character to us.

We Need to See Ourselves as God's Adopted Children

We are God's spirit-born sons and daughters.

Being a child of God makes us either a prince or a princess. We have become a being of worth and value. Christ's presence within us gives us worth. We are placed in Christ and Christ is placed in us, making us one with Him. Some other exciting truths that result from our new standing as children of God are that:

- We are totally forgiven by our Father—Ephesians 1:3-7; 2:4-5
- We have His Holy Spirit to teach and remind us—John 14:26
- Our Father loves us the same as He loves Jesus—John 16:27, 17:23
- Our Father has made us acceptable and delights in us—Zephaniah 3:17; Romans 15:7; Colossians 1:22
- Our Father is committed to transforming us—Romans 8:29, Philippians 1:6

Abba - daddy

Our protector, King, provider, comforter.

He loves us unconditionally.

He desires the best for us.

He is trustworthy, forgiving, merciful, kind, and compassionate.

© COPYRIGHT 1998, 2001, 2005, 2007 SCOPE MINISTRIES INTERNATIONAL INC.

We need to acknowledge our adoption as God's beloved children and relate to Him as our Heavenly ABBA.

We must choose to renew our minds about God.

We need to think in day-to-day situations according to our new beliefs about God as our Father. We need to view our circumstances in light of our loving Heavenly Father's care, putting our trust in Him and His ultimate purposes for us (Romans 8:28; Jeremiah 29:11).

We must choose to act and react according to Who God is.

Depending on the Holy Spirit, we learn to act on our new thoughts and beliefs. This is how we live in a faith relationship with God.

NOTE:

It is important that we not blame our earthly parents for our wrong view of God. Our real enemy is Satan, the father of lies. The good news is that our Heavenly Father has made possible knowing Him as He really is through Jesus Christ. However, there are not three easy steps to a good Father/God concept. Knowing God as He really is is a life—long process which involves more than having the right knowledge about God. It is experientially knowing and trusting His true character in the midst of life's circumstances. Remember, we can accomplish this only through the empowering presence of the Holy Spirit in our lives.

SUMMARY:

1. How we view God affects the quality of our lives.

2. Our experiences with our earthly dads have influenced our concept of God as father.

3. We can know our Heavenly Father as He really is through Jesus and through renewing our minds with Scripture.

4. We must choose to renew our minds about God and relate to Him as His dearly loved children.

© COPYRIGHT 1998, 2001, 2005, 2007 SCOPE MINISTRIES INTERNATIONAL INC.

A Life Transformed, con't.

God began to expose the darkness in my soul and my mind and my body, and He began to reveal Himself to me as He truly is. I met the real Jesus in whom there is no darkness at all, and He gave me a safe way to think about Him - as a bright light.

Gradually, God's truth began to push out the deeply rooted lies about who He is and who I am. I had believed that He was punishing me by withholding good things from me. Now I know that He loves me, that He knows best what I need, and He gives it to me. I thought that He had abandoned me while I was being abused and that He would abandon me again. Now I know that He was with me when I was abused and that He will give me justice. I am sure that He will never leave me.

He restored my childhood to me — in a sense — by using children in my life to show me how to relate to Him. I began to talk to Him, sharing more and more with Him. I began to trust Him in little things, and I became willing to receive from Him in little ways. I began to express my emotions to Him no matter how raw or immature they seemed. I learned that even when I was angry with Him, I was still safe just being with Him and letting Him love me.

Many beliefs I had about me changed too. I no longer believe that I am an orphan, repulsive to God, worthless, dirty, marked, and defiled. I now believe that I am chosen, accepted, loved, cleansed, forgiven, and holy.

As I changed on the inside, I changed on the outside, but I didn't even see the changes at first. I learned to listen to God through journaling and music. I began to experience freedom in worship and praise. I broke the code of silence and was able to shout to the Lord with joy. I would catch myself laughing. I could call God Father.

I no longer believed that I had to make myself clean and worthy so that I could be good enough to receive His love. My desire to receive His love was stronger than my desire to hurt or punish myself. I was finally free to receive His love.

As I began to receive His love, I no longer had to seek it from other people. I'm not afraid that I'll lose the relationship if I don't do everything right. I don't have to take responsibility for everything. I don't have to control and manipulate others and circumstances. Instead of my neediness being the driving force in relationships, now love is.

My journey continues. God is my Father, and I know that He really loves me. To paraphrase 1 Peter 2:9, God has called me out of my darkness, and now I live in His wonderful light.

Cyndee - Assistant Bookkeeper

© COPYRIGHT 1998, 2001, 2005, 2007 SCOPE MINISTRIES INTERNATIONAL INC.

4.10

© COPYRIGHT 1998, 2001, 2005, 2007 SCOPE MINISTRIES INTERNATIONAL INC.

Getting to Know Our Heavenly Father - Day One

Goal: To recognize how your earthly father (or other authority figure) has influenced your emotional perception of God as your Heavenly Father.

1. Write a description of who your earthly father is to you.

2. Write who God the Father is to you (based on your emotional—**not** intellectual understanding of God).

© COPYRIGHT 1998, 2001, 2005, 2007 SCOPE MINISTRIES INTERNATIONAL INC.

3. Do you see any correlation between the way you view your earthly father and the way you view God as your Father? If so, in what ways?

4. Until we recognize the lies we're believing about God, we will probably not trust Him enough to turn to Him in a time of need or develop a close, intimate relationship with Him. Below are some common wrong perceptions we have about God.

   Evaluate your emotional perception of God (**not** what you know to be true) by circling the number that best describes your thoughts and feelings.

   0 = never 1 = seldom 2 = sometimes 3 = often 4 = usually 5 = always

Generally, in my relationship with God I feel:

Nothing (I don't feel His presence at all)	0	1	2	3	4	5
Abandoned (I have to do things myself)	0	1	2	3	4	5
Alone (I'm all by myself for solutions and strength)	0	1	2	3	4	5
Unsure (of what He thinks of me or where I stand with Him)	0	1	2	3	4	5
Uneasy (I don't know what to expect)	0	1	2	3	4	5

Generally I feel God is:

Inconsiderate (He doesn't take into account my feelings and forces me to do things I don't want to do or doesn't let me do things I want to do)	0	1	2	3	4	5
Hard to please (No matter what I do, it isn't good enough; or, I can't know what is expected from me; He's hard to please)	0	1	2	3	4	5
Conditionally loving (His love for me is based on my obedience)	0	1	2	3	4	5
Unloving (He sees my situation and allows me to suffer)	0	1	2	3	4	5
Angry/Judgmental (He is quick to punish me when I don't measure up; turns His back on me when I fail)	0	1	2	3	4	5

4.12

© COPYRIGHT 1998, 2001, 2005, 2007 SCOPE MINISTRIES INTERNATIONAL INC.

Impatient (He wants things done now!)	0	1	2	3	4	5
Critical (Most of what He thinks or says to me is negative)	0	1	2	3	4	5
Punishing (He's mad and withdraws or punishes me when I sin)	0	1	2	3	4	5
Hard to hear (I don't hear from Him, or I vaguely hear from Him)	0	1	2	3	4	5
Non-communicative (He doesn't talk to me much or at all)	0	1	2	3	4	5
Hard to understand (can't quite figure Him out—complicated)	0	1	2	3	4	5
Not helping me (I'm left to do it in my own strength)	0	1	2	3	4	5
Irresponsible (He's allowing all sorts of bad things to happen)	0	1	2	3	4	5
Slow (He takes His time changing me or getting things done)	0	1	2	3	4	5
Uncaring (He really doesn't care)	0	1	2	3	4	5
Tolerating my presence (He doesn't prefer me)	0	1	2	3	4	5

5. Now list the characteristics of God for which you circled 3 or higher on question 4.

6. What does the following verse tell you about your Heavenly Father?

> No man has ever seen God at any time; *the only unique Son, or* the only-begotten God, Who is in the bosom [in the intimate presence] of the Father, He has declared Him [He has revealed Him and brought Him out where He can be seen; He has interpreted Him and He has made Him known].   John 1:18 Amplified

© COPYRIGHT 1998, 2001, 2005, 2007 SCOPE MINISTRIES INTERNATIONAL INC.

4.13

7. What does Jesus claim in the following verses?

> Jesus said to him, "I am the Way and the Truth and the Life; no one comes to the Father except by (through) Me.
>
> If you had known Me [had learned to recognize Me], you would also have known My Father. From now on, you know Him and have seen Him."
>
> Philip said to Him, "Lord, show us the Father [cause us to see the Father—that is all we ask]; then we shall be satisfied."
>
> Jesus replied, "Have I been with all of you for so long a time, and do you not recognize *and* know Me yet, Philip? Anyone who has seen Me has seen the Father. How can you say then, Show us the Father?
>
> Do you not believe that I am in the Father, and that the Father is in Me?"
>
> John 14:6-10a Amplified

8. According to these verses, how can we know what our Heavenly Father is like?

© COPYRIGHT 1998, 2001, 2005, 2007 SCOPE MINISTRIES INTERNATIONAL INC.

Getting to Know Our Heavenly Father - Day Two

Goal: To recognize and strengthen the areas where your concept of your Heavenly
Father is weak or distorted.

1. Relational Evaluation: This exercise allows you to evaluate your relationship with
   God as your Heavenly Father. Because it is subjective, there are no wrong answers.
   On a scale of 1-10, rate how real this characteristic is to you in your relationship with
   your Heavenly Father. Remember you are evaluating how much you experience this
   characteristic of God.

   Do you see your Heavenly Father as One who is:

Characteristic	Never . . . . Always
___ Loving	1 2 3 4 5 6 7 8 9 10
___ Caring	1 2 3 4 5 6 7 8 9 10
___ Forgiving	1 2 3 4 5 6 7 8 9 10
___ Compassionate	1 2 3 4 5 6 7 8 9 10
___ Giving	1 2 3 4 5 6 7 8 9 10
___ Understanding	1 2 3 4 5 6 7 8 9 10
___ Accepting	1 2 3 4 5 6 7 8 9 10
___ Satisfies	1 2 3 4 5 6 7 8 9 10
___ Persistently pursuing	1 2 3 4 5 6 7 8 9 10
___ Reasonable	1 2 3 4 5 6 7 8 9 10

2. Psalm 103 contains many characteristics of our Father-Savior. With each
   characteristic, provide the corresponding verse. Next, rate yourself as to how
   real this characteristic is to you in your relationship with God.

Characteristic	Verse	Never . . . . Always
___ Pardons	_____	1 2 3 4 5 6 7 8 9 10
___ Heals	_____	1 2 3 4 5 6 7 8 9 10
___ Redeems	_____	1 2 3 4 5 6 7 8 9 10
___ Lovingkindness	_____	1 2 3 4 5 6 7 8 9 10
___ Compassion	_____	1 2 3 4 5 6 7 8 9 10
___ Satisfies	_____	1 2 3 4 5 6 7 8 9 10
___ Renews	_____	1 2 3 4 5 6 7 8 9 10
___ Righteous	_____	1 2 3 4 5 6 7 8 9 10
___ Gracious	_____	1 2 3 4 5 6 7 8 9 10
___ Sovereign	_____	1 2 3 4 5 6 7 8 9 10

© COPYRIGHT 1998, 2001, 2005, 2007 SCOPE MINISTRIES INTERNATIONAL INC.

A rating of 1 to 6 probably indicates a wrong concept of God as Father-Savior. From this list and the list in question 5, Day One, identify the characteristics you need to experience more fully in your relationship with God and check them on the list below.

Loving — John 3:16; 1 Corinthians 13:4-8; 1 John 4:10
____ My Father-Savior loves me for who I am.
____ His love for me is unconditional and unceasing.

Caring — Matthew 6:26; 10:29-31; 1 Peter 5:7
____ My Father-Savior cares for me always.
____ His major concern is my well-being.

Forgiving — Psalm 103:12; Colossians 1:14; Hebrews 10:17
____ My Father-Savior has forgiven me unconditionally.
____ His forgiveness of my sins includes forgetfulness.

Compassionate — Exodus 33:19; Deuteronomy 4:31; Psalm 103:4-5
____ My Father-Savior is full of compassion toward me.
____ His compassion affirms me and supports me.

Giving — Psalm 37:4; Romans 8:32; James 1:17
____ My Father-Savior gives me the desires of my heart.
____ His giving nature withholds no good thing from me.

Understanding — Job 12:13; Psalm 139:1-2; Isaiah 40:28
____ My Father-Savior understands my thoughts and my actions.
____ His understanding of me gives me strength and comfort.

Accepting — Psalm 139:1-6; Romans 15:7
____ My Father-Savior accepts me totally and unconditionally.
____ His acceptance of me is based on who I am and not on what I do.

Satisfies — Psalm 107:9; Matthew 6:33; John 14:14; Ephesians 3:19
____ My Father-Savior fulfills my every need.
____ His grace provides a canopy of satisfaction for me.

Persistently pursuing — Luke 19:10; 1 Timothy 1:15; 2:4; Titus 2:11
____ My Father-Savior is the Hound of Heaven.
____ He moved Heaven and earth to bring me to Him.

Reasonable — Proverbs 3:5-6; Isaiah 1:18; Ephesians 3:12
____ My Father-Savior is completely approachable.
____ His attitude toward me is one of favor and good will.

4.16

© COPYRIGHT 1998, 2001, 2005, 2007 SCOPE MINISTRIES INTERNATIONAL INC.

Pardons — Psalm 103:3; Isaiah 43:25; 55:7

___ My Father-Savior offers me full and free pardon.

___ He does not take into account the wrongs I have done to Him.

Heals — II Chronicles 7:14; Psalm 147:3; Isaiah 53:5

___ My Father-Savior is a God Who heals.

___ His concern for my health and well-being is overwhelming.

Redeems — Job 19:25; Psalm 19:14; Isaiah 63:16

___ My Father-Savior has redeemed me from all my sin.

___ His redemption of me is for all eternity.

Lovingkindness — Psalm 86:15; 117:2

___ My Father-Savior expresses His lovingkindness to me always.

___ His lovingkindness to me sustains me through everything.

Renews — Isaiah 40:31; II Corinthians 4:16; Titus 3:5

___ My Father-Savior renews me day by day.

___ He imparts His strength and power to me.

Righteous — Jeremiah 9:23-24; Psalm 11:7; 1 Corinthians 1:30

___ My Father-Savior is righteous in all that He does with me.

___ He imputes righteousness to me, making me righteous.

Gracious — Nehemiah 9:31; Psalm 86:1,15; Ephesians 1:7-8

___ My Father-Savior is always gracious to me.

___ He lavishes His graciousness on me as His child.

Sovereign — Psalm 24:8; Psalm 103:19; Revelation 1:8

___ My Father-Savior is sovereign over all.

___ He is King of kings and Lord of lords, and I am His child.

Now that you know the characteristics which need to be strengthened in your understanding of God, select one verse for each of those characteristics. Begin renewing your mind about Who your Father is by meditating each day on these verses. Spend some time now writing what your wrong thoughts have been and then write the right thoughts. Spend time talking to God and making a conscious choice to put off the wrong thoughts.

© COPYRIGHT 1998, 2001, 2005, 2007 SCOPE MINISTRIES INTERNATIONAL INC.

Wrong Thoughts about God Put Off	Right Thoughts about God Put On
Example: I don't see how God could possibly love me.	Example: My Father's love is unconditional and unchanging. It is not based on who I am, but Who He is.

© COPYRIGHT 1998, 2001, 2005, 2007 SCOPE MINISTRIES INTERNATIONAL INC.

Getting to Know Our Heavenly Father - Day Three

Goal: To know the character and heart of God the Father through His Son, Jesus Christ.

1. Describe how you view Jesus as a person.

2. What do the following verses tell you about Jesus?

> I and the Father are One.   John 10:30 Amplified

> [Now] He is the exact likeness of the unseen God [the visible representation of the invisible]; He is the Firstborn of all creation.   Colossians 1:15 Amplified

> For in Him the whole fullness of Deity (the Godhead) continues to dwell in bodily form [giving complete expression of the divine nature].   Colossians 2:9 Amplified

3. Compare your view of Jesus with your view of God the Father from Day One. What are the similarities and/or differences?

© COPYRIGHT 1998, 2001, 2005, 2007 SCOPE MINISTRIES INTERNATIONAL INC.

Often our view of Jesus is very different from our view of God the Father. This may be because we have developed our view of Jesus more from the stories in the Gospels, but we have based our view of God the Father more on our past experiences.

4. Read the following Scriptures and write how each verse describes Jesus.

Luke 19:10 _____

Matthew 9:10-13 _____

Matthew 9:36 _____

Matthew 11:28-30 _____

Matthew 23:37 _____

John 8:1-11 _____

John 10:11 _____

5. Seeing the Father through Jesus and learning to relate to Him in a personal and intimate way is vital. Spend a few minutes thanking God for Who He is and what He is really like. Ask God to reveal Himself to you more clearly and enable you to have a deeper, more intimate relationship with Him as your Father. Remember that His ability and desire to reveal Himself to you is greater than your ability and desire to see Him differently.

6. Continue to meditate on verses pertaining to God's character from Day Two.

© COPYRIGHT 1998, 2001, 2005, 2007 SCOPE MINISTRIES INTERNATIONAL INC.

Getting to Know Our Heavenly Father - Day Four

Goal: To begin recognizing and receiving your Heavenly Father's thoughts towards you.

> Many, O Lord my God, are the wonderful works which You have done, and Your thoughts toward us; no one can compare with You! If I should declare and speak of them, they are too many to be numbered.   Psalm 40:5 Amplified

> How precious *and* weighty also are Your thoughts to me, O God! How vast is the sum of them! If I could count them, they would be more in number than the sand.
> Psalm 139:17-18a Amplified

1. Read out loud the paraphrased, personalized verses on the next page, placing your name in the blanks.

2. Meditate on one of these verses during the next few days. Receive this as your Heavenly Father's thoughts toward you each morning before you start your day and each night before you go to sleep.

© COPYRIGHT 1998, 2001, 2005, 2007 SCOPE MINISTRIES INTERNATIONAL INC.

MY HEAVENLY FATHER'S THOUGHTS TOWARD ME

For I AM the Lord! Your Lord, _____, I AM merciful and gracious; slow to become angry and overflowing with lovingkindness and truth, maintaining lovingkindness toward you. I have forgiven your wickedness, rebellion and sin.   Exodus 34:6

For the Spirit which you received (at the moment of new birth) is not a spirit of slavery to return you to bondage to fear; rather you have received from Me the Spirit of adoption! I have made you My child and in the bliss and security of that position, _____, you can cry "Abba" or "Father" (Daddy)! The Holy Spirit Himself witnesses to your spirit telling you this is so, assuring you that you are My child.   Romans 8:15-16

_____, My child, do not dread, neither be afraid, for I AM the Lord your God (your Father) Who goes before you in your trouble; I will fight for you, just as I did the nation of Israel when I brought them out of Egypt. I will carry you just like I did them, just as a man carries his son.   Deuteronomy 1:29-31

This is what I, the Lord Who created you, Who formed you says; Fear not, _____, for I have redeemed you. I have bought you back for Myself by paying the price of My life instead of leaving you captive. I have called you personally by name, and you are Mine. Therefore, when you walk through the waters of trouble, I, your Father, will be with you, and as you go through the rivers, they will not overwhelm you; when you walk through the fire you shall not be burned or scorched, nor shall the flame touch you. Fear not because I, your Father, am with you. You are precious in My sight, and honored, and I love you!   Isaiah 43:1-4

Listen to Me, _____, I the Lord, your Father, have borne you from your birth; I carried you from the womb. Even to your old age I will remain the same, for I AM the source of supply for your every need; even until your hair is white with age, I, your Father will carry you, _____, and deliver you! Isaiah 46:3-4

And the Lord, your Father, declares to you: Can a woman forget her nursing child and have no compassion on the son of her womb? Yes, she may forget, yet your Father will not forget you, _____. See, I have indelibly tattooed a picture of you on the palm of each of My hands.   Isaiah 49:15-16

I, the Lord, your Father, have loved you, _____, with a love that never ends; therefore, with My favor and merciful kindness I have taken the initiative and have drawn you to myself.   Jeremiah 31:3

Fear not, _____, and don't let your hands sink down and don't be discouraged, for I AM with you in everything! I AM the Mighty One, the Savior Who saves! I AM rejoicing over you with joy! I rest in the silent satisfaction of your being My child and in the love that I have for you. I will never make mention of your past sins or even recall them. I delight in you and rejoice over you with singing!   Zephaniah 3:16-17

Dear Child, I made you alive when you were dead in your sins; those sins in which you, at one time, walked habitually. You were then destined for my wrath like the rest of mankind. But I, being rich in mercy and in order to satisfy the great and wonderful and intense love that I have for you, made you alive together in fellowship and in union with My Son Jesus, by giving you His very life. All because of My grace and mercy, which you did not deserve, you have been delivered from My righteous judgment. Not only have I made you alive to Me, _____, but I have raised you up with Jesus and have seated you with Him in the heavenly sphere, by virtue of your being IN Christ Jesus. I did this for you to demonstrate clearly for all eternity the immeasurable, limitless, surpassing riches of My free grace, given to you out of the kindness and goodness of My heart. For it is by My free and gracious love that you have been delivered from judgment and made a partaker of My salvation in Christ, which you have received by faith. Always remember your salvation is not of your own doing; you did not obtain it by your own striving or performance, but it is a free gift from Me, your Heavenly Father.   Ephesians 2:4-10

© COPYRIGHT 1998, 2001, 2005, 2007 SCOPE MINISTRIES INTERNATIONAL INC.

Getting to Know Our Heavenly Father - Day Five

Goal: To understand how to live and walk as God's child.

1. Read the article, "FatherCare" on page 4.27. Underline the important sentences that speak to you. Write out the main idea or thought you received from this article.

2. Ask God to reveal to you who/what you have turned to to meet your deepest need. Fill in the blanks below.

   I have primarily depended upon _____ to meet my need for love.

   I have tried to _____ in order to feel like I belong.

   I have depended on _____ to give me a sense of well-being.

   I have depended upon _____ to make me feel secure.

   I have looked to _____ for approval.

   I have tried to gain acceptance from _____ by _____.

   I have worshiped (valued) _____ more than God.

3. Pray the following prayer out loud to God.

Dear Heavenly Father, I have come to realize that I do not know You as You really are, and because of this, I have not experienced the kind of intimacy that You desire to have with me. I have looked to myself, others, and things to meet my deepest needs. I now desire for You to meet these needs by interacting with You daily in a close and intimate way. I want to know You as fully as possible, but I don't know how to get to know You. So, Father, I'm asking You to reveal Yourself to me through Your Word and in my daily life. Open my eyes that I might see Your glory, majesty, and goodness. Open my mind and heart to understand and to receive Your perfect unconditional love for me.

© COPYRIGHT 1998, 2001, 2005, 2007 SCOPE MINISTRIES INTERNATIONAL INC.

© COPYRIGHT 1998, 2001, 2005, 2007 SCOPE MINISTRIES INTERNATIONAL INC.

Getting to Know Our Heavenly Father - Lesson Four

Name _____ Date _____

Answer the following questions. To turn in page to small group leader, use identical perforated page in back of book.

1. What corrupted beliefs about God as Father did you recognize through this lesson?

2. How would knowing and relating to God as your Father affect your life (emotionally, relationally, behaviorally)?

3. How would relating to God as an unconditionally loving and perfect Father affect your life?

4. What from this week's assignment was most meaningful to you?

5. What characteristic(s) of God need strengthening in your life?

6. Mark the graph to indicate how much of this week's assignment you completed.

None	50%	100%

© COPYRIGHT 1998, 2001, 2005, 2007 SCOPE MINISTRIES INTERNATIONAL INC.

Record Your Prayer Requests:

_____

_____

_____

_____

_____

_____

_____

_____

_____

_____

_____

_____

_____

_____

_____

_____

_____

_____

_____

_____

_____

_____

© COPYRIGHT 1998, 2001, 2005, 2007 SCOPE MINISTRIES INTERNATIONAL INC.

FatherCare

Adapted from "FatherCare"
by Jim Craddock

Life is made up of relationships—some are good, some are bad, but all are necessary. The Bible, God's inspired textbook on relationships, reveals that the basic common denominator inherent in all relationships is man's relationship to God, the father/child relationship. It was this father/child relationship that made Adam's interaction with God so unique, and it was the father/child relationship that was lost at the Fall, thereby making man's life so desperate.

History shows us that men have always sought God. From the earliest and most primitive of cultures, there has been a pattern of worship, of man's attempt to restore the lost father/child relationship. However, man is not capable of restoring this lost relationship. It has to be done by God. From God's perspective the restoration of the father/child relationship, so that we can know God as our Father, was so critically important that He stepped out of Heaven in the Person of Jesus Christ to initiate and accomplish this.

The Bible demonstrates that all Jesus did, all that He said, was for this one single purpose of revealing God as our Father. What man lost at the Fall—the father/child relationship—God was determined to restore.

At the same time, the restoration of the father/child relationship is so terribly threatening to Satan that he has made every attempt to hinder and confuse the process of that restoration (2 Corinthians 4:4). For a child of God to know God as Father brings that child into such intimacy with God, producing such worship of God and service for God, that the whole hierarchy of the evil one is threatened.

Because of Satan's master strategy of fostering hindrances and confusion, the vast majority of Christians have either an erroneous or at the least a very vague concept of God as their Father.

This ignorance of God and Who He is as Father causes most of a Christian's emotional and spiritual problems. Studying how Christ revealed the Father can revolutionize your life, because it brings you into an intimacy with God as your Father that you have not experienced before.

Why Is It Important to Know God As Father?

First, it is important to know God as Father because the Bible commands that we know God.

That the God of our Lord Jesus Christ, the Father of glory, may give to you a spirit of wisdom and of revelation in the knowledge of Him.
Ephesians 1:17 NAS

But from there you will seek the Lord your God, and you will find *Him* if you search for Him with all your heart and all your soul. Deuteronomy 4:29

I have manifested Your name [I have revealed Your very Self, Your real Self] to the people whom You have given Me out of the world. They were Yours, and You gave them to Me …
John 17:6 Amplified

To know God intimately, as God desires us to know Him, we need to know Him as Father. It is one thing to know God through His attributes, but it is quite another to know Him as Father. Knowing God only through His attributes tends to produce a sterile, non-intimate relationship, while knowing Him as Father creates an awesome intimacy.

It is astounding to read the Scripture and realize that God, the absolute Sovereign of the universe, desires that we know Him, and He made it possible for us to do so. I repeat, Christ's primary purpose of coming to this sin-ridden planet was to reveal God as Father, so that we, as His children, might enjoy that father/child relationship that once existed between God and Adam.

Not only are we commanded to know God, but knowing God as Father is also important for giving meaning to our lives.

© COPYRIGHT 1998, 2001, 2005, 2007 SCOPE MINISTRIES INTERNATIONAL INC.

J.I. Packer wrote:

"Knowing about God is crucially important for the living of our lives. As it would be cruel to an Amazonian tribesman to fly him to London, put him down without an explanation in Trafalgar Square and leave him as one who knows nothing of English or England to fend for himself, so we are cruel to ourselves if we try to live in this world without knowing about the God whose world it is and who runs it. The world becomes a strange, mad, painful place, and life in it a disappointing and unpleasant business, for those who do not know about God. Disregard the study of God, and you sentence yourself to stumble and blunder through life blindfolded, as it were, with no sense of direction and no understanding of what surrounds you. This way you can waste your life and your soul."

Third, it is important for the Christian to know God as Father for emotional and spiritual well-being. A person cannot and will not trust a stranger. If God as Father is a stranger to us, for whatever the reason, we cannot and will not trust Him (Psalm 9:10). If we don't trust Him, we will doubt Him. As we try to live for God, our doubts about God produce a contradiction in our lives that creates tremendous emotional and spiritual stress (James 1:6). I have never ministered to someone who was suffering from emotional stress and turmoil who also had a good, Biblical concept of God as Father.

No relationship is more crucial to children than the parent/child relationship. Unfortunately, in our culture, we have forgotten how important the father/child relationship is. The average father spends approximately six minutes a day with his children. We live in a society that not only condones, but encourages absentee fatherhood.

What is a true father? William Barclay writes:

"Fatherhood describes an intimate, loving, continuous relationship in which father and son grow closer to each other every day." This "Fatherhood" describes God's relationship to us. A true father, a perfect father, a caring father is one who has the ability and desire to meet his children's deepest needs.

However, we usually do not experience God as this kind of Father because we have developed our concept of His Fatherhood from our experiential relationships with our earthly fathers. Unfortunately, we developed erroneous concepts of a true father, because there is no absolutely perfect human father who can provide a role model for us.

What a refreshing and astounding difference to realize that God is our Father and that He is never absent but always available to us every moment of every day. Our Heavenly Father is a true father, a perfect father, a caring father who has the ability and desire to meet our deepest needs. What are our deepest needs?

Let's look at six of them:

• The need to worship

• The need to be loved and to belong

• The need for well-being

• The need to feel secure

• The need for approval

• The need for acceptance

The Need to Worship

Most people would probably not list worship as one of their deeply felt needs, but it is man's most vital need because man was created for worship and to worship.

The word "worship" comes from the Anglo-Saxon word "weorthscipe," which evolved into the word "worthship" and then into "worship." Worship is ascribing worth to someone or something. Man was not designed to live independently from God but to fellowship intimately with and depend totally upon God. In order to live life as it was meant to be lived, to its fullest, man must ascribe to God His infinite, ascendant, absolute worth: His "first-place-ness." Man must worship. Without worship, we do not have God in His rightful place and, therefore, everything else in life is totally out of place. Right worship is ascribing to God His worth and worthiness.

Worship and intimacy are related. Only through right worship can we come to know God and experience His love and care. When His Spirit indwells us at our rebirth in Christ,

4.28

© COPYRIGHT 1998, 2001, 2005, 2007 SCOPE MINISTRIES INTERNATIONAL INC.

He gives us the ability to worship Him rightly, to place Him in His rightful position, to honor Him, and therefore, to return to our deep dependence upon Him in every aspect of our lives, in other words, to be in an intimate, right relationship with our Father.

In an age when "self-worth" is considered to be man's basic need, we need to realize that true worth—a true understanding of who we really are—can come only through right worship. Worship that is based on a true understanding of who God really is, the One of ultimate worth.

The Need to Be Loved and to Belong

To be loved is a very basic, deeply felt need in all of our lives. We crave love, but not a conditional love based on what we have or on what we are able to achieve. We crave an unconditional love based on who we are. Our ability to love and be loved is directly related to our knowledge of God as our Father. The Bible explains it best:

We love, because He first loved us.

I John 4:19 NAS

God's love for us is always based on Who He is—His holy and unchanging character. God's love always gives unselfishly what is needed. But His love is not limited to an eternal decision to do us good. He also has chosen to passionately delight in who we are as His children.

When my son Danny was a preschooler, he invariably had a crush on one or more of the young women on our staff, depending upon who was the cutest and most responsive. One Sunday afternoon, we hosted a rather formal tea to introduce new staff members. One young woman, Arlys, was dressed in the prettiest, filmiest, whitest dress you have ever seen.

As the adults were chatting, Danny came in with his dust cloud, looking as though he just invented 12 new ways to incorporate dirt and mud into his four-year-old body. Out of the corner of his eye, as he was heading out the front door, he glimpsed this lovely girl in white. In a second, he was in her lap, hugging the life out of her.

I almost fainted. All I could see was a dirty, grimy little guy who was messing up the whitest dress in the room. But all Arlys could see was a little guy who needed loving, and she just loved and hugged him as though he were the only little guy in all the world.

God taught me something in that moment. We tend to look at ourselves as though we are dirty, grimy sinners, but God, as our Father, sees us only as little guys and gals who need lots of loving. That is why His love is INCREDIBLY MAGNIFICENT!

Belonging to God allows us to fulfill the flip side of this need, that of belonging to others. In Genesis 2, God said that it wasn't good for man to be alone. The word "alone" in the Hebrew means to be isolated. If we are rightly related to God, enjoying the intimacy of right worship, then He becomes the prime mover in bringing other people into our lives to fulfill the need for belonging. How? He does this through the Church—a family of like-minded people, born of His Spirit, enjoying oneness in His Spirit, learning to care for one another. Here is where our need to belong can be and should be met.

The Need for Well-Being

Our Lord made it quite clear in Matthew 6 that a sense of well-being comes not through what we have or what we can get, but from Who our Father is!

. . . do not be anxious for your life, *as to what you shall eat, or what you shall drink; nor for your body, as to what you shall put on. Is not life more than food, and the body than clothing? Look at the birds of the air, that they do not sow, neither do they reap, nor gather into barns, and yet your heavenly Father feeds them. Are you not worth much more than they?. . . Do not be anxious then, saying, 'What shall we eat?' or 'What shall we drink?' or 'With what shall we clothe ourselves?' For all these things the Gentiles eagerly seek; for your heavenly Father knows that you need all these things. But seek first His kingdom and His righteousness; and all these things shall be added to you.*

Matthew 6:25b-26; 31-33 NAS

Our Father promises to meet all of our needs. As we relate to our Father, He opens our eyes to see His abundant provision, to see that our well-being is a need He eagerly desires to fulfill.

© COPYRIGHT 1998, 2001, 2005, 2007 SCOPE MINISTRIES INTERNATIONAL INC.

The Need to Feel Secure

A father is one who provides security. God our Father guarantees personal security. This personal sense of security is affirmed and reinforced by the term "Abba Father" in the Bible (Mark 14:36; Romans 8:15; Galatians 4:6). The word "abba" is a transliteration of an Aramaic word that is the first word a little baby calls its father. Our modern-day counterpart is "da da," and the best translation of the word "abba" is "daddy." God is our "Daddy"!! When we know God as our Abba Father, then we have that profound sense of personal security and safety. No matter what we face, the obstacles that lie in our paths, the struggles in our lives, our Father is there!!! He will never leave us nor forsake us! (Hebrews 13:5)

The Need for Approval and Significance

Approval comes in many forms, and we all desire it. Everyone desperately seeks parental approval, and the lack of it creates real problems. The drive for approval is so strong that people will neglect their families, their health, all that they have—to gain approval.

Why is significance so important to us? Because we want deeply to "be somebody," to stand apart from the crowd, to leave an indelible mark on history, to stand approved before men. What gives us significance? In our age, we base significance upon performance, on what we achieve, what we have and what other people think of us. Notice that this

significance is based only on external factors, not on internal ones.

How do we, as Christians, gain a sense of God's approval and our significance? Is it through performance or achievement? Is it doing, is it having, or is it through some other means? Obviously, it is through God's means and not through man's efforts. The Bible tells us that God gives His approval unconditionally in Christ (Colossians 1:22)! Our Father is far more concerned with who we are than with what we do. In other words, approval and significance is related to BEING, not doing. Real, lasting approval comes from a relationship with the Father that assures us we are His children.

God created man to be loved, accepted, approved, and understood unconditionally. In each one of us there is an expectation and need to be received unconditionally. However, we are born into a world system that receives no one unconditionally, but only conditionally based on what a person is able to do, achieve, or have. Every person born into this world discovers that there is a direct contradiction between the desire to be received unconditionally and the world's refusal to honor this need. This contradiction produces enormous stress, especially in light of the tremendous drive that we all have for approval.

At the Fall, man's concept of God was shattered and replaced with a distorted mindset. Man then had no

absolute basis of worth, so his own identity was shattered. Because man had no basis of unconditional worth, he had to compensate. He did this by adopting a compensation system of self-imposed standards which would allow him to gain conditionally what was denied him unconditionally.

He tried to gain worth and significance through his performance rather than in what God says about Him, which was God's original plan before sin entered the picture. Therefore, a person doesn't consider himself worthy enough to receive anything unconditionally, so we try harder to be better and do more to make ourselves worthy of approval. However, we can never do enough, achieve enough, or have enough to satisfy our longing for approval and acceptance.

The good news is that our Father, who created us to be received unconditionally, does receive us unconditionally. His approval is given on the basis of who He has made us to be in Christ, not on the basis of what we do. He loves us, accepts us, and He approves of us as His children.

The Need for Acceptance

Approval and acceptance are very closely related. If we feel approved, we will feel accepted. Unfortunately, many Christians do not feel approved or accepted by God. We have mistakenly believed that God does not love us but that He only loves Christ in us. We have reasoned that because of sin there is no good

© COPYRIGHT 1998, 2001, 2005, 2007 SCOPE MINISTRIES INTERNATIONAL INC.

thing in us. Therefore, God in His holiness, can look at us only through "rose-colored glasses"—the rose-colored glasses being the blood of the Lord Jesus.

Nothing could be further from the truth. The truth is that God not only loves the Christ in us, but He loves us!!! He accepts us unconditionally because of what Christ did on the cross. Because we are acceptable to God, His Spirit lives in us and makes us righteous. God, our Father, accepts us with all our hang-ups, with all our sins, with all our weaknesses, as a person, unconditionally.

Relationship

As previously defined, a father has children and meets the needs of those children. However, another facet of fatherhood, *relationship*, is also crucial to both father and child. A relationship involving three factors: a consistent relationship, a growing relationship and an intimate relationship.

A true father/child relationship is always a continuing relationship. We see this in the parable of the prodigal son (Luke 15:11-32). None of the son's attitudes or actions affected the relationship of the father to the son. The parable teaches that nothing can affect the consistency of our Father's relationship with us. This is important because every child needs a parent that remains unchangeable even in the face of a changeable child. As a parent, we are not to respond in kind to our children's outbursts or inconsistent behavior. We are to be unmoveable and unchangeable in

our love. Unfortunately, we fall short of this, but our Father in heaven does not! (It is important to remember that although nothing affects God's relation to us, sin in our lives can and will affect our relationship with Him.)

Although the love of our earthly parents falters at times, the love of our Heavenly Father is consistent. If we are faithless, He is faithful (2 Timothy 2:13). If we are impossible, He is kind. If we are angry with Him, He is patient. We desperately need the security of a Father Whose love, kindness, acceptance, and approval are consistent and not subject to the whims of vacilating emotions. We have that kind of Father!

Not only is our relationship with our Heavenly Father a consistent one, it must be a growing one—one that grows deeper every day. There is one relationship that we have with our children as babies and quite another as they enter into puberty and then adulthood.

Although the consistency of our Father's relationship with us depends completely on Him, the growth of that relationship depends a great deal on us. In his book, *Enjoying Intimacy With God*, J. Oswald Sanders graphically describes the various positions of the disciples with Christ:

"Each of the disciples was as close to Jesus as he chose to be, for the Son of God had no favorites... It is a sobering thought that we too are as close to Christ as we really choose to be."

Intimacy develops from a growing

relationship with our Father. This intimacy with the Father is not a luxury, but a necessity for our well-being. The more we see our Heavenly Father for who He really is, the more our love for Him deepens and the more we become like Him. This positive cycle conforms us into Christ-likeness.

Although God our Father initiated our relationship with Him and now sustains it, we have to respond to Him. As to God's part, J.I. Packer puts it well:

"What matters supremely, therefore, is not, in the last analysis, the fact that I know God, but the larger fact which underlies it—the fact that **He knows me**. I am graven on the palms of His hands; I am never out of His mind. All my knowledge of Him depends on His sustained initiative in knowing me. I know Him because He first knew me and continues to know me."

The Bible calls God's part of the relationship "grace," and our part, "faith." Grace has been called "the divine adequacy." Faith is the human response to our Father's adequacy. As we grow in awareness of His adequacy, we grow in our experience of the love and care and peace of the Father.

Who then is a father? One who begets children, who raises and nourishes them, who meets their needs, and who encourages a consistent, growing, intimate relationship with them. A father is one who loves his children dearly and who tenderly

© COPYRIGHT 1998, 2001, 2005, 2007 SCOPE MINISTRIES INTERNATIONAL INC.

watches over them, cares for them, understands them, talks with them, listens to them, and is vitally concerned for them. This is our Heavenly Father.

How are we to grow in relationship with the Father, Who is Spirit (John 4:24), when we as flesh and blood, can't identify with a Spirit? The Father revealed Himself as flesh and blood in His Son Jesus. Jesus said, "If you have seen Me, you have seen the Father." We can know God as Father, through Jesus Christ Who reveals Him.

By observing Jesus in the Gospels, we can see our Father's compassionate response to sinners, the broken-hearted, the sick, and the religious. We can know His sacrificial love as we witness Jesus' excruciating death on the cross. His forgiving heart is wonderfully revealed by Jesus' final words, "Father forgive them; for they do not know what they are doing" (Luke 23:34).

There is nothing more satisfying than experientially knowing God as Father. By studying the life of Christ, we can see in detail the Father at work here on earth. In Jesus we can

see all the characteristics of our perfect Father. It is in Jesus loving that we see a loving Father. It is in Jesus caring that we see a caring Father. It is in Jesus approving that we experience a Father's approval. It is in Jesus' kindness that we see a kind Father. It is in Jesus' gentleness that we see a gentle Father. It is in Jesus' acceptance that we feel a Father's acceptance. It is through a patient Jesus that we see a patient Father. It is in Jesus that our knowledge of our Heavenly Father can be complete.

© COPYRIGHT 1998, 2001, 2005, 2007 SCOPE MINISTRIES INTERNATIONAL INC.

Living By the Spirit

If any man is thirsty, let him come to Me and drink. He who believes in Me, as the Scripture said, 'From his innermost being shall flow rivers of living water.'

John 7:37b - 38 NAS

Lesson 5

A Life Transformed

My parents divorced when I was a baby. When my mother abandoned us, and my father couldn't take care of us, I was sent to a boarding school for Indian children when I was five years old. I felt like an orphan and as if I never belonged to anyone, especially when my brother and sister went to live with my mother for a while but I never did.

When I was 12 years old, I became a Christian, but nothing changed. I still felt lonely and unwanted, like an orphan, and I thought that God was distant and uncaring. No one told me that the Christian life could be different.

Many years later I learned that when I became a Christian, the Holy Spirit came to live in me. I realized that I had been living as if I had a dead spirit and as if I were still separated from God, as if I were still a spiritual orphan. I had read in John 14 that Jesus Christ said that the Holy Spirit would teach me, so I started asking the Holy Spirit, "Will you teach me about myself so that I can understand my life and know who I am?"

to be continued...

© COPYRIGHT 1998, 2001, 2005, 2007 SCOPE MINISTRIES INTERNATIONAL INC.

Living By the Spirit - Lesson Five

The Person of the Holy Spirit

We have already discovered how our corrupted beliefs about ourselves and about God affect the quality of our lives. This lesson will help us discover how to live life by the Spirit rather than by the flesh. We were created to contain the Spirit of God and to live by His life. Only as we live by the Spirit do we experience our new identity and enjoy a satisfying relationship with God.

The Holy Spirit is a person.

The Holy Spirit is the third person of the Trinity. God is revealed in three persons: Father, Son, and Holy Spirit. The Holy Spirit is identical in essence to God the Father and God the Son. He is a person, not an "it" or a "power." He has a mind (knows and communicates God's thoughts [1 Corinthians 2:10-11]), will (distributes gifts as He wills [1 Corinthians 12:11]), and emotions (can be grieved [Ephesians 4:30], expresses joy [Luke 10:21]).

The Holy Spirit is the Spirit of Christ living in us.

Jesus promised to send the Holy Spirit to live in those who receive Him.

> But the one who joins himself to the Lord is one spirit with Him.
> 1 Corinthians 6:17 NAS

The word "one" in "one spirit" is the same word used for the "one flesh" relationship between husband and wife. The two shall become "one flesh" (Genesis 2:24) means that they no longer function as two separate, independent people. Likewise, we have become one with Christ's Spirit so that when we live and walk by the spirit, Christ is living through us.

> . . . it is no longer I who live, but Christ lives in me; and the *life* which I now live in the flesh I live by faith in the Son of God . . .
> Galatians 2:20b NAS

The Holy Spirit is our Helper.

In John 14:16, Jesus described the Holy Spirit as "another Helper," meaning another of the very same kind. The Holy Spirit is to us all that Jesus was to His disciples and more. He does for us what Jesus would do for us if He were physically present. He is our permanent resident Counselor, Comforter, Helper, Intercessor, Advocate, and Strengthener.

> And I will ask the Father, and He will give you another Comforter (Counselor, Helper, Intercessor, Advocate, Strengthener, and Standby), that He may remain with you forever.
> John 14:16 Amplified

Counselor

Helper

Intercessor

Revealer

Strengthener

Comforter

Teacher

© COPYRIGHT 1998, 2001, 2005, 2007 SCOPE MINISTRIES INTERNATIONAL INC.

Three Person

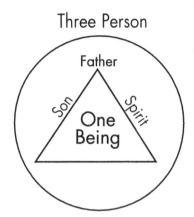

The Holy Spirit is our Comforter.

Our Heavenly Father is the God of all comfort. He has given us His Spirit to comfort us as we experience life. We need God's comfort when we feel rejected, sad, lonely or depressed. We need God's comfort when we experience trials or when we lose a friend or loved one. God cares about how we feel and has not left us alone.

The Holy Spirit is our Teacher.

Jesus has not left us to figure out life on our own. He has given us the Holy Spirit to teach us the truth about God, ourselves, life and others. He not only teaches us but also He reminds us of the truth when we need to apply it to our lives. He gives us God's perspective, wisdom, and understanding.

> But the Comforter (Counselor, Helper, Intercessor, Advocate, Strengthener, Standby), the Holy Spirit, Whom the Father will send in My name [in My place, to represent Me and act on My behalf], He will teach you all things. And He will cause you to recall (will remind you of, bring to your remembrance) everything I have told you.   John 14:26 Amplified

The Roles of the Holy Spirit

Imparts Life — (John 6:63) The Holy Spirit gives us Eternal Life, which is God's quality of life. He has given us everything we need to live life to its fullest. The Holy Spirit has deposited God's resurrection life in our spirit. When we live by the Spirit, we experience God's quality of life.

Imparts Hope — (Romans 15:13) The Holy Spirit is God's active agent for change. He is the "down payment," assuring us that God will complete the good work He started in us through the regenerating work of the Holy Spirit.

Imparts Spiritual Gifts — (Romans 12:5-8) The Holy Spirit has given spiritual gifts to each believer so that they are equipped to minister to others.

Reveals Truth — (John 16:13) The Holy Spirit guides us into all truth. Truth taught by the Holy Spirit is the unveiling of the unseen reality. He longs to do this because the truth will set us free (John 8:32).

Reveals Jesus — (John 16:14) The Holy Spirit makes Christ real to us. Anyone can learn information about Jesus, but only the Holy Spirit can make Jesus known to us in a personal, intimate way.

Reveals God's Thoughts — (1 Corinthians 2:10-13) The Holy Spirit puts God's thoughts in our minds and reveals to us the things freely given to us by God. Since we have the mind of Christ, we can receive God's wisdom for daily living. The Holy Spirit makes an intimate relationship with God possible.

Reveals God's Love — (Romans 5:5; John 4:8-10, 18-19) The Holy Spirit makes God's love known to us. Only as we experience His unconditional love are we freed from fear and able to trust His ways. The more God's love is revealed to us by the Holy Spirit, the more we love God.

Reveals Things to Come — (John 16:13) At times the Holy Spirit even shows us what lies ahead, preparing us for future events. The Holy Spirit gives us practical guidance in our daily lives.

Empowers Us With Supernatural Life — (Ephesians 1:17-20; 3:16) The Holy Spirit empowers us to face all of life's obstacles with confidence and hope. He empowers us to rejoice in our trials and to love the most difficult people. The Holy Spirit gives us spiritual gifts to empower us to serve and minister to others.

Empowers Us to Love Others — (Galatians 5:22) The Holy Spirit is God and God is love, therefore, the fruit of the Spirit is love. The Holy Spirit empowers us to do what God commands: to love one another as He has loved us.

© COPYRIGHT 1998, 2001, 2005, 2007 SCOPE MINISTRIES INTERNATIONAL INC.

Our Choice

The memory of our old way of living still influences us on a daily basis.

Our old ways of thinking, our old habits and emotional responses are very familiar to us, but the thoughts and ways of the Spirit can seem foreign. Even the Apostle Paul had to learn not to put confidence in his old ways (flesh).

The flesh can be defined as the natural drives, desires, thoughts, and capabilities of the soul and body, energized by indwelling sin. As Christians, our identity is **NOT** in our flesh, but in our spirit. Jesus said that the flesh profits nothing, but the Spirit gives life.

> It is the Spirit who gives life; the flesh profits nothing; the words that I have spoken to you are spirit and are life.
> John 6:63, NAS

> However, you are not in the flesh but in the Spirit, if indeed the Spirit of God dwells in you. Romans 8:9a NAS

We are tempted to rely on our own natural abilities and strengths.

> But I say, walk by the Spirit, and you will not carry out the desires of the flesh. For the flesh sets its desire against the Spirit, and the Spirit against the flesh; for these are in opposition to one another, so that you may not do the things that you please.
> Galatians 5:16-17 NAS

Living by the flesh is trying to meet our needs apart from God. The flesh can appear good and respectable, but it can never produce God's quality of life.

> But the fruit of the Spirit is love, joy, peace, patience, kindness, goodness, faithfulness, gentleness, self-control; against such things there is no law. Galatians 5:22-23 NAS

Remember our example of the tree and the fruit of the Spirit.

Produces a transformed and empowered life.

↑

Reveals truth to our minds.
Motivates us to do God's will.
Fills us with love, joy and peace.

↑

Christ in Us

It is important that we realize and believe that we have already been given everything we need for life and Godliness through the presence of the Holy Spirit in our spirit. This is the mystery of the Gospel; Christ in us, the hope of glory (Colossians 1:27). The tree illustrates the ministry of the Holy Spirit in the soul of the believer. What the Holy Spirit does for our soul produces a change in our behavior.

© COPYRIGHT 1998, 2001, 2005, 2007 SCOPE MINISTRIES INTERNATIONAL INC.

Many times we attempt to produce the fruit of the Spirit by relying on our own natural abilities and strengths. We can compare this to tying fruit on the tree instead of growing fruit. We know that, if we want apples on a tree, we can buy apples and tie them on the tree. The apples will look good at first, but within a few days they will rot. The fruit will not last. To grow real fruit on the tree, we have to feed and water the roots.

Often, as Christians, we attempt to tie spiritual fruit on our spiritual tree (ourselves). We attempt to produce the "fruit of the Spirit" (love, joy, peace, patience, kindness goodness, faithfulness, gentleness, and self-control) through our own self-effort. We may look good for a short amount of time but our fruit does not last. To produce lasting fruit, we have to water and feed our roots spiritually by believing in Jesus and depending on the Holy Spirit. We do not and cannot produce fruit by trying harder, but the Holy Spirit grows His fruit in us as we yield to His work in our life.

> Remain in [continue to believe and rely on] Me, and I will remain in [dwell and fill] you. No branch can bear fruit by itself; it must remain in the vine. Neither can you bear fruit unless you remain in Me. . . You did not choose Me, but I chose you and appointed you to go and bear fruit—fruit that will last.
>
> John 15:4, 16 Amplified

Transformation occurs through living by the Spirit, not by improving our flesh.

Living by the Spirit is a radically different way of life. It is much more than changing our behavior. It is learning to live moment-by-moment by faith in Christ's life within us, which will ultimately change our behavior.

We choose to walk relying on the Holy Spirit.

The flesh sets its desire against the Spirit and the Spirit against the flesh. When we choose to live by the flesh (our old natural way of living independently of God), the Holy Spirit will bring this to our attention. God desires that we walk by the Spirit even more than we desire it. When we realize we are living by the flesh, **we have to make a choice:** to continue in that direction or to turn to God, rejecting the "deeds of the flesh" and once again allowing Him to live His life through us. Galatians 5:16 promises that as we walk by the Spirit, we will not carry out the desires of the flesh.

> For the flesh sets its desire against the Spirit, and the Spirit against the flesh; for these are in opposition to one another, so that you may not do the things that you please.
>
> Galatians 5:17 NAS

Our self-sufficiency or living by the flesh eventually leads to misery and frustration. The only solution is to declare the flesh absolutely worthless, placing no confidence in it. How can we know when we are walking by the Spirit? The following list can help us recognize what it means to walk by the Spirit instead of relying on the flesh.

The key is to not focus on trying to improve or get rid of the flesh, but to live and walk by faith in the Spirit, allowing Him to change us.

5.6

© COPYRIGHT 1998, 2001, 2005, 2007 SCOPE MINISTRIES INTERNATIONAL INC.

Spirit Walk	Flesh Walk
Relate to Jesus by faith John 7:37-38; Colossians 2:6	Rely on self and others Jeremiah 17:5-6
Trust in the character of God Proverbs 3:5-6; Jeremiah 24:7	See God in an inaccurate way Romans 1:25; 1 Corinthians 15:34
Praise and thank God Ephesians 5:18-19; Psalms; Hebrews 13:15	Pessimistic, discontent, and ungrateful Romans 1:21; James 4:14,16
Consideration and love for others Ephesians 5:21; Romans 12:10	Act envious, jealous, selfish 1 Corinthians 3:3; James 4:1-2
Request God's wisdom 1 Corinthians 2:10-13; James 1:5	Rely on own understanding Isaiah 55:8-9; 1 Corinthians 1:27; 3:18-20;
Believe my new identity 2 Corinthians 5:17; Colossians 3:10	Believe my old identity Ephesians 4:22; Colossians 3:9
Security in my relationship with God Romans 8:16; Galatians 4:7-8	Lack assurance of salvation 1 John 2:28-29; 1 John 4:17
Abide in God's love Romans 5:5; Ephesians 3:16-19; 1 John 3:1	Fear God's punishment 1 John 4:18; 1 John 2:28
Rest in God's acceptance Romans 15:7; Ephesians 1:4	Work for God's acceptance Galatians 2:16, 21; Galatians 5:1-6
Trust Christ to live through me Matthew 11:18-20; Hebrews 4:10	Strive to do good in my own strength Romans 7; Galatians 3:2-3; Colossians 2:20-23
Rely on the Holy Spirit to teach John 14:26; John 16:13	Rely on my own ability to learn John 5:38-40; 1 Corinthians 8:1-2
Acknowledge God's presence and activity in my daily life. 2 Corinthians 4:18; Hebrews 11:6	Do not recognize God's involvement in my daily life Romans 1:28; Hebrews 3:7-10
Base my worth on who Christ has made me to be Philippians 2:5-6; James 4:10; 1 Peter 5:6	Base worth on performance, appearance, and others' opinions Jeremiah 9:23-24; Romans 12:16; James 4:5-6

© COPYRIGHT 1998, 2001, 2005, 2007 SCOPE MINISTRIES INTERNATIONAL INC.

Walking By the Spirit

Walking by the Spirit can be compared to turning on a light switch. The life of the Holy Spirit is always available to us, but we must choose to turn on the switch and to allow His power to work in our lives. In this way we cooperate with Him and He is able to transform our lives.

Walking by the Spirit means we are moment by moment being motivated, led, and empowered by the Holy Spirit.

- The Holy Spirit reveals God's love to us personally so we are motivated to trust and obey God.
- The Holy Spirit brings God's thoughts to our mind so we can follow His leading.
- The Holy Spirit empowers us to love others, even our enemies and people who have hurt us.

This new way of walking involves making decisions in the midst of daily life and circumstances.

We choose to set our mind on the things of the Spirit.

This is like choosing to change channels on a TV which only has two channels. Channel One is the "flesh" channel and Channel Two is the "Spirit" channel. "Setting our mind on the things of the Spirit" is choosing to listen to Channel Two. The thoughts of the Spirit are always consistent with God's Word. Walking by the Spirit means listening and acting on the thoughts prompted by the Spirit. This is what it means to walk by faith, not by sight, not relying on our own understanding but responding by faith to the Word of God.

> For those who are according to the flesh set their minds on the things of the flesh, but those who are according to the Spirit, the things of the Spirit. For the mind set on the flesh is death, but the mind set on the Spirit is life and peace. Romans 8:5-6 NAS

We choose to allow the Holy Spirit to guide all areas of our life.

Our journey in the Spirit involves progressively yielding to the Spirit in all areas of life:

- Physical—our physical appetites and desires
- Family—relationships with parents, spouse, children, etc.
- Finances—the managing of money
- Work—relationships with boss and co-workers; work ethics
- Ministry—relating to the Body of Christ and with those who don't know Christ
- Social—friendships.
- Recreation—use of leisure time

© COPYRIGHT 1998, 2001, 2005, 2007 SCOPE MINISTRIES INTERNATIONAL INC.

Therefore, I urge you, brothers, in view of God's mercy, to offer your bodies as living sacrifices, holy and pleasing to God—this is your spiritual act of worship. Romans 12:1 NIV

Being Filled With the Spirit

Living by the Spirit is not optional, but essential if we are going to experience intimacy with God and become outwardly all that we already are inwardly in Christ. Relying on the Holy Spirit is vital to our everyday life. It is important to realize and remember that:

- We are powerless to live the Christian life on our own. Only Jesus can live the Christian life through us. (John 15:5)
- His Spirit indwells us and supplies everything we need for life and Godliness. (II Peter 1:3)

God commands us to be filled with the Spirit.

This command to "be filled" literally means to "keep on being filled." This is our continual, ongoing need. It is not an option. Every child of God is to be filled continually with the Holy Spirit.

> And do not get drunk with wine, for that is dissipation, but be filled with the Spirit. Ephesians 5:18 NAS

Being filled is having our soul flooded with the presence of God.

It is allowing the Holy Spirit to renew our mind (thoughts and beliefs) with God's Word, to direct our will, and to express God's feelings. The Holy Spirit reveals to us the heart of the Father: His thoughts, His will, His feelings.

We do not have to be filled with the Spirit to know that God loves us, but **we need to be filled in order to experience God's love and to love others**. We do not have to be filled in order to know that we are forgiven, but **we must be filled in order to forgive others**. We don't have to be filled in order to know that we are accepted by God, **but we need to be filled in order to accept others**.

Jesus promised to fill us with the Spirit.

Jesus promised never to leave us nor forsake us. He promised to live in and through us by His Spirit. Being filled with the Spirit satisfies our souls.

> Blessed are they which do hunger and thirst after righteousness: for they shall be filled. Matthew 5:6 NAS

Jesus described the Spirit-filled life as drinking life-giving water.

> If any man is thirsty, let him come to Me and drink. He who believes in Me, as the Scripture said, 'From his innermost being shall flow rivers of living water.' But this He spoke of the Spirit, whom those who believed in Him were to receive; for the Spirit was not yet *given*, because Jesus was not yet glorified. John 7:37b-39 NAS

Our spirit is made new *permanently* by the Holy Spirit at salvation, but the filling of our souls with the Holy Spirit is a *present and ongoing process.*

© COPYRIGHT 1998, 2001, 2005, 2007 SCOPE MINISTRIES INTERNATIONAL INC.

"If any man is thirsty . . ." communicates our need and desire to be filled with God's Spirit. "Let him come and drink . . ." is Jesus' invitation to relate to Him and talk to Him by faith. "Drink" refers to our believing and receiving His life as ours. *Thirst, come, drink, believe* are all in the present tense. This means we are not to come to Jesus just once at salvation, but we are to keep coming to Jesus because we have the continuing need to be filled with the Spirit. **Our part is to believe God's Word and rely on the Holy Spirit.**

Just to believe that we have the Holy Spirit living in us is not enough. We must trust Him to fill our soul with Christ's life in each situation and circumstance of life.

We experience a greater fullness of the Holy Spirit by exercising faith in Who God is and who He has made us to be. Our faith is not merely in the facts or even in God's promises, but in the Person of Jesus. He is our life, and He fills our soul with everything we need for abundant life.

The more we know God, the more we experience a Spirit-filled life.

Even a brand new "baby" Christian is filled with the Spirit. For example: a seven-pound baby and a 200-pound man both have lungs filled with air. What is the difference? One just has a greater capacity. Both are filled, yet one is more filled than the other because his capacity is so much greater. The same is true of our spiritual life and growth. A newborn babe in Christ is made new and filled with the Spirit. Both he and the mature believer of many years are the temple of the Holy Spirit. The difference is their "lung capacity," or level of faith in Who God is and who they are in Him.

Being filled with the Holy Spirit does not mean we will be sinless and perfect or that we will never struggle. It *does* mean that we will live in a vital and personal relationship with God and will allow Jesus to live through our soul and body (Galatians 2:20). When we are filled with the Spirit, others are touched by His presence in our lives!

Developing a thirst is the main prerequisite for being filled with the Spirit.

This means recognizing our need for the Holy Spirit's fullness. Our thirst leads us to:
- desire to be filled
- agree with God concerning any area of our lives which we have been controlling
- yield control of our life to Him (Romans 12:1)
- ask God to fill us with His Spirit (Luke 11:13, Ephesians 5:18)
- believe that He is filling us
- live dependent upon Him

© COPYRIGHT 1998, 2001, 2005, 2007 SCOPE MINISTRIES INTERNATIONAL INC.

When we are living dependent on the Holy Spirit, we are focused on receiving, relating, and responding to God. It is like a ballroom dance. The Holy Spirit leads and we follow. The Holy Spirit prompts us in our thoughts and we simply respond, believing He will empower us to do God's will. This is a moment-by-moment relationship.

A Spirit-filled life is a moment-by-moment relationship with Jesus. It is like a ballroom dance. The Holy Spirit leads and we follow.

SUMMARY:

1. The Holy Spirit is to the Christian everything Jesus was to the disciples: Helper, Comforter, Teacher, and Friend. He comes to live in us at salvation and will never leave or forsake us.

2. To be filled with the Spirit means to be motivated, led, and empowered by the Holy Spirit, allowing Him to live through us.

3. Daily, we have to choose between living by our spirit and living by our flesh. The flesh is the memory of our old way of living—relying on our own natural abilities and strengths.

4. A Spirit-filled life is a moment-by-moment relationship with Jesus, relying on the Holy Spirit to lead and empower us in our daily lives.

© COPYRIGHT 1998, 2001, 2005, 2007 SCOPE MINISTRIES INTERNATIONAL INC.

A Life Transformed, con't.

One day while I was driving and enjoying the beautiful clouds, the Holy Spirit told me, "Ruby, you are a child of God. That's who you are." He showed me that I am loved and very special to Him. He showed me that I am free from the bondage of my wrong belief that I am an orphan. That was the beginning of understanding my identity in Christ and the beginning of a relationship with God that is more than knowing that I'll go to heaven when I die.

The Holy Spirit has changed me. I used to be really quiet and withdrawn, and I didn't want people around me because I thought that if they knew me they wouldn't want me. Now I am more outgoing and confident and joyful because I'm not as afraid of rejection as I used to be. I know who I am in Christ, and I know that He loves me unconditionally regardless of my mistakes.

The Holy Spirit has taught me. When I first started co-leading small group studies, I depended upon the other leader in the group to help me because I believed that I wasn't smart enough to do it by myself. The first time I had to lead a group by myself, I thought, "I can't do this because I don't understand the material. I'm not living it." The Holy Spirit responded, "Yes, you do, and yes, you are." I know that the Holy Spirit speaks only the truth, so I was really excited to realize that I truly do understand the material.

Another time I asked the Holy Spirit to show me a wrong belief in my life. He brought to my mind a scene from the movie *Annie*. She's in a room with a long row of beds, much like the boarding school where I grew up. Annie thought that she had to be tough and take care of herself. The Holy Spirit showed me that this is how I used to be: tough — so that I wouldn't feel emotions — and really independent from God. I was so encouraged when God showed me how much I've changed.

The Holy Spirit is changing how I interact with my children. He showed me that it's not my job to change them. I have a daughter who's married to an alcoholic who verbally abuses her. I used to get angry with her and tell her that she didn't need a husband like that. By not accepting her, I alienated her and my grandchildren because she didn't want to tell me what was going on in their lives when she knew I wouldn't like it.

Now the Holy Spirit is enabling me to give her the freedom to make her choices and to accept her unconditionally, and she's beginning to trust me more. I'm no longer trying to control the situation, but it is still an area of my life that's hard, and I have to depend constantly on the Spirit. I tell Him, "You know how I used to be. I need you to remind me when I start withdrawing from her that I don't have to be that way anymore."

Through the Holy Spirit, I am experiencing the joy, freedom, and love that God has for me. He interacts with me in the most personal ways, and the more I know God, as He really is, the more I want to be with Him. The more I am with Him, the more I become like Him. That's the very best work of the Spirit!

Ruby - Biblical Personal Guidance Minister

© COPYRIGHT 1998, 2001, 2005, 2007 SCOPE MINISTRIES INTERNATIONAL INC.

Living By the Spirit - Day One

Goal: To understand the person of the Holy Spirit.

The Holy Spirit is God within us. He is more than a "power." He is a person Who has a mind (knows and communicates God's thoughts), a will (distributes gifts as He wills—1 Corinthians 12:11), and emotions (can be grieved, made sorrowful—Ephesians 4:30). He is called the "Spirit of Truth" in John 15:26.

1. In John 14:26, what is the Holy Spirit called?

2. In John 15:26, what is the Holy Spirit called?

3. Who is sending Him?

4. In Romans 8:2, what is the Holy Spirit called?

5. How does Isaiah 11:2 describe the Holy Spirit?

6. Galatians 5:22-23 lists some of the fruit of the Spirit. What emotions does this list indicate that the Holy Spirit has?

© COPYRIGHT 1998, 2001, 2005, 2007 SCOPE MINISTRIES INTERNATIONAL INC.

7. Write each of the nine characteristics of the fruit of the Spirit out in this manner:

    1) The Holy Spirit is love.

    2)

    3)

    4)

    5)

    6)

    7)

    8)

    9)

8. Based on what you've just read about the Holy Spirit, write your own description of Who the Holy Spirit is to you personally.

9. Is this the type of person you could trust? Why or why not?

10. According to 1 Corinthians 6:19, what is your body?

11. According to Romans 12:1, what are you to do?

12. Spend a few minutes expressing to God your desire for the Holy Spirit to live through you. Pray Romans 12:1 back to God, offering your body (life) to Him.

© COPYRIGHT 1998, 2001, 2005, 2007 SCOPE MINISTRIES INTERNATIONAL INC.

Living By the Spirit - Day Two

Goal: To understand the Holy Spirit's role in your life.

1. What does John 6:63 tell us the Spirit does?

2. According to John 14:17, where does the Holy Spirit live?

3. Read the following verses and write what the Holy Spirit will do for you.

    a) John 14:26

    b) John 16:13

    c) Romans 5:5

    d) Romans 8:15

    e) Romans 8:16

    f) Romans 8:27

    g) Romans 15:13

4. Read John 15:1-5. The word "abide" means to dwell or make yourself at home. Abiding in Jesus is simply giving oneself to Him to be ruled and taught and led, thereby resting in His unconditional love. According to verse 4 and 5, how much of the Christian life can you accomplish on your own?

5. In what ways have you tried to live the Christian life on your own?

© COPYRIGHT 1998, 2001, 2005, 2007 SCOPE MINISTRIES INTERNATIONAL INC.

6. Write down some personal examples of how the Holy Spirit has been working in your life until now (reflect on your answers to question 3).

7. Write a thank-you note to the Holy Spirit, expressing your gratitude for all He has already done for you.

© COPYRIGHT 1998, 2001, 2005, 2007 SCOPE MINISTRIES INTERNATIONAL INC.

Living By the Spirit - Day Three

Goal: To recognize your need to walk by faith and depend moment-by-moment on the Holy Spirit.

Jesus described the Spirit-filled life as thirsting and drinking and walking. Each of these activities is repetitive in nature.

> If we live by the Spirit, let us also walk by the Spirit.   Galatians 5:25 NAS
>
> As you have therefore received Christ . . . so walk in Him. Colossians 2:6 NAS

1. How did you receive Christ? How are you to walk?

2. We exercise faith in Christ not only at salvation but also daily, moment-by-moment. With each new situation or need, we need to express faith in Christ, Who is our life. Read Galatians 2:20. How does Paul say he now lives?

3. Read John 7:37-39. Thirst expresses our continuous need and desire to know God. How often during a day do you get thirsty? How often do you think of trusting Jesus?

4. The following verses express the psalmist's longing for God. Write your own psalm expressing your thirst to God.

> As the deer pants for the water brooks,
> So my soul longs for Thee, O God.
> My soul thirsts for God, for the living God.
> Psalm 42:1-2a, NAS

© COPYRIGHT 1998, 2001, 2005, 2007 SCOPE MINISTRIES INTERNATIONAL INC.

5. Drinking expresses receiving by faith. Every time we are thirsty (long for God) we acknowledge His presence (by talking to Him). Then, by trusting in Jesus, our soul is filled with His life-giving Spirit.

> If any man is thirsty, let him come to Me and drink. He who believes in Me, as the Scripture said, 'From his innermost being shall flow rivers of living water.'
> John 7:37b-38 NAS

6. Read John 4:5-24 about Jesus and the Samaritan woman. How was the woman trying to satisfy her thirst (her inward needs)? What did Jesus offer her?

7. Read John 5:38-40. Jesus was addressing the religious leaders who knew the Scriptures well. In fact, they had memorized most of it. What were these religious people missing? Why?

8. How have you tried to satisfy your thirst? (relationships, approval of others, material possessions, job, fame, etc.)

9. Write Galatians 2:20, personalizing it and putting it into your own words.

10. Express to Jesus your desire to trust Him moment by moment to satisfy your deepest needs and desires.

© COPYRIGHT 1998, 2001, 2005, 2007 SCOPE MINISTRIES INTERNATIONAL INC.

Living By the Spirit - Day Four

Goal: To understand the negative consequences of choosing to live according to the flesh and the value of living by the Spirit.

Living by the flesh is simply living by our own natural abilities, energy, and strength to meet our needs apart from God. Although the flesh might even appear very good and respectable, it can never produce God's quality of life.

After God promised Sarah and Abraham a son, Sarah persuaded Abraham to father a child by her handmaid, Hagar. This produced Ishmael, who persecuted Isaac, the son promised by God. These two sons represent the difference between living by the flesh and living by the Spirit.

1. Read Galatians 4:22-24; 28-29. Ishmael represents depending on our own energy, natural ability and strength. Isaac, the son of promise, represents the supernatural life of the Spirit. In what ways have you tried to fulfill God's plan for your life through your own energy, natural ability, and strength?

2. Through the life of the Apostle Peter, we can see the contrast between the flesh and the Spirit. Before the Holy Spirit was given, Peter was earnest in his efforts to follow Christ, but all his human effort ended in his denying Christ. Read Matthew 26:26, 31-35.

3. After the Holy Spirit was given on the day of Pentecost, Peter courageously and boldly proclaimed the Gospel. Even when experiencing physical suffering and persecution, Peter rejoiced in the Lord and continued to proclaim Him to others. Read Acts 4:13; 5:27-29.

4. Read Philippians 3:3-6. Describe the Apostle Paul's flesh.

5. Read John 6:63. What did Jesus say about the Spirit and the flesh?

© COPYRIGHT 1998, 2001, 2005, 2007 SCOPE MINISTRIES INTERNATIONAL INC.

6. Read 1 Corinthians 2:7-13. What does the Spirit reveal to your mind?

7. Looking back over today's answers, what personal benefit do you think you would receive by being motivated, led, and empowered by the Holy Spirit?

8. How would living by the Spirit change you in the midst of your present struggles and how you view your present circumstances?

9. In what areas do you need to receive God's wisdom?

10. In what areas do you need to receive God's strength?

11. In what ways do you need to be comforted by God?

12. Spend some time thanking God for being your resident Counselor, Teacher, Comforter, Helper, and Strengthener. Ask Him to remind you of how He has been all of these to you in the past. Ask Him to make you more aware of His presence in the future.

© COPYRIGHT 1998, 2001, 2005, 2007 SCOPE MINISTRIES INTERNATIONAL INC.

Living By the Spirit - Day Five

Goal: To recognize and correct any wrong beliefs that hinder you from experiencing a Spirit-filled life.

Living life by the Spirit requires living by faith (taking God at His Word). It means believing that the Holy Spirit indwells you and desires to live through your soul and body (Romans 8:15; 1 Corinthians 3:16).

Christ is the only Person capable of living the Christian life! No matter how sincere and determined our self-efforts are, we fail to love God and others as God has instructed us. However, the Holy Spirit fulfills God's righteous requirements by filling our souls with Christ's life. By faith, we accept that, in Christ, God has fulfilled all His righteous requirements for holiness and that Christ now lives in us and is our life.

In faith, we ask the Spirit to fill us (Ephesians 5:18), trusting Him to give us the power to live an abundant and Godly life. In faith, we accept that God has given us new hearts that desire to please Him, has poured out His love into our hearts, and has written His commandments on our hearts (Ezekiel 36:26-27; Romans 5:5).

1. According to the following verse, what is God's will concerning how you are to walk?

> Therefore be careful how you walk, not as unwise men, but as wise, making the most of your time, because the days are evil. So then do not be foolish, but understand what the will of the Lord is. And do not get drunk with wine, for that is dissipation, but be [continually] filled with the Spirit. Ephesians 5:15-18, NAS

To be filled with the Spirit means to be stimulated, empowered, and influenced by the Holy Spirit who lives in you. To be filled, we must surrender control of our lives to the Holy Spirit (Romans 12:1) and allow Him to live through us. This is not a one-time experience but a day-to-day, moment-by-moment lifestyle.

2. Read Ephesians 5:15-18 again.

We are filled with the Holy Spirit by faith. Christ lives through you by the power of His Holy Spirit.

3. Read Galatians 2:20. Ask Him to begin teaching you how to live by faith in the Spirit.

© COPYRIGHT 1998, 2001, 2005, 2007 SCOPE MINISTRIES INTERNATIONAL INC.

4. Read the chart, "Common Wrong Beliefs About the Spirit-filled Life." Write out the wrong beliefs that best represent your thinking, then read the corresponding truth and Scriptures.

5. Choose to put off the lies you have believed about the Spirit, and replace them with the truth based on Scripture. Ask the Holy Spirit to remind you when the lies influence your thoughts again.

Being "filled" with the Holy Spirit is not a one-time experience, but a day-to-day, moment-by-moment lifestyle. To be filled, we must surrender control of our lives to the Holy Spirit.

6. Read the following verses, then take a few minutes to express to God your decision to yield control of your life to Him and to be filled with His Spirit.

> Or do you not know that your body is a temple of the Holy Spirit who is in you, whom you have from God, and that you are not your own? For you have been bought with a price: therefore glorify God in your body.   1 Corinthians 6:19-20 NAS

> But if the Spirit of Him who raised Jesus from the dead dwells in you, He who raised Christ Jesus from the dead will also give life to your mortal bodies through His Spirit who indwells you. So then, brethren, we are under obligation, not to the flesh, to live according to the flesh—for if you are living according to the flesh, you must die; but if by the Spirit you are putting to death the deeds of the body, you will live.
>
> Romans 8:11-13 NAS

© COPYRIGHT 1998, 2001, 2005, 2007 SCOPE MINISTRIES INTERNATIONAL INC.

Common Wrong Beliefs About the Spirit-filled Life

Lie	Truth
I live my life with God as my helper. I can't expect God to do everything. Implication: God helps those who help themselves.	God wants to live His life through me by means of the Spirit. He says that I can do NOTHING apart from Him! John 15:5; Acts 17:28; Galatians 2:20
I can control my life better than the Holy Spirit. If I let the Spirit control my life, then my life would be out of control Implication: My control is better than God's control.	When I try to control my life, I actually become out of control. Living by my laws and standards activates the principle of sin, and I inevitably end up doing the opposite of what I want to do. By allowing the Spirit to live through me, I am empowered with self-control. Romans 7:4, 8, 15; Galatians 5:16, 22-23; 2 Timothy 1:7
Living by faith in the Holy Spirit is foreign to me, unnatural, contrary to how I best operate. Implication: God is unwise and doesn't know what is best for me.	I am primarily a spiritual being. Living by faith in the Spirit is consistent with who I really am. Living by faith may feel awkward initially because it has not been the way I have been living my life. However, God calls me to walk by the Spirit because He knows that is how I have been designed by Him to live. It is how I best operate. Romans 8:14-16; Galatians 2:20
If I submit to the Spirit, I'll have to give up _____. I won't enjoy life as much. Implication: God doesn't know or care about my desires. He may withhold something from me that I really want and that would be terrible. My enjoyment in life is based on external things.	Fullness of joy comes from knowing God and living conscious of His presence. The Holy Spirit enables me to experience and know God intimately, which results in unequaled joy and peace. My Heavenly Father cares about my needs and desires. He delights in giving to me and is infinitely wise in knowing the perfect gifts and perfect time to give those gifts to me. Psalm 16:11; Matthew 7:7-11; Romans 8:31-32; James 1:17
The Spirit-filled life is unclear and confusing. I cannot live by the Spirit; it is too hard. Implication: God is telling me to do something and not telling me how to do it. He is unclear and confusing.	God is not a God of confusion, but of peace. He commands me to be filled with the Spirit, and His commandments are not burdensome. God desires more than I do that I learn to live and walk by the Spirit. I can trust Him to teach me and clarify the truth to me. Matthew 11:28-30; 1 Corinthians 14:33; Ephesians 5:18; 1 John 5:3
I will be obnoxiously over-spiritual, do crazy-looking things, and alienate people if I am filled with the Spirit. Implication: God will make me weird and obnoxious.	The Holy Spirit is God. God is not obnoxious, overly pushy, or insensitive to people. He desires to draw people to Himself, not alienate them. The Spirit lives uniquely through the personality of each person. The Holy Spirit is in the process of conforming all of us to the image of Jesus; therefore, comparing ourselves to others is non-productive. 1 Corinthians 13:4-8; 2 Corinthians 3:18, 10:12

© COPYRIGHT 1998, 2001, 2005, 2007 SCOPE MINISTRIES INTERNATIONAL INC.

The underlying wrong belief in all of these lies is that God does not have my best interests at heart, does not know what is best for me, and/or does not want to be intimately involved in my life. Therefore, He cannot be trusted, and I will not yield my life to Him.

The underlying truth undergirding all of these truths is that God is perfect in His love toward me, and perfect in His wisdom in knowing me completely and knowing what is best for me. He desires to be intimately involved in every aspect of my life. Because God is trustworthy, I can choose to yield myself to Him and walk in the power of His Spirit.

© COPYRIGHT 1998, 2001, 2005, 2007 SCOPE MINISTRIES INTERNATIONAL INC.

Living By the Spirit - Lesson Five

Name _____ Date _____

Answer the following questions. To turn in page to small group leader, use identical perforated page in back of book.

1. What encouraged you most about this week's study on the Holy Spirit?

2. List any fears or concerns you have about surrendering control of your life to the Holy Spirit.

3. What do you feel would keep God from filling you with His Spirit?

4. How would living by the Spirit affect your life and your current struggles?

5. Mark the graph to indicate how much of this week's assignment you completed.

| None | 50% | 100% |

© COPYRIGHT 1998, 2001, 2005, 2007 SCOPE MINISTRIES INTERNATIONAL INC.

Record Your Prayer Requests:

_____

_____

_____

_____

_____

_____

_____

_____

_____

_____

_____

_____

_____

_____

_____

_____

_____

© COPYRIGHT 1998, 2001, 2005, 2007 SCOPE MINISTRIES INTERNATIONAL INC.

Be Transformed

Part Two

Common Obstacles We Encounter

Controlling Emotions

These things I remember, and I pour out my soul within me . . .
Why are you in despair, O my soul? And *why* have you become
disturbed within me? Hope in God, for I shall again praise Him *for*
the help of His presence.

Psalm 42:4a, 5 NAS

Lesson 6

A Life Transformed

When I was a child, my family didn't communicate well. Because my mother and father had marriage problems, my mom was usually depressed. When I was mad or sad, she would walk away while I was talking to her or send me to my room. I learned that it didn't do any good to express my emotions. I bottled them up inside, and became emotionally numb.

Things got even worse in high school when my family experienced some tragedies. All of us had problems but no one ever talked about anything. My mother always said, "Talk only about good things," so we were silent instead. That was when my emotions really went crazy and I tried to suppress them. Instead they dominated my life. I escaped the hurt at home through drugs, guys, school, and performance. I was really depressed and sick a lot, so I tried to do things to feel better, but I never really dealt with my emotions.

I thought that God was just like my parents and didn't really care, but, when I first became a Christian in college, I found that He really does care. It was a very emotional time because I started expressing myself to God. I cried out to Him a lot, and I felt relieved to tell Him everything.

After a few rough times, though, I returned to my old pattern of suppressing my emotions. The more I tried ignoring them, the more they controlled me. I turned to some of the things I had done in the past to make myself feel better.

to be continued...

© COPYRIGHT 1998, 2001, 2005, 2007 SCOPE MINISTRIES INTERNATIONAL INC.

Controlling Emotions - Lesson Six

When renewing our minds, one of the greatest obstacles we may encounter is our emotions. It is often easier to believe the lies about God and ourselves because of how we feel. For example, we may find it difficult to believe that God has forgiven us or unconditionally loves us because we do not "feel" forgiven or unconditionally loved.

Our society highly values "positive" emotions such as happiness and peace, yet it ignores or despises the "negative" emotions of depression, anger, and fear. However, the Bible is filled with examples of both pleasant and unpleasant or "less acceptable" feelings.

We are Emotional Beings

God is a spiritual being. (John 4:24)

Although the Bible clearly states that God is Spirit, He does express emotionally. He expresses emotions of grief (Genesis 6:6), anger (Psalm 106:40), joy and excitement (Zephaniah 3:17), and love and compassion (Isaiah 54:10). Jesus expressed anger as He drove the moneychangers from the Temple. He showed compassion toward the multitude who had been without food for three days. Because we are made in His image, we also have the ability to feel a wide range of emotions.

Jesus' soul was deeply grieved to the point of death.

Sin has affected us emotionally.

Before man experienced sin, his emotions expressed the heart of his Creator. As Adam received revelation from God, his thoughts and emotions reflected the love, joy, and peace of God. When man became disconnected from God, his mind became darkened, and his thoughts no longer reflected the truth about God. This gave rise to the "renegade" emotions such as fear, anger, guilt, and sadness. Living independently of God's truth, man's reason and emotions became his final authority for what he would believe. Because we have all been affected by sin, we often allow our emotions to control our beliefs and behavior.

Emotions are morally neutral and are part of our soul.

Emotions are not necessarily sinful, but our response to our emotions may be sinful. We need to acknowledge our emotions, even the "negative" ones, but not allow them to dictate our behavior or what we believe.

Renegade emotions, although they are negative and harmful, are still just a part of our emotion spectrum. And as such, they should be addressed as Paul addresses anger in Ephesians 4:31. For example, many people consider anger to be a sin. However, the Bible tells us to "be angry and sin not" (Ephesians 4:26, KJV). Anger is not a sin but an emotion. Conversely, few of us would ever say that happiness is a sin. But consider a situation where I felt my rights had been violated by a co-worker and I felt angry. Later when I heard that he had been fired, I would feel happy and satisfied.

© COPYRIGHT 1998, 2001, 2005, 2007 SCOPE MINISTRIES INTERNATIONAL INC.

Our emotions motivate us and can positively aid our performance.

When we experience negative emotions, often we are motivated to seek positive change. For example, anger over an unjust law might motivate a person to seek to change that law. Our performance in sports, in a musical performance, or in a job situation can be heightened by our emotions. Emotions are the product of our thoughts and beliefs, and they powerfully influence our ability to be motivated.

Emotional pain often motivates us to seek help and pursue change.

Emotional pain is to our soul what physical pain is to our body. We could not physically survive very long if our nervous system gave us no sensation of pain. In the same way, emotional pain warns us of a problem so that we can take action. If we ignore physical pain and do not deal with the cause, we can create significant physical problems. For example, if we ignore a toothache, a tooth could become abscessed and poison the bloodstream. Likewise, if we do not deal with emotional pain, we make problems worse. When experiencing emotional pain, we need to determine the cause of the pain and take steps to deal with it.

Our emotions help us express God's character.

Both pleasant and unpleasant emotions are part of God's character. Jesus was called "a man of sorrow, acquainted with grief." He experienced a depth of distress and agony on the cross that we will never have to experience. When Lazarus died, Jesus wept intensely. However, in that same moment, He also experienced compassion for Mary and Martha. He rejoiced greatly when the 70 disciples returned from their journey into the towns and villages he was about to visit (Luke 10:21). Because we are made in the image of God, we demonstrate many facets of His personality. We have the same ability to feel grief, distress, and other unpleasant emotions, but also love, compassion, mercy, joy, and peace.

Our emotions enable us to enjoy God.

The Westminster Catechism defines our purpose as: "The chief end of man is to glorify God and enjoy Him forever." Scripture uses words such as delight, rejoice, pleasure, peace, and joy to describe our emotional response to God. Experientially knowing and loving God involves our whole being, including our emotions.

> I have set the Lord continually before me; Because He is at my right hand, I will not be shaken. Therefore my heart is glad, and my glory rejoices;. . . In Thy presence is fullness of joy; In Thy right hand there are pleasures forever.
>
> Psalm 16:8-9a, 11b NAS

How does God respond to our "negative" emotions? What is His attitude toward us in the midst of our struggles? How can we keep from being controlled by our emotions? How can we again experience and express the heart of our Heavenly Father? **In this lesson we will look at three characteristics of emotions: They are messengers, they are messy, and they are manageable.**

© COPYRIGHT 1998, 2001, 2005, 2007 SCOPE MINISTRIES INTERNATIONAL INC.

Our Emotions are Messengers

Our emotions tell us what is occurring in our soul.

Imagine yourself on the highway when the red light marked "oil" on your dashboard lights up. Do you ignore it and keep driving your car for the next few days? Do you reach into the glove box, pull out a screwdriver and disconnect the light so you don't have to see it anymore? Do you pull into a service station and ask the attendant to repair your red "oil" light? No! The problem is not the light. The light is only a messenger telling you about a deeper problem in the engine. It's the engine that needs your attention; the light just tells you that.

This illustration helps us better understand how our emotions are messengers. The red "oil" light plays a role much like the role our emotions play in our lives. Most people seek counseling because they are unhappy, frustrated, depressed, or anxious. Their emotions are telling them that there is something "wrong" that needs to be acknowledged and addressed. Therefore, our emotions alert us to "look under the hood" . . . to find the thoughts, beliefs and perceptions that are underlying the emotions. Then we can seek new ways to think, believe, and perceive life—ways which are based on the truth of God's Word.

Our emotions are messengers reminding us to relate to God.

As messengers, our emotions (especially the painful ones) remind us to communicate with God about all that concerns us. God cares how we feel, but even more importantly, God cares about how we are thinking, what we are believing and how we are interpreting the circumstances of life.

> Casting the whole of your care [all your anxieties, all your worries, all your concerns, once and for all] on Him, for He cares for you affectionately *and* cares about you watchfully.
> 1 Peter 5:7 Amplified

> Cast your burden on the Lord [releasing the weight of it] and He will sustain you; He will never allow the [consistently] righteous to be moved (made to slip, fall, or fail). Psalm 55:22 Amplified

God desires for us to relate to Him as emotional beings and to communicate honestly to Him what is happening in our souls. We need to relate to God in order to gain His perspective and receive His comfort and peace.

Fear and Anxiety	Shame	Inadequacy or Fear of Failure	Loneliness	Anger
Remind us of our need to acknowledge and live consciously aware of our Savior's presence. For the One Who is perfect Love has promised, "I will never, no never, leave you nor forsake you." Fear is faith in a lie rather than the truth. It means our focus is on something or someone other than God.	Reminds us that our identity and worth is not determined by our performance and what others think but only by the love and sacrifice demonstrated by our Creator Father. It is only as we look into His face that we can accurately see who we are and what we are worth.	Reminds us that apart from our indwelling Lord we can do nothing. It reminds us that we are created for a dependent relationship—as little children—and that we need to rely on our Father's infinite wisdom and strength.	Reminds us of our most vital need of intimate companionship with our Father God. It is the call of our soul to reach out to the Father of mercy and God of all comfort. He longs to reveal Himself to the lonely.	Anger is a messenger, reminding us that we live in a fallen world and life is not fair. It reminds us of our need to release God's mercy and forgiveness to others, yielding our rights and expectations to God, Who works everything together for our good.

© COPYRIGHT 1998, 2001, 2005, 2007 SCOPE MINISTRIES INTERNATIONAL INC.

6.5

Emotions can be messy when they seem more true than God's Word.

All that we feel, both pleasant and unpleasant emotions, are to be expressed to God. We are told in Scripture to pray about everything with thanksgiving. Often we feel comfortable only going to God with our pleasant emotions. However, in the Psalms we see many examples of unpleasant emotions prompting heart-felt worship and trust in God, the One Who alone can meet all our deepest needs.

Our Emotions Can be Messy

Our emotions can be messy when they seem more true to us than the Word of God.

They can disrupt our lives when we allow them to control us. Our emotions are messy when they become the final authority in our lives to control our behavior. For example, if I am angry with my co-worker, and I choose to gossip, slander, or seek revenge, I am being controlled by messy emotions.

When we act and react based on how we feel about what is happening in our lives, our emotions become the primary influence in our life, overriding God's Word. For example, many Christians have thoughts like, "I don't feel close to God, so I guess He must be mad at me (or there must be sin in my life)." On the other hand, a Christian might justify sin with, "I don't feel guilty, so it must not be wrong." In both cases, the feeling, not God's Word, dictates the person's thinking and beliefs about God and sin.

Often, when we feel depressed, this feeling fuels more negative thoughts which produce deepening feelings of depression. Sometimes young men don't understand their unmet emotional needs for normal father-son affection. These feelings may become twisted and affect their sexual choices, leading them to choose a homosexual lifestyle. Sexually promiscuous young women typically are trying to change their feelings of unworthiness and meet their need for intimacy and affection. In each case, the determining factor is the desire to seek emotional satisfaction (or avoid pain) rather than to face the message of the emotion and deal with the underlying false beliefs. Emotions can be messy!

What Other Factors Affect Our Emotions?

Wrong teaching or poor modeling about our emotions.

Our culture has influenced our ability to deal properly with our emotions. Children are told not to cry or be angry. Men are often taught not to be fearful or emotional. Many men who have struggled with fear are embarrassed to share this with others or to acknowledge their angry feelings to themselves or God. Tears are seen as a sign of weakness.

Our physical health and needs can affect us emotionally.

Hormonal changes, stress, fatigue, poor eating or sleeping habits, or lack of exercise can affect us emotionally. When Elijah was physically exhausted, his interpretation of life's circumstances was grossly inaccurate (1 Kings 19). When thoughts and interpretations are inaccurate, strong feelings can easily follow.

© COPYRIGHT 1998, 2001, 2005, 2007 SCOPE MINISTRIES INTERNATIONAL INC.

Our pride can make dealing with our emotions difficult.

Acknowledging feelings of jealousy, fear, anger, or resentment is difficult. Thoughts such as, "Shouldn't I be above that? Why did I let that bother me?" keep us from dealing with the real cause of our feelings. It hurts our pride to admit to such "unspiritual" feelings.

Our Emotions are Manageable

We need to take our messy emotions to God.

We do not have to be enslaved to the dictates of our feelings. God desires to help us handle our emotions. The Psalms are evidence that David and others felt free to approach God with their emotions. Psalms 13, 55, and 73, are good examples of how we can do this. The acrostic "REED" helps us remember how to manage our emotions.

Suppressed emotions will eventually emerge and be harder to handle.

Recognize our emotions.
We need to acknowledge them, not ignore them. We need to learn to verbalize how we feel. Some people have to develop a vocabulary to express how they feel. Sometimes a friend or Biblical Spiritual Advisor can help by giving us objective feedback about the emotions that we are experiencing but can't identify. (See a list on page 6.23.)

Express our emotions to God.
Many people are afraid they may offend God if they tell Him how they feel, especially if it is about Him. However, He knows about our feelings and is not offended by them. Our feelings do not change the character of God! When we read the Psalms, we realize that He has heard everything many times before.

We must avoid denying or repressing our feelings. If we deny our feelings and turn them inward, we are essentially lying to ourselves, God, and others. "Stuffing" our emotions can result in physical illness, intense and explosive emotional outbursts, disjointed thoughts and words, or destructive behavior. Besides, we can't suppress our emotions forever. Eventually they will emerge and will be even harder to address.

Dumping emotions on others can wound the person and damage the relationship.

On the other hand, expressing our emotions to others can potentially wound them and damage our relationships. We may get our feelings off our chest and feel some temporary relief, but we are not addressing the issues behind the emotions.

God cares about how we feel, and more importantly, why we feel the way we do. When we express our emotions to God, we are being honest with ourselves and with Him. His Spirit and His Word can then direct our thoughts, beliefs, behavior, and eventually, our feelings.

Evaluate what our emotions are telling us.
We need to reflect on how our emotions, behavior, and thinking are related. Just as David asked himself, "Why are you in despair O my soul?" Psalm 42:5 NAS, we need to ask God to show us what wrong beliefs or thoughts are feeding our emotions.

Decide to replace our thinking and behavior with God's Truth.
Questions we can ask ourselves: How does what I think and how I behave compare with God's Word? What needs to change? Remember we have a new identity and destiny. We do not have to stay stuck in old patterns of living. We can choose to act and react according to our new Biblical thinking. This adjustment of thoughts and beliefs in the light of God's truth is the "renewing of the mind" process that is commanded in Romans 12:2.

© COPYRIGHT 1998, 2001, 2005, 2007 SCOPE MINISTRIES INTERNATIONAL INC.

> Do not be conformed any longer to the pattern of this world, but be transformed by the renewing of your mind.
>
> Romans 12:2 NIV

Renewing our minds according to God's reality results in our being transformed. As our thinking and beliefs are corrected, our emotions eventually change also.

One word of caution. "REED" is not "four easy steps" to managing your emotions. It is a springboard for interacting actively with God about your deeply felt personal desires and needs. It is important to remember that, as Christians, we are in a vital moment-by-moment relationship with the living God. We often try to define the "Christian life" as a series of principles to be followed rather than as a constant conversation with, a total dependence upon, and an active trust in God Himself.

God truly wants to be involved with us in our emotions, in our concerns, in our personal life—more so than our closest friend. He is so much more than a friend, because not only does He empathize, comfort, and advise, but He also transforms us through His Spirit and His Word!

Conclusion: The world around us is clamoring for good feelings while indulging emotions in its search for happiness. Yet, people are not satisfied. They are never quite fulfilled. They are always wanting more. We must live by faith rather than feelings, remembering Jesus' words:

> Blessed *and* fortunate *and* happy *and* spiritually prosperous. . . are those who hunger and thirst for righteousness,. . . for they shall be completely satisfied.   Matthew 5:6 Amplified

---

In our pursuit of God, He will give us something far greater than temporal happiness: a joy that is rooted in His unchanging character.

┌─ **SUMMARY:** ─────────────────────────────

God's Word shows us that:

1. God never condemns or belittles us because of our emotional struggles. Both pleasant and unpleasant emotions are a normal part of the Christian life.

2. Emotions are messengers of our internal beliefs about God, self, and others.

3. Emotions are messy when they become the final authority in our lives to control our beliefs and behavior.

4. Emotions are manageable when we express them to God and allow Him to renew our thinking.

└──

© COPYRIGHT 1998, 2001, 2005, 2007 SCOPE MINISTRIES INTERNATIONAL INC.

A Life Transformed, con't.

When I learned that my emotions revealed my false beliefs, the Holy Spirit revealed experiences and situations in my life when I had developed false beliefs about God, myself and others. Although this was painful, it was also a relief to be freed from the lies that I had believed for years. God's truth brought healing.

I learned that emotions are natural because God has created me in His image with emotions like He has. That gave me the freedom to face my emotions for the first time in my life. I always knew that God had emotions like joy and peace, but I was so relieved to learn that He also has emotions like anger. I no longer feel guilty for having emotions like that.

I've learned to recognize the clues when I'm suppressing emotions: drinking coffee, smoking cigarettes, eating when I'm not hungry, cleaning when things aren't dirty, shopping when I don't need anything, writing to-do lists, doing things just to be busy so I don't think. Now when I start to feel like doing one of these things, I talk to God about how I feel and I ask Him, "What is bothering me? Why do I feel this way?" I read the Word to see what He says. After He reveals my wrong beliefs, then I renew my mind with His truth. I say verses out loud when I began to feel like hiding or stuffing my emotions. I often write Scripture verses like Philippians 4:6-7 NIV.

"Don't be anxious about anything, but in everything, by prayer and petition, with thanksgiving, present your requests to God. And the peace of God, which transcends all understanding will guard your hearts and your minds in Christ Jesus."

I've always known those verses, but now I use them. Instead of trying to handle the problem myself, I turn to God, and He keeps His promise. He does give me His peace!

Over a year ago, I was really hurt by a friend of mine. I tried to contact her by phone and mail, but she didn't respond. I kept turning to God with my emotions when I felt rejected and disliked. I kept trusting Him and praying for her. Recently she sent me a letter asking for forgiveness. If I had continued to let that hurt dominate me, I could have been bitter and unable to give her grace and forgiveness. Instead, our friendship is restored, and God was glorified in it.

I am so grateful I've learned to let my emotions take me to God instead of away from Him. Now I can handle the hurts in my life constructively instead of destructively.

Tammy - Customer Service Representative

© COPYRIGHT 1998, 2001, 2005, 2007 SCOPE MINISTRIES INTERNATIONAL INC.

© COPYRIGHT 1998, 2001, 2005, 2007 SCOPE MINISTRIES INTERNATIONAL INC.

Controlling Emotions - Day One

Goal: To recognize how you deal with your negative emotions, and to begin to interact with God concerning them.

1. What emotions were expressed in your home as you were growing up?

    Which ones were "acceptable"? Which ones were "unacceptable"?

2. Presently, what emotions are you comfortable in expressing?

    Uncomfortable expressing?

    Comfortable with others expressing?

    Uncomfortable with others expressing?

3. What are your "red flags" that indicate you may be feeling an emotion but not acknowledging it? (Examples: yelling, physical stress, short temper, withdrawal, compulsive behavior such as overeating, etc.)

© COPYRIGHT 1998, 2001, 2005, 2007 SCOPE MINISTRIES INTERNATIONAL INC.

4. Review your answers from Week 1, Day 1. How were your problems affecting you emotionally?

5. Our emotions are messengers alerting us to something in our thoughts and beliefs. What are some thoughts and beliefs that your emotions may reveal?

6. When our emotions are more real to us than God's truth and we base our decisions and responses upon them, then our emotions are messy. Possible responses to these negative emotions include denying, "stuffing," venting on others, and expressing them to God. How have you handled these negative emotions in the past? (Example: When I feel depressed, I ignore it by eating or watching TV.)

7. How did these emotions affect your behavior and/or choices?

8. Take a few moments to interact with God. First, compare your, beliefs, thoughts, and behaviors with God's Word. Ask the Holy Spirit to reveal to you any inconsistencies, and confess (agree with God) those that He reveals. Then, decide how you need to change your thoughts, beliefs, and behavior to be consistent with God's truth. Next, ask the Holy Spirit to help change your behavior and to continue to reveal incorrect beliefs and thoughts. Remember, each time you experience a negative emotion or the Holy Spirit reveals a wrong belief or thought, you need to replace that belief or thought with God's truth.

© COPYRIGHT 1998, 2001, 2005, 2007 SCOPE MINISTRIES INTERNATIONAL INC.

Controlling Emotions - Day Two

Goal: To recognize the emotional side of God in Scripture.

1. Read the following verses, and list the emotions that God expresses.

    Genesis 6:5-6

    Psalm 145:8

    Psalm 149:4

    Isaiah 57:16

    Isaiah 62:5

    Mark 10:21

    Luke 13:34

    Luke 22:44

    John 11:33-36

    Hebrews 5:7

2. Compare and/or contrast these verses with how you have previously viewed God.

© COPYRIGHT 1998, 2001, 2005, 2007 SCOPE MINISTRIES INTERNATIONAL INC.

3. Read the following verses to learn how God feels about your emotions. Write how God feels about or responds to your emotions.

    Psalm 51:17

    Psalm 56:8

    Matthew 11:28

    John 20:24-28

    Hebrews 4:15-16

    1 Peter 5:7

4. Compare and/or contrast these verses with how you have previously thought that God feels about your emotions.

© COPYRIGHT 1998, 2001, 2005, 2007 SCOPE MINISTRIES INTERNATIONAL INC.

Controlling Emotions - Day Three

Goal: To see the Biblical pattern for managing your emotions.

1. The Biblical pattern for REED (what to do with emotions) is especially noticeable in Psalms 55 and 73.

> **R**ecognize your emotions.
> **E**xpress them to God (don't ignore them, stuff them or lash out toward others).
> **E**valuate (ask the Holy Spirit to show you) what your emotions and thoughts reveal about what you are believing.
> **D**ecide to agree with God about the truth (believe), and act in faith on that truth.

REED applies to both positive and negative emotions. However, all emotions are actually positive, because they help us turn to God and evaluate our thinking and beliefs.

2. Read Psalm 73 in the chronological order provided below and answer the questions.

RECOGNIZE: (verses 2-14) What emotions does the Psalmist experience?

EXPRESS: (verses 16, 21-22) How does the Psalmist express his emotions to God? List some of the statements he makes.

EVALUATE: (verses 17-20, 1, 23-27) What beliefs do his emotions reveal?

© COPYRIGHT 1998, 2001, 2005, 2007 SCOPE MINISTRIES INTERNATIONAL INC.

DECIDE: (verse 28) How does the Psalmist choose to act on the truth (rather than on his emotions)?

3. Ask the Holy Spirit to remind you to practice REED in your communication with God.

© COPYRIGHT 1998, 2001, 2005, 2007 SCOPE MINISTRIES INTERNATIONAL INC.

Controlling Emotions - Day Four

Goal: To begin using the REED method of managing your emotions.

1. Emotions, both pleasant and unpleasant, are a normal part of the Christian life. Think back to the last time you were struggling with negative emotions. Use the chart on page 6.23 to help you recognize your feelings and list them below.

2. Now express your feelings to God by writing the thoughts that prompted you to feel this way. Be as honest as possible. God already knows and accepts you. He never condemns or rejects you because of your emotional struggles.

3. Emotions are the result of thoughts and beliefs. Now, evaluate your thoughts by answering the following questions:
   A. What beliefs do your thoughts reveal about God, yourself, and your circumstances?

   B. What is the truth according to God's Word? (Refer to the "Father/God" Bible study, pages 4.15-4.18, and the "Creating a Christian Identity" sheet page 3.28 for the truth).

© COPYRIGHT 1998, 2001, 2005, 2007 SCOPE MINISTRIES INTERNATIONAL INC.

4. Next, decide to reject the lies you've been thinking and to replace them with the truth. Make a deliberate choice to walk by faith, accepting God's Word as your final authority. Ask God what steps of faith (action) He wants you to take.

5. For the rest of this week practice the REED method whenever you encounter negative or painful emotions. You may want to journal (write) your thoughts and feelings using the worksheet on pages 6.25 and 6.26.

© COPYRIGHT 1998, 2001, 2005, 2007 SCOPE MINISTRIES INTERNATIONAL INC.

Controlling Emotions - Day Five

Goal: To recognize and express your fears to God and learn to trust in Him when you are afraid.

One of our most painful emotions is fear—which is often disguised as worry, anger, or depression. It is one of the most difficult emotions to acknowledge. Often we've been taught that fear is a sign of weakness; therefore, we've learned to suppress it.

1. King David, a man after God's heart, often experienced fear. Read Psalm 56.

2. What did David fear? (see verses 2, 5-6)

3. What did David do when he was afraid? (see verses 1, 3-4, 9-13)

4. Think of a specific situation which causes you to be afraid. It might be a future event, or it may be the fear of failure or rejection. Use the REED method for taking this fear to God.

   RECOGNIZE: Ask God to help you identify what you are afraid of. Acknowledge your fear to yourself and God.

   EXPRESS: Write to God what you fear and why you are afraid.

© COPYRIGHT 1998, 2001, 2005, 2007 SCOPE MINISTRIES INTERNATIONAL INC.

EVALUATE: Consider what your thoughts and feelings tell you about your beliefs about this issue. What beliefs about God does your fear reveal? How does what you think and believe compare with God's Word?

DECIDE: Choose to agree with God's truth about this issue. Then, choose to act on that truth, knowing that the Holy Spirit will empower you.

Example: "Father, I am afraid my husband may lose his job. It's hard for me to trust You in this area when I think of our family's needs. Thank You for listening and caring about how I feel. I know You promise to meet all our needs (Philippians 4:19), so I am casting all my cares on You (1 Peter 5:7). Therefore, I choose to go about my day, not focusing on the potential problem, but trusting You to work this out for our good and to meet our needs in Your way and in Your timing."

© COPYRIGHT 1998, 2001, 2005, 2007 SCOPE MINISTRIES INTERNATIONAL INC.

Controlling Emotions - Lesson Six

Name _____ Date _____

Answer the following questions. To turn in page to small group leader, use identical perforated page in back of book.

1. What negative emotion did you experience most this past week? What kind of thoughts usually produced this emotion?

2. What did these thoughts tell you about what you were believing?

3. What new insight or perspective did God give you when you expressed your feelings honestly to Him?

4. How will practicing REED improve your relationship with God and your quality of life?

5. Mark the graph to indicate how much of this week's assignment you completed.

None	50%	100%

© COPYRIGHT 1998, 2001, 2005, 2007 SCOPE MINISTRIES INTERNATIONAL INC.

Record Your Prayer Requests:

© COPYRIGHT 1998, 2001, 2005, 2007 SCOPE MINISTRIES INTERNATIONAL INC.

How Do You Feel?

Lonely			Belonging		
left out	isolated	separate	popular	important	influential
friendless	withdrawn	rejected	famous	well-known	valuable
forsaken	lonesome		needed	accepted	worthwhile
lost	insignificant			attached	

Angry			Peaceful		
furious	mad	frustrated	calm	collected	composed
hacked off	hard	boiling	quiet	sedate	cool
aggravated	irritated	indignant	serene	content	tranquil
	distant	annoyed			

Sad			Happy		
dejected	depressed	gloomy	joyful	glad	bright
unhappy	cheerless	glum	ecstatic	pleased	vivacious
dreary	blue	downcast	cheerful	delighted	elated
woeful	grieving	heavy	upbeat	light	bouncy

Afraid			Secure		
anxious	fearful	scared	safe	optimistic	hopeful
frightened	shocked	terrified	protected	sure	confident
alarmed	unnerved	timid	stable	poised	assured
jumpy	tight	shaky			

Hateful			Loving		
hostile	critical	jealous	tender	accepting	loyal
unfriendly	quarrelsome	spiteful	affectionate	kind	sympathetic
mean	nasty	harsh	warm	devoted	caring
	shameful			forgiving	

Inadequate			Powerful		
weak	bashful	inept	strong	great	sure
small	meager	powerless	energetic	dominant	aggressive
useless	deficient	vulnerable	assertive	pushy	confident
			upbeat	assured	intoxicated

Guilty			Innocent		
ashamed	damned	judged	pardoned	set free	naive
criticized	doomed	trapped	pure	released	acquitted
cursed	dirty	embarrassed	forgiven	exonerated	justified
			clean	fresh	

© COPYRIGHT 1998, 2001, 2005, 2007 SCOPE MINISTRIES INTERNATIONAL INC. (Adapted from chart titled "How Do You Feel?" author unknown)

6.23

6.24

© COPYRIGHT 1998, 2001, 2005, 2007 SCOPE MINISTRIES INTERNATIONAL INC.

Taking My Emotions to God

RECOGNIZE: Acknowledge your emotions; don't suppress them. Ask the Holy Spirit to help you identify what emotions you are feeling.

EXPRESS: Write to God what you feel and why.

EVALUATE: Consider what your emotions are telling you about your thinking on the issue. Ask the Holy Spirit to reveal to you any false beliefs about yourself or about God. How does what you think and believe compare with God's Word?

DECIDE: Choose to agree with God's Word. Then choose to act on that truth, relying on the Holy Spirit to empower you.

© COPYRIGHT 1998, 2001, 2005, 2007 SCOPE MINISTRIES INTERNATIONAL INC.

Taking My Emotions to God

RECOGNIZE: Acknowledge your emotions; don't suppress them. Ask the Holy Spirit to help you identify what emotions you are feeling.

EXPRESS: Write to God what you feel and why.

EVALUATE: Consider what your emotions are telling you about your thinking on the issue. Ask the Holy Spirit to reveal to you any false beliefs about yourself or about God. How does what you think and believe compare with God's Word?

DECIDE: Choose to agree with God's Word. Then choose to act on that truth, relying on the Holy Spirit to empower you.

© COPYRIGHT 1998, 2001, 2005, 2007 SCOPE MINISTRIES INTERNATIONAL INC.

Expectations, Anger, and Bitterness

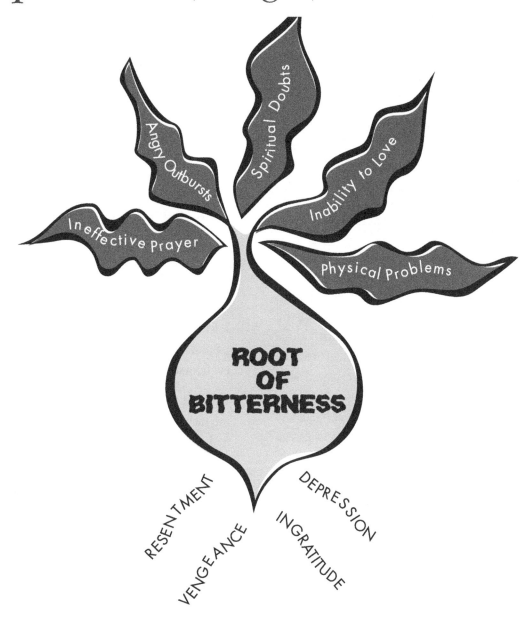

See to it that no one misses the grace of God and that no bitter root grows up to cause trouble and defile many.

Hebrews 12:15 NIV

Lesson 7

A Life Transformed

In April 1995 my life appeared to be great. I was married to a wonderful man, and we had two precious children. We were financially stable. I had many friends. My career was progressing. We attended a friendly church.

But underneath the smile was a pain so deep that depression had nearly overtaken me. I felt as though I had fallen into a deep, dark hole. The harder I tried to climb out, the deeper I sank. At times, just getting up each morning was nearly impossible. At work I would sit at my desk and stare at my computer for hours. Even at home, I was so depressed that all I wanted to do was sleep.

My facade of happiness covered an emotional pain that was deeply rooted in my childhood. I was the youngest of six children. My parents were successful people who were extremely active in church. On the surface, my family life appeared normal, but the "game" my brother, seven years older, played with me was far from normal. From the time I was five until I was 11 years old, my older brother frequently asked me to go to the game room above our garage where he sexually abused me.

I knew that at least part of the reason for my depression was the abuse. I had lived with flashbacks and pain for many years with memories haunting me daily. I thought that I deserved this because I blamed myself for the abuse, and I thought it was my fault that it had lasted so long.

I knew that I couldn't continue my life this way and that I had to be free from depression.

I contacted Scope Ministries and asked for help. I confided my struggles to a sweet lady who, week after week, lovingly responded to my pain with Scriptures. The Word of God started seeping into my spirit to begin healing me. During the next six months, I talked with her weekly, I read scores of books, I listened to many tapes, and I memorized many scriptures. I'll never forget the day that I realized that the abuse was not my fault.

At this point, one of my greatest fears was confronting my brother. We both had spent many years pretending that the abuse never happened. After six months of dealing with this agonizing issue, I felt that I needed to confront him and face the painful results of the abuse in my life. I was ready for confrontation and forgiveness and healing.

I needed to confront my brother because, even with the memories, I still had some doubt that the abuse had really occurred. By acknowledging it, I removed all my doubts that it really happened.

It was one of the toughest things I've ever done, but I wrote him a letter and then waited to see if and how he would respond. Would he deny it? Trivialize it? Blame me? I really just didn't know.

to be continued...

© COPYRIGHT 1998, 2001, 2005, 2007 SCOPE MINISTRIES INTERNATIONAL INC.

Expectations, Anger, and Bitterness - Lesson Seven

As we saw in the previous lesson, our "unpleasant" emotions can be an obstacle in believing God's truth. Actually, they are merely acting as messengers, alerting us to what we are thinking and believing. It is important that we recognize what we are feeling and evaluate what is taking place in our soul (mind, will, and emotions).

One "unpleasant" emotion that everyone experiences is anger. It is one of the strongest of emotions. The Bible says "be angry, and *yet* do not sin" (Ephesians 4:26). God is holy, and Jesus is without sin, yet the Bible records both expressing the emotion of anger.

The *New World Dictionary* defines anger as "a feeling of displeasure resulting from injustice, injury, mistreatment, opposition, etc., and usually showing itself in a desire to fight back at the supposed cause of this feeling; intense displeasure or exasperation; an emotional state of hostility, indignation, and revenge."

Expectations and Anger

Anger is a normal part of our total emotional spectrum.

Anger can be likened to power, sex, or fire. These things are neither inherently right nor wrong, but they become right or wrong only as they are used properly or abused. To determine if the anger we feel is appropriate, we must identify the basis of our anger and evaluate how we express it.

The Apostle Peter, at the time of Jesus' arrest, is a good example of an **inappropriate response** caused by the emotion of anger.

> And behold, one of those who were with Jesus reached and drew out his sword, and struck the slave of the high priest, and cut off his ear. Then Jesus said to him, "Put your sword back into its place; for all those who take up the sword shall perish by the sword." Matthew 26:51-54, NAS

Peter's anger was based on his love for Christ, but he failed to control the expression of his anger. Anger was not the problem, but the expression of his anger was inappropriate.

The cause of anger is blocked or unmet expectations.

An expectation is something we are looking forward to or assume will take place. Throughout life, we all develop expectations which are usually produced by comparing ourselves with others ("They get to . . ., so why can't I?") or from commitments people make or imply. Some expectations result from valid needs in our lives such as the need to feel loved, accepted, and secure. When these expectations are not met in the ways that we desire, the emotional reaction is often anger.

© COPYRIGHT 1998, 2001, 2005, 2007 SCOPE MINISTRIES INTERNATIONAL INC.

We Can Prevent Inappropriate Expressions of Anger

First, we need to yield our expectations and rights to God.

Anger becomes a problem when we deal with it improperly. A way to safeguard against responding in anger is to yield our expectations to God. In yielding, we choose to let God meet our needs in the ways He sees best instead of the way we want to see things done. We choose to trust and look to Him as the source of our contentment instead of looking to circumstances and people to give us joy. We need to acknowledge our anger to ourselves and God.

Sometimes anger masks other painful emotions such as fear and hurt. For example, it often feels better to be mad than to deal with the pain that is causing the emotion. It is less painful to "cover up" the real problems with an inappropriate expression of anger. Likewise, if I am afraid of something, I may express inappropriate anger rather than admit to being fearful. It is vital that we express our anger to God and allow Him to show us the cause of our anger. If we choose to deny or suppress our anger, it will manifest itself in our behavior, eventually affecting our emotional and/or physical health.

The following diagram is helpful in understanding the downward progression of emotions when we fail to deal properly with unmet expectations and unresolved anger.

Expectations	Anger	Bitterness				
Needs	Prevention:	Cure:	Resentment			
Comparisons	Yield expectations as act of trust in God.	Forgiveness		Vengeance		
Verbal Commitments					Ingratitude	
						Depression

Unsurrendered Anger Leads to Bitterness

When we don't address our anger properly, it will turn into bitterness. The Bible talks about this as developing a root of bitterness. The Biblical definition of bitterness is "resentfulness" or "harshness" and is referred to specifically in Ephesians 4:31 and Hebrews 12:15. To deal with anger and bitterness, we must choose to forgive others for what has happened and release them from our expectations. It is *God's* job to deal with the actions of other people, not ours.

© COPYRIGHT 1998, 2001, 2005, 2007 SCOPE MINISTRIES INTERNATIONAL INC.

> Let all bitterness and wrath and anger and clamor and slander
> be put away from you, along with all malice.
> Ephesians 4:31 NAS

> See to it that no one comes short of the grace of God; that no
> root of bitterness springing up causes trouble, and by it many
> be defiled. Hebrews 12:15 NAS

Bitterness is the result of a perceived right that has been violated.

If we don't exercise true forgiveness, we will hold the offender responsible (guilty) for his wrong. We then begin to accumulate fault in our mind towards him which we will bring up when the situation calls for it. When we don't forgive, we secretly await the "joy" of seeing the offender punished by God. This is a form of vengeance.

Bitterness causes emotional, physical and spiritual bondage.

When we are bitter towards a person, we may think we are hurting that person, but in reality we are hurting ourselves. Bitterness creates a feeling of distance in our fellowship with God. Emotionally, it can cause anxiety, stress, and depression. Physically, it can cause anything from headaches and fatigue to ulcers and arthritis. Unresolved anger also gives Satan an opportunity to wreak havoc in our lives.

> . . . do not let the sun go down on your anger, and do not give
> the devil an opportunity. Ephesians 4:26b-27 NAS

Bitterness affects not only us but will contaminate all our relationships.

Bitterness is like a cancer. Just as cancer will eventually spread throughout our entire body, bitterness will eventually affect all our relationships. A bitter person becomes critical, cynical, hateful, and harsh.

In His love, God desires to free us from this renegade emotion. His solution is forgiveness. He clearly instructs us to love our enemies and do good to those who mistreat us (Luke 6:27-28). It is our nature as God's children to forgive others as God has forgiven us.

> And be kind to one another, tender-hearted, forgiving each other,
> just as God in Christ also has forgiven you. Ephesians 4:32 NAS

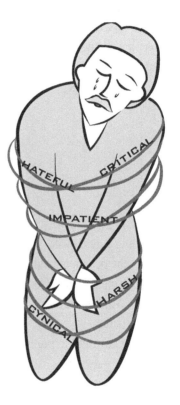

Forgiveness Frees Us From Anger and Bitterness

We must choose to forgive those who have blocked our expectations or injured us. If we do not deal with the bitterness, its roots grow into resentment, vengeance, and depression. We will become unable to be satisfied, and we will focus totally on our unmet expectations and the ones who failed to meet them. This blinds us as to how God is meeting our needs.

© COPYRIGHT 1998, 2001, 2005, 2007 SCOPE MINISTRIES INTERNATIONAL INC.

FORGIVENESS IS NOT:
ignoring/disregarding the
    wrong done
tolerating the person
excusing the person
forgetting about the
    wrong done
letting time pass
allowing abuse
being nice to the person
keeping silent
saying, "I forgive you."
based on feelings

FORGIVENESS IS:
canceling a debt owed
giving the person to God
yielding our rights to God
trusting God to redeem
    the situation
yielding our right to punish
not seeking revenge
    or getting even
not judging or condemning
not keeping score
extending mercy and grace
making a conscious choice

Forgiveness is a characteristic of our new identity in Christ.

God's forgiveness of us motivates and allows us to forgive others.

> . . . bearing with one another, and forgiving each other, whoever
> has a complaint against anyone; just as the Lord forgave you, so
> also should you.   Colossians 3:13, NAS

Forgiveness is more than an outward behavior.

Forgiveness is not ignoring, disregarding, tolerating, excusing, overlooking or closing our eyes to the wrong another person has done against us. It is not simply letting time pass after the offense has been committed. It is not trying to forget that the offense happened or pretending that it didn't. It is not just resigning ourselves to the other person's actions by saying, "Well, that's just the way he is." Forgiveness is not putting ourselves in the position to be abused or victimized again.

Forgiveness is a deliberate decision to cancel the debt owed.

Forgiveness is foregoing what we feel is due us and declaring the person no longer guilty toward us. It involves relinquishing the right to punish or to get even. It is relinquishing the right to judge or condemn the person for what they have done. Forgiveness is giving up the demand that they make right the wrong done.

The process of forgiveness includes:

1. Acknowledging the offense to God.

2. Expressing to God how it made you feel.

3. Expressing to God your decision to cancel the debt.

   • Giving up the right to punish or get even.

   • Giving up the right to judge or condemn.

   • Giving up the demand that they make right the wrong done.

4. Accepting the person just as they are.

   • Yield expectations to God.

   • Trust God to meet your needs.

   • Pray God's best for that individual.

5. Being willing to risk being hurt again.

   • Take down any walls of self-protection.

   • Trust God to heal and protect you should you be hurt again.

Forgiveness requires our trust in God's character.

We must trust in God's faithfulness to work everything out for good, even our injury and pain.

© COPYRIGHT 1998, 2001, 2005, 2007 SCOPE MINISTRIES INTERNATIONAL INC.

> And as for you, you meant evil against me, *but* God meant it for
> good . . .   Genesis 50:20a, NAS

> And we know that God causes all things to work together for
> good to those who love God, to those who are called according
> to *His* purpose.   Romans 8:28, NAS

Even after we have made the choice to forgive, the emotions of anger and bitterness may still linger. Our emotions will eventually reflect God's heart of mercy and compassion as we continue to renew our minds with truth and reaffirm our decision to forgive.

What if our bitterness is toward God?

Even when we are angry at God, He does not condemn or become angry with us. He is committed to us and always responds with mercy and love. Therefore, when we are angry with God, we need to choose to trust in God's loving and merciful character. We must trust that He is working all the circumstances in our life for our good (Romans 8:28) and that He will provide for our every need (Philippians 4:19). We need to express honestly our anger to Him and to allow Him to show us the wrong beliefs we have about Him. There are many examples of this in Scripture. David, a man after God's own heart, freely expressed his anger toward God in Psalm 13:1-6 NAS.

> How long, O Lord? Wilt Thou forget me forever?
> How long wilt Thou hide Thy face from me?
> How long shall I take counsel in my soul,
> *Having* sorrow in my heart all the day?
> How long will my enemy be exalted over me?

After expressing His anger, David chose to trust in God's character.

> But I have trusted in Thy lovingkindness;
> My heart shall rejoice in Thy salvation.
> I will sing to the Lord,
> Because He has dealt bountifully with me.

Forgiveness is primarily for our benefit.

Forgiving others has many benefits in our life. Getting rid of unforgiveness and bitterness can feel like having a heavy burden or weight taken off our shoulders. God desires that forgiveness become a part of our lifestyle. A few of the personal benefits that are often experienced through forgiveness are:

- Emotional healing;
- Healthier relationships;
- Increased intimacy with God;
- Physical healing; and
- Freedom from spiritual oppression

© COPYRIGHT 1998, 2001, 2005, 2007 SCOPE MINISTRIES INTERNATIONAL INC.

Conclusion:

Expectations, anger, and bitterness all need to be recognized and acknowledged to God. As we interact with our Heavenly Father, He will reveal to us the cause so we can apply His solution. Although anger is common to all as a result of the Fall, it is not the norm for the Spirit-filled Christian. Christ has truly set us free from being controlled by anger and bitterness. The more we learn to walk by the Spirit, the more love will be the controlling factor in our lives.

SUMMARY:

1. Anger can result from blocked or unmet expectations or goals. God's solution for anger is to yield our expectations and rights to God. Unresolved anger leads to bitterness.

2. Bitterness can result from a perceived right that has been violated. God's solution for bitterness begins with understanding and receiving God's complete forgiveness.

3. By receiving God's forgiveness of us we can make a deliberate choice to forgive others.

A Life Transformed, con't.

To my relief, he wrote me, admitting the abuse. He said that I would probably never be able to forgive him, but that he wished that somehow I could.

Because my brother lives out-of-state, I didn't expect to see him for a while, but just a week after I received his letter, my father passed away unexpectedly. I knew that he would be in town for the funeral, and I was uneasy because I didn't know what to expect. He asked me to talk, and when we got together, I felt for the first time that I could truly forgive. It wasn't a forgiveness that I was mustering within myself but a forgiveness that only the Holy Spirit could produce within me. I knew that, because Christ forgave me when I didn't deserve it, I could forgive my brother even though he didn't deserve it.

When I told my brother that I forgave him for the abuse, he broke into tears. I was crying too as I hugged him. I knew that I needed to forgive him even more than he needed me to forgive him. At that precise moment, a heavy weight lifted from my shoulders. All the years of painful memories were washed away.

Many things have changed in my life since that moment. Through forgiveness, I let go of the bitterness that I had carried for so many years. Now I no longer experience flashbacks, and when I do remember the abuse, it is without the pain that used to engulf me. As I let go of my anger, God replaced my depression with His peace. Now my everyday struggles don't overwhelm me like before.

Now I am better able to express my love to my family. Instead of assuming that my husband and children know that I love them, I try to tell them more often. It's been difficult because I was never taught to say those three little words, "I love you," but it's been rewarding.

I am so grateful to the Lord for healing my emotions. I can't explain how different I feel each day when I wake up. It is such a sweet release to be at peace.

Marge - Writer/Editor

© COPYRIGHT 1998, 2001, 2005, 2007 SCOPE MINISTRIES INTERNATIONAL INC.

Expectations, Anger, and Bitterness - Day One

Goal: To gain a Biblical perspective of anger and recognize the underlying cause of it.

When you acknowledge and take responsibility for your anger, victory over the anger becomes a distinct probability rather than a remote possibility. You may have "reason" for your anger, but do you have the "right" to stay angry? Have you reserved for yourself the "right" to be angry? No matter the reason for your anger, you must understand that you CHOOSE to stay angry.

1. To gain a Biblical perspective of anger, write out the main point of the following passages.

   Proverbs 29:11

   Proverbs 19:11

   Proverbs 29:22

   Ephesians 4:26-27

   Colossians 3:8-9

   James 1:19-20

2. List at least five expectations you have of yourself or others which, when not met, make you feel angry (irritated, frustrated, outraged, etc.). Circle the "+" if you think these expectations are presently being met, and circle the "-" if you think they are not being met.

a) _____ + -

b) _____ + -

c) _____ + -

d) _____ + -

e) _____ + -

© COPYRIGHT 1998, 2001, 2005, 2007 SCOPE MINISTRIES INTERNATIONAL INC.

3. Everyone has needs. When our needs are not met, we often feel hurt or angry. Listed below are a number of needs that we have. Circle the "+" if you think the need is being met, and circle the "-" if you think the need is not being met. Circle the letter that corresponds with the person(s) you think should meet this need: (Y) Yourself, (S) Spouse, (P) Parent, (O) Others.

1) To be loved	Y S P O	+ -
2) To be needed	Y S P O	+ -
3) To be understood	Y S P O	+ -
4) To be wanted	Y S P O	+ -
5) To be cared for	Y S P O	+ -
6) To have significance	Y S P O	+ -
7) To be approved of	Y S P O	+ -
8) To be secure	Y S P O	+ -
9) To belong	Y S P O	+ -
10) To be fulfilled	Y S P O	+ -

4. One of the major causes of anger is thinking that our "rights" have been denied. Which of the "rights" listed below do you think of as being your personal "right"? Circle the "-" if the right is being denied, and list by whom the right is being denied.

By Whom

1) To be treated fairly	- _____
2) To make my own decisions	- _____
3) To date	- _____
4) To have self-expression	- _____
5) To do my own thing	- _____
6) To be obeyed	- _____
7) To have my own money	- _____
8) To have privacy	- _____
9) To my own opinion	- _____
10) To have my own friends	- _____
11) To be protected	- _____
12) To be free	- _____
13) To be appreciated	- _____
14) To be heard	- _____
15) To receive affection	- _____

5. Read Philippians 2:5-11. What rights do you think Jesus surrendered? Are you willing to yield your rights and trust God to meet your needs and exalt you in His way and in His time? As you pray about this, ask God to empower you to surrender all of your rights to Him.

© COPYRIGHT 1998, 2001, 2005, 2007 SCOPE MINISTRIES INTERNATIONAL INC.

Expectations, Anger, and Bitterness - Day Two

Goal: To learn to prevent and deal with anger by recognizing and yielding
expectations to God.

When an expectation is blocked or unmet, often our immediate emotional response is anger. Ephesians 4:26-27 tells us to, "be angry, and yet do not sin; do not let the sun go down on your anger, and do not give the devil an opportunity (foothold)." Unresolved anger leads to bitterness, and bitterness to resentment, vengeance, ingratitude, and depression.

1. Read over the "Expectations, Anger, and Bitterness" worksheet on page 7.21.
    Describe a situation that causes you continual anger.

2. What expectations are unmet? If you don't know, refer to Day One answers.

3. Choose to yield your expectations to God, and trust Him to meet your need in
    whatever way HE sees best. How would this change your response to the situation
    or person?

© COPYRIGHT 1998, 2001, 2005, 2007 SCOPE MINISTRIES INTERNATIONAL INC.

Anger as an emotion is not sinful. The wrong beliefs, attitudes, and actions which follow are what are sinful and need to be changed.

> And do not grieve the Holy Spirit of God, by whom you were sealed for the day of redemption. Let all bitterness and wrath and anger and clamor and slander be put away from you, along with all malice. And be kind to one another, tender-hearted, forgiving each other, just as God in Christ also has forgiven you.
>
> Ephesians 4:30-32 NAS

4. What beliefs, attitudes, or actions do you need to change? Whom do you need to forgive?

5. Write a prayer asking God to enable you to forgive and to accept those who are not fulfilling your expectations.

© COPYRIGHT 1998, 2001, 2005, 2007 SCOPE MINISTRIES INTERNATIONAL INC.

Expectations, Anger, and Bitterness - Day Three

Goal: To understand God's forgiveness of you and to recognize obstacles to
forgiving others.

1. Often we have misconceptions about what forgiveness really involves. Read the list
    of "Common Misconceptions Regarding Forgiveness" on page 7.22, and check those
    that you have used to define forgiveness in the past.

2. Forgiving others is difficult until we have received God's total forgiveness for
    ourselves. Is there anything that you have done that still causes you to feel shame
    or guilt?

3. Read Matthew 18:21-35. Jesus taught this parable to demonstrate four important
    aspects of forgiveness:

    1) Forgiveness is a gift we do not deserve.
    2) It is erasing or foregoing what we feel is due us, canceling the debt owed, and yielding our rights and
       expectations.
    3) Once received from God, it is to be given to others.
    4) Unforgiveness results in personal torture and inner torment.

4. In Christ there is complete forgiveness.

    > And when you were dead in your transgressions and the uncircumcision of your flesh,
    > He made you alive together with Him, having forgiven us ALL our transgressions,
    > having canceled out the certificate of debt consisting of decrees against us *and* which
    > was hostile to us; and He has taken it out of the way, and nailed it to the cross.
    > Colossians 2:13-14, NAS (emphasis added)

© COPYRIGHT 1998, 2001, 2005, 2007 SCOPE MINISTRIES INTERNATIONAL INC.

In the Roman courts of law, when a person was charged with a crime, a "certificate of debt" was written against him. This indictment stated the charge or charges against the person, and a due penalty was demanded. If the person charged was found guilty, he was removed to prison. The "certificate of debt" was nailed to his prison door. Once he had completed his sentence he was freed, and the words "paid in full" were stamped on the certificate of debt. The last words of Jesus on the cross were "It is finished." Incredibly, the word "finished" is the same word that was stamped on the certificate of debt, "paid in full"! Jesus paid in full the penalty for all our sins.

> By this will we have been sanctified through the offering of the body of Jesus Christ once for all. And every priest stands daily ministering and offering time after time the same sacrifices, which can never take away sins; but He, having offered one sacrifice for sins for all time, SAT DOWN AT THE RIGHT HAND OF GOD, . . . For by one offering He has perfected for all time those who are sanctified. "AND THEIR SINS AND THEIR LAWLESS DEEDS I WILL REMEMBER NO MORE." Now where there is forgiveness of these things, there is no longer *any* offering for sin. Since, therefore, brethren, we have confidence to enter the holy place by the blood of Jesus.
>
> Hebrews 10:10-12, 14, 17-19 NAS (emphasis added)

Is there any sin that Jesus hasn't forgiven? What?

5. It is essential and imperative that you accept what God says and receive His total and complete forgiveness. Verbalize your gratitude to Him (be specific).

© COPYRIGHT 1998, 2001, 2005, 2007 SCOPE MINISTRIES INTERNATIONAL INC.

Expectations, Anger, and Bitterness - Day Four

Goal: To begin resolving any unforgiveness and bitterness in your life.

Forgiveness is a decision, a choice based on an act of the will, not a feeling. It is a rational choice I make because I have been totally and completely forgiven by God. I have been made a forgiving person by nature in Christ. Therefore, not to forgive is to act contrary to my identity in Christ. Therefore, forgiveness includes:

a. Acknowledging the hurt.

b. Acknowledging how I felt.

c. Releasing the person from the debt owed me. (Saying in effect: "You never have to make it up to me or repay me. You are now free. You are forgiven. I release you...the debt is canceled.")

d. Accepting the person unconditionally, just as he is, and letting God change him. It requires releasing the person from the responsibility to love and accept me. I look to Christ alone to meet my need for security and significance and yield the right to judge the other person.

e. Being willing to risk being hurt again in the future should God allow it. In other words, I take down my wall of self-protection and trust Christ as my Wisdom and Protection should I get hurt again.

1. Some reasons why we fail to forgive are listed on page 7.23. Circle the number of each one that applies to you.

2. Describe an incident in your past that causes ongoing hurt.

© COPYRIGHT 1998, 2001, 2005, 2007 SCOPE MINISTRIES INTERNATIONAL INC.

3. On a separate piece of paper list each person who has contributed to your hurt, specifically stating the offense and the resulting emotions. The following outline may be helpful.

    1) "God, it hurt me when . . . " (Be specific).

    2) "And I felt . . . "

    3) "I now choose to forgive _____ . "

    4) "I accept _____ unconditionally, which means my love and acceptance of _____ does not depend on _____ or _____ performance now or in the future. I accept _____ just the way _____ is . . . even if _____ never changes...even if _____ gets worse."

    5) "I release _____ from the responsibility to meet my needs for love and acceptance. I choose to trust Jesus alone as the only one who can truly meet all my needs."

    6) "I am willing to risk being hurt again by _____ and trust Jesus as my Wisdom and Protection in the future about _____ and this matter."

    7) "God, I give You permission to change or to not change my feelings, according to Your time schedule."

Remember, forgiveness is primarily for your benefit. Revealing to the offender that you have forgiven _____ is not necessary or desirable unless he requests your forgiveness.

4. Now after you have walked through the steps of forgiveness, destroy this list.

© COPYRIGHT 1998, 2001, 2005, 2007 SCOPE MINISTRIES INTERNATIONAL INC.

Expectations, Anger, and Bitterness - Day Five

Goal: To recognize and remove a root of bitterness.

Bitterness is to the soul what cholesterol is to the arteries. Bitterness blocks the flow of the living water, limiting our capacity to be filled with the Holy Spirit.

> And do not grieve the Holy Spirit of God, by whom you were sealed for the day of redemption. Let all bitterness and wrath and anger and clamor and slander be put away from you, along with all malice.   Ephesians 4:30-31 NAS

> Pursue peace with all men . . . See to it that no one comes short of the grace of God; that no root of bitterness springing up causes trouble, and by it many be defiled.
>   Hebrews 12:14a, 15 NAS

The root of bitterness is invisible, but it produces visible fruit such as:

- Withdrawal from God
- Inability to love others
- Spiritual doubt and unbelief
- Depression
- Physical problems

The solution for bitterness is forgiveness. Cleansing our hearts of bitterness is often a long process when there has been an accumulation of unresolved anger and hurt. The following exercise may take some extra time to complete. No matter how long it takes, it will be worth it. Gaining freedom from bitterness will bring new freedom and joy in your life.

1. Ask the Holy Spirit to bring to your mind each event in your past that still stands out as an unpleasant or painful experience. Make a list on a separate piece of paper, writing down just a few words to identify the incident.

2. Below each incident list each person who contributed to your hurt.

3. List each wrong you suffered from each person.

© COPYRIGHT 1998, 2001, 2005, 2007 SCOPE MINISTRIES INTERNATIONAL INC.

4. Review the handout, "Reasons Why We Don't Forgive" on page 7.23. Note which ones apply in each situation.

Remember, forgiveness is primarily for your benefit. Now it is your nature to forgive as God has forgiven you.

5. One by one, verbalize to God your decision to forgive each person. Yield your "right" to punish the person in any way. Trust God to deal with each one as He sees best (Romans 12:19). *

6. Thank God for His faithfulness to use even the most hurtful incidents in your life for your ultimate good (Genesis 50:20; 1 Thessalonians 5:18; Romans 8:28).

7. Ask God to help you see each person who has hurt you the way He does and to empower you to love each one unconditionally (Matthew 5:43-48; Luke 6:27-38).

8. When you have completed this exercise, write "Paid In Full" across your list, and destroy it.

* If you still find this too painful or difficult, you may need a trusted friend, pastor, or Biblical personal guidance minister to pray with you.

© COPYRIGHT 1998, 2001, 2005, 2007 SCOPE MINISTRIES INTERNATIONAL INC.

Expectations, Anger, and Bitterness - Lesson Seven

Name _____ Date _____

Answer the following questions. To turn in page to small group leader, use identical perforated page in back of book.

1. About what have you been the most angry?

2. What expectations or rights are you holding onto that are contributing to this anger?

3. How are unforgiveness and bitterness affecting your life and relationships?

4. Have you forgiven those who have hurt you? If not, what do you think are the obstacles to forgiving them?

5. Whom did God lead you to forgive through this assignment?

6. Mark the graph to indicate how much of this week's assignment you completed.

None	50%	100%

© COPYRIGHT 1998, 2001, 2005, 2007 SCOPE MINISTRIES INTERNATIONAL INC.

Record Your Prayer Requests:

_____

_____

_____

_____

_____

_____

_____

_____

_____

_____

_____

_____

_____

_____

_____

_____

_____

_____

_____

_____

© COPYRIGHT 1998, 2001, 2005, 2007 SCOPE MINISTRIES INTERNATIONAL INC.

Expectations, Anger, and Bitterness Worksheet

Expectations	Anger	Bitterness				
Needs	Prevention:	Cure:	Resentment			
Comparisons	Yield expectations as act of trust in God.	Forgiveness		Vengeance		
Verbal Commitments					Ingratitude	Depression

Throughout life, we all develop expectations. They are usually produced by comparing ourselves with others ("They get to, so why can't I?") or from commitments people make or imply. Some expectations result from valid needs in our lives, such as being loved, accepted, and feeling secure. When those expectations are not met in the ways we want them to be met by others or by God, the emotional reaction is often anger.

The Bible says to "be angry, and yet do not sin" (Ephesians 4:26). Anger becomes a problem when we deal with it improperly. A way to safeguard against responding in anger is to yield our expectations to God. In yielding, I choose to let God meet my needs in the ways He sees best, not in the ways in which I want to see things done. I decide to trust Him and look to Him as the source of my contentment, joy, and security, instead of looking to circumstances or to other people.

However, what if I don't recognize an expectation I have and I get angry? What if the anger remains in my heart and turns into bitterness? To deal with anger and bitterness, I can choose to forgive others for what has happened and release them from my expectations. God will deal with them, so I defer that right to Him. If I do not deal with the bitterness, its roots grow down deeper and deeper into resentment, vengeance, and depression (Hebrews 12:15). I become unable to be satisfied and focus totally on the unmet expectation and the one who failed to meet it. I become unable to see how God is meeting my needs. But, what if the anger is at God? Then, I must make a choice to trust in God's loving and merciful character, that He is working all circumstances in my life for the good (Romans 8:28) and that He will provide my every need (Philippians 4:19) in His way.

ASSIGNMENT:

1. List any incident in your past that causes ongoing hurt. List each person who has contributed to your hurts.

2. Ask God to make you willing to forgive these people, and even yourself, and to trust Him to work all together for good.

3. By faith, choose to forgive the offenders by an act of your will, apart from what your emotions or reason are telling you. Verbalize this choice to God. Trust God to change your feelings of anger and hurt in His timing.

© COPYRIGHT 1998, 2001, 2005, 2007 SCOPE MINISTRIES INTERNATIONAL INC.

COMMON MISCONCEPTIONS REGARDING FORGIVENESS

I feel like I have forgiven _____ because:

_____ I don't feel angry anymore. Forgiveness is not feeling angry anymore.

_____ I am able to justify, understand, and explain away this person's hurtful behavior. I can see some of the reasons why he did it.

_____ I am able to put myself in his shoes and see things from his point of view.

_____ I am able to separate the person from their behavior. Forgiveness is being able to say, "What a person does and who he is, are two different things."

_____ I am giving him the benefit of the doubt. He didn't mean it. Forgiveness says no one is perfect, so you need to cut people some slack.

_____ I am saying to myself "time heals all wounds." I am willing to be patient and go on with my life. Forgiveness is a process that takes a lot of time.

_____ I am willing just to forget about it. Forgiving is forgetting...it is saying, "Let's just forget about it."

_____ I am able to pray for the person who has hurt me. I have asked God to forgive him.

_____ I am waiting for him to come to me and ask for my forgiveness. Once he does this, I will forgive him. I am willing to forgive.

_____ I have confronted this person about his behavior.

_____ I am able to say that I haven't really been hurt that badly. I just pretend that the hurt was really not that big of a thing.

_____ I am able to act as if it never happened.

_____ I have attempted reconciliation. Forgiveness says that the broken relationship must be restored.

_____ I am willing to go to the person and tell him that I forgive him.

_____ I am willing to be nice, take him a gift, and "turn the other cheek."

_____ I am trying to behave in a forgiving manner.

_____ I am trying to pretend that everything is OK and go on with my life and not bring the matter up again.

In short, forgiveness is none of the above items. Some of these may help in the process of getting ready to forgive, or they may be products of the forgiveness process, but they are not actually the same as forgiveness.

© COPYRIGHT 1998, 2001, 2005, 2007 SCOPE MINISTRIES INTERNATIONAL INC.

Reasons I Don't Forgive

1. Pride: forgiving someone makes me look weak. I want to be strong and superior. I'm right and I don't have to give in. *But pride is what keeps me in bondage and hinders growth.*

2. I don't want to give up my excuse-making system. *At first, freedom can be scary. I am out of my comfort zone. I will be learning a whole new way of living if I learn to forgive.*

3. If I were to forgive I would feel out of control. I want to feel in control and be able to manipulate others by holding the debt against them. *The truth is I am out of control when I cling to my hurt. I am the one in bondage.*

4. If I forgive, I may get hurt again. *The truth is I am going to get hurt again by others regardless of what I do. So the issue is, "What is the best response?" to these upcoming hurts so that I am not living in fear and being controlled by others.*

5. If I ignore it, the problem will go away. *The problem just gets buried and resurfaces later. Unresolved baggage from the past is brought into the present.*

6. Revenge: the person has to pay for it. He needs to be punished and learn a lesson. I want to hang on to the right to be a judge. *I'm not God, and trying to play God will get me in trouble. Vengeance belongs to the Lord.*

7. Failure to understand God's love and forgiveness for me. *I cannot give a gift to someone unless I first have something to give.*

8. Seems too easy and unfair. It seems I'm overlooking or condoning his sin. *No, in fact I am charging and documenting the debt and recognizing that Jesus died on the cross for that sin.*

9. Waiting for the person to come to me first. *It rarely happens.*

10. The person isn't sorry for what he's done. *Chances are he'll never be sorry. Forgiveness is primarily for my benefit. I don't need to wait.*

11. If I choose to forgive, I'm acting like a hypocrite because I don't "feel" loving and forgiving. *The truth is I'm a hypocrite if I don't forgive because my real nature in Christ is now a forgiving nature.*

12. Waiting for a "convenient" time and a "feeling." *It will never be convenient. I will never "feel" like forgiving.*

13. Thinking it takes too much time. I don't have time to forgive. *I can't afford <u>not</u> to forgive. I am the one in torment and in suffering.*

14. Fear of feelings that might be stirred up. *God knows how to gently get out the feelings that need to be healed. I won't die or go crazy.*

© COPYRIGHT 1998, 2001, 2005, 2007 SCOPE MINISTRIES INTERNATIONAL INC.

7.24

© COPYRIGHT 1998, 2001, 2005, 2007 SCOPE MINISTRIES INTERNATIONAL INC.

The Performance Treadmill and Guilt

But the Law does not rest on faith [does not require faith, has nothing to do with faith], for it itself says, He who does them [the things prescribed by the Law] shall live by them [not by faith].

Galatians 3:12 AMP

Lesson 8

A Life Transformed

During the summer after my third year of university studies, I was sitting in a Bible study when the leader showed a cartoon of a woman being taken to the insane asylum. Her pastor said to another member of the church, "We're really going to miss that woman. She did everything in this church."

Although I laughed with everyone else in the group, on the inside I felt like that woman. I was physically ill, emotionally drained, and spiritually dry because my life was so overloaded. I knew I couldn't continue to live the way I had been living ever since I was in high school. That's when I began to get the idea that I was loved and accepted only if I was successful. Although I didn't recognize this belief then, it began to affect my outlook on life.

I felt like I never measured up. I worked and worked, but I always felt that I needed to do one more thing to be really good. I wanted people to accept and approve of me, and I really wanted God's acceptance and approval, but I wasn't sure how to get it. I thought that God was disappointed in me and that He never totally approved of me. I carried a load of guilt and anxiety.

My belief that both people and God loved and accepted me because of my actions became even more dominant during my college years. I was very involved in the leadership of a Christian student organization, plus I was attending the university on an academic scholarship, and I was determined to graduate with a 4.0 GPA and honors.

I felt I would go crazy any minute.

to be continued...

© COPYRIGHT 1998, 2001, 2005, 2007 SCOPE MINISTRIES INTERNATIONAL INC.

The Performance Treadmill and Guilt - Lesson Eight

Jesus promised us abundant life, but a common obstacle to enjoying it is living by our self-effort rather than living by faith in the Holy Spirit. Living motivated by the emotion of guilt leads us to try harder to do better. This performance-based view of the Christian life is a common wrong belief about the source of our identity and worth. Our attempt to gain our identity and worth apart from who God made us to be is described as living on the "Performance Treadmill."

The Performance Treadmill

Living by law, legalism, and/or standards puts us on the "Performance Treadmill." Attempting to live the Christian life by the law, legalism, or standards can cause many devastating problems:

- Physically—headaches, high blood pressure, fatigue, stomach disorders, digestive problems, sleep disorders.

- Behaviorally—critical spirit, workaholism, compulsive religious activity, chemical dependence, compulsive behaviors, perfectionism, high control, deeds of the flesh, suicide.

- Emotionally—stress, anger, fear of failure and punishment, guilt, anxiety, depression, hopelessness, despair, nervous breakdown.

- Mentally—poor concentration, chronic worrying, negativism, low self-esteem, self-condemnation, self-pity, lack of assurance of salvation, pride, judging, self-righteousness, wrong thinking about God, comparing self to others.

- Relationally—dependence on the approval of others, conditional love for others, rejection of others who do not measure up, unresolved conflict, criticizing, anger.

Every Christian can gain freedom from the "Performance Treadmill" by evaluating our understanding of the following three ideas: Law, Legalism, and Standards.

Law Produces Religion, Not Relationship

The Law is holy, righteous, and good (Romans 7:12).

The Law reveals that perfect obedience is the minimum standard of a righteous and holy God. The word "Law" is used over 400 times in the Bible. The Law demands perfect obedience.

© COPYRIGHT 1998, 2001, 2005, 2007 SCOPE MINISTRIES INTERNATIONAL INC.

> I would not have known about covetousness [would have had no consciousness of sin or sense of guilt], if the Law had not [repeatedly] said, You shall not covet . . . The Law therefore is holy, and [each] commandment is holy and just and good.
>
> Romans 7:7b, 12 Amplified

Living by the Law is trying to earn salvation.

Scripture clearly teaches that no one is made right with God by keeping the Law but we still choose to believe that we must do something for God. This produces religion (man's attempt to make himself acceptable to God), not relationship (Galatians 3:8-14).

> Now it is evident that no person is justified - declared righteous and brought into right standing with God - through the Law...
>
> Galatians 3:11a Amplified

The Law causes sin to increase (Romans 5:20).

The flesh is hostile to God's Law and is not capable of keeping it. Living under the Law brings death. If we could keep the Law, it would not have been necessary for Christ to die (Galatians 2:21b).

> Once I was alive, but quite apart from *and* unconscious of the Law. But when the commandment came, sin lived again and I died (was sentenced by the Law to death). And the very legal ordinance which was designed *and* intended to bring life actually proved [to mean to me] death. For sin, seizing the opportunity *and* getting a hold on me [by taking its incentive] from the commandment, beguiled and entrapped and cheated me, and using it [as a weapon], killed me.
>
> Romans 7:9-11 Amplified

The Law was intended to be a thermometer, not a thermostat. A thermometer measures or reveals the temperature, but a thermostat controls it. The Law, like a thermometer, reveals our standing in relation to God's standards, but it does not produce the ability to achieve those standards.

The Law was given by God to expose and reveal our sinful condition.

God never intended for us to live by the Law, because we can never completely fulfill its requirements. Its purpose is to lead us to Christ (Galatians 3:24). Christ kept the Law perfectly and has redeemed us from the curse of the Law.

When we try to keep the Law, we try to earn our salvation by what we do, by "working to do good." However, Christ is the only Person Who has kept the Law perfectly, and He has redeemed us from its curse. He offers us salvation not as something to be earned by keeping the Law but as a free gift from God, which we receive by faith in Christ. Accepting this work of grace in our life results in eternal life.

We can gain freedom from the "Performance Treadmill" by evaluating our understanding of the following three ideas: law, legalism, and standards.

© COPYRIGHT 1998, 2001, 2005, 2007 SCOPE MINISTRIES INTERNATIONAL INC.

Understanding what happens at salvation helps us to understand how the law relates to legalism and standards. At salvation, we exchange our attempts at righteousness (doing good apart from God) for Christ's righteousness, His "garment of salvation" (Isaiah 61:10).

> For all of us have become like one who is unclean, and all our righteous deeds are like a filthy garment . . . Isaiah 64:6a NAS

Christ took our sin and gave us His righteousness, and, on that basis, we are made acceptable to God. We may not always feel righteous or act righteously, but we are righteous because of Christ.

> He made Him who knew no sin *to be* sin on our behalf, that we might become the righteousness of God in Him.
>
> 2 Corinthians 5:21 NAS

Legalism Produces Self-Righteousness, Not Love

Using the Law properly is good, but using the Law wrongly leads to legalism.

Legalism is trying to earn acceptance or blessing from God by obeying the Law.

We focus on our ability which causes us to measure our spirituality (acceptability to God) on the basis of what we do rather than on the basis of who God has made us to be in Christ.

This problem of trying to live the Christian life in bondage to the law is not new. It was so prevalent in the early Church that Paul wrote a lengthy letter to the church at Galatia to address this issue.

> You foolish Galatians, who has bewitched you, before whose eyes Jesus Christ was publicly portrayed *as* crucified? This is the only thing I want to find out from you: did you receive the Spirit by the works of the Law, or by hearing with faith? Are you so foolish? Having begun by the Spirit, are you now being perfected by the flesh? Galatians 3:1-3 NAS

> For if a law had been given which was able to impart life, then righteousness would indeed have been based on Law.
> Galatians 3:21b NAS

Legalism distorts God's Law in order to make it possible to keep.

Jesus amplified the Law (revealed its proper interpretation) so we could realize that we are not able to keep it. The Pharisees of Jesus' day had created hundreds of additional laws to ensure they did not break God's Law. Jesus summed up the Law as "Love God with all your heart, mind, soul, and strength, and love your neighbor as yourself" (Matthew 22:37). Legalism can never fulfill this commandment (Matthew 5:17-48).

© COPYRIGHT 1998, 2001, 2005, 2007 SCOPE MINISTRIES INTERNATIONAL INC.

Legalism causes us to be self-focused and produces self-righteousness.

Self-righteousness is "self" trying to achieve what we perceive to be God's expectations of us, and produces failure and spiritual burnout (Romans 7:9-11, 18-24).

The chart below helps us see the relationship between the Law, legalism and standards.

We believe that if we try hard enough, that if we are "working to do good," then we can achieve God's expectations. We will then be more spiritual and we will be a "better Christian." We believe that we will earn God's blessings in our life.

Trying harder or working to do good may include reading the Bible more, praying more, being at church more, teaching a Sunday school class or sharing your faith. All of these activities are good things which can enhance our relationship with God, but if our motive is to live up to our perception of God's expectation of us, then we are destined to fail. When we have problems in life, we believe that we are being punished by God or that God did not protect us because we were not doing enough. We decide that the Christian life is too hard and we quit trying, or we keep trying harder until we burn out. If we believe that we did try hard and we did do enough, then we are angry at God because He didn't do His part to bless us or protect us. But if we received the righteousness of Christ at salvation, how much more spiritual can we be? How can we possibly do more to be a better Christian when we *already* have Christ's righteousness? The solution is to realize that God's grace gives us the blessings in our life. Our spirituality is Christ working through us, not all of those things we do as a Christian. No longer do we "work to do good" in order to earn something from God. Instead, we receive His grace and focus on developing an intimate relationship with Him and allowing Him to live through us. Then our Christian life becomes a joy instead of a burden.

	CORRUPTED BELIEF	RESULT
LAW	Salvation is earned by doing good.	Separation from God
LEGALISM	Spirituality is achieved by doing good.	Self-righteousness, burnout, failure
STANDARDS	Worth is determined by the good we do.	Pride, fear of rejection and failure, low self-esteem

© COPYRIGHT 1998, 2001, 2005, 2007 SCOPE MINISTRIES INTERNATIONAL INC.

Standards Produce Bondage, Not Freedom

Living by standards is our attempt to find worth and identity apart from a relationship with Jesus.

We were created with a need for unconditional acceptance. However, the world system does not accept us on the basis of who we are but on the basis of what we do. Because the world bases worth on performance, we have adjusted to performance-based acceptance in an effort to gain a sense of worth. Our desire for acceptance, approval, and worth is so strong that when it is unfulfilled, we create standards. We then attempt to achieve these standards in order to give us the sense of acceptance and approval that we so strongly desire. The things that give us the acceptance and approval we desire become part of our lifestyle.

These standards that govern our lives are just as demanding as any law of God. They demand perfect performance, produce guilt, create a sense of fear and dread, enslave us, and destroy relationships. Standards force us to try to become the person we think others want us to be. **We can not be ourselves.** We become phony. The fear of rejection and disapproval is so strong that it continually reinforces the standards we have adopted. Because our standards demand perfection, we have no alternative but to try to be perfect.

As we again refer to the chart below, we realize the problem is trying to achieve our worth through what we do, "working to do good." But if we received the righteousness of Christ at salvation, how much more worthy can we be? Our worth does not come from what we do but from who God has made us to be. So, we can exchange the performance treadmill of trying to do more or better for the peace of knowing that we have great worth and value through Jesus.

> Our worth does not come from what we do, but from who God has made us to be.

TRUTH	APPLICATION	RESULT
Salvation is a gift of God's grace.	Place faith in Christ alone.	Eternal Life
Spirituality is Christ living in me.	Depend on Holy Spirit to live through me.	Freedom and joy in life
Worth is based on who God has made me to be.	Accept by faith new identity in Christ.	Security and peace in life

© COPYRIGHT 1998, 2001, 2005, 2007 SCOPE MINISTRIES INTERNATIONAL INC.

Standards are any objective measure or ideal that we or others must meet in order to be acceptable.

The personal standards we hold have many sources:
- church or organized religion;
- family;
- culture or society;
- peers ; and
- comparing ourselves with others.

Living by standards affects how we view ourselves and others.

Judging ourselves by standards produces either pride or shame. It also causes us to judge others as unacceptable when they do not meet our standards. We often try to achieve the standards of others to gain their love and acceptance.

Dudley Hall, in his book *Grace Works*, explains what happens when we live by our own standards instead of Christ's righteousness.

> "If you are looking for your own individual identity, you will forever be self-conscious; always conscious of your performance and your failure, always regretting that you didn't do better or gloating over the fact that you did pretty well after all. You will be acutely aware of other people's failures, so you will constantly battle judgmentalism. And you will be very alert to how you are perceived by others, so you will struggle with fear of rejection and a people-pleasing spirit (attitude)."

The performance treadmill produces a cycle of "Trying Harder" and "Giving Up."

When we attempt to achieve our standards or the standards of others, we receive positive messages which motivate us toward more self-effort. However, eventually we become tired, and we fail to measure up, leading us to "Give Up." In the "Give Up" stage, we receive messages that shame us and reinforce our wrong beliefs about ourselves. The pain from guilt and shame then motivates us once again to "Try Harder" to meet our standards. Eventually, we get tired again and give up again. We continue to repeat this cycle until we realize that we are not really accomplishing our goal of gaining acceptance, approval, and worth. God desires for us to cease striving and to rest in His unconditional acceptance.

By trusting in the Holy Spirit to live through us, we enjoy the rest Jesus promised in Matthew 11:28-30.

> Come to Me, all who are weary and heavy-laden, and I will give you rest. Take My yoke upon you, and learn from Me, for I am gentle and humble in heart; and you shall find rest for your souls. For My yoke is easy and My load is light.
>
> Matthew 11:28-30 NAS

© COPYRIGHT 1998, 2001, 2005, 2007 SCOPE MINISTRIES INTERNATIONAL INC.

The following diagram, adapted from Jeff VanVonderen's book, *Tired of Trying to Measure Up*, illustrates the cycle that the performance treadmill creates.

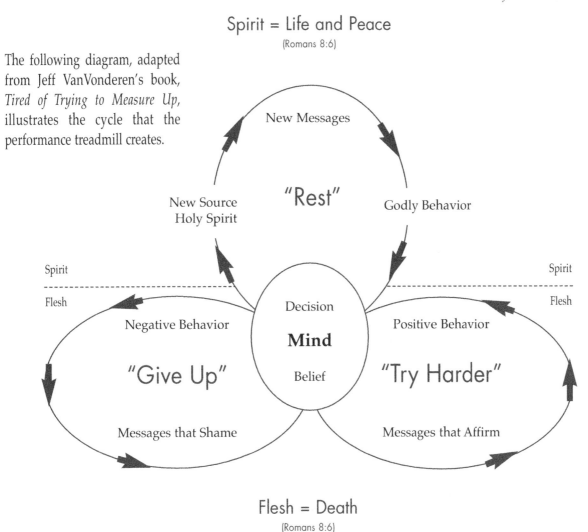

Spirit = Life and Peace
(Romans 8:6)

New Messages

"Rest"

New Source
Holy Spirit

Godly Behavior

Spirit

Flesh

Negative Behavior

Decision

Mind

Belief

Positive Behavior

Spirit

Flesh

"Give Up"

"Try Harder"

Messages that Shame

Messages that Affirm

Flesh = Death
(Romans 8:6)

When we find ourselves on the performance treadmill, we need to ask ourselves:

- Am I still trying to be good enough to go to Heaven?
- Am I trying to get God's approval, love, and acceptance by doing good for Him?
- Do I feel that God doesn't love me when I fail, or that He couldn't possibly like me?
- What are the standards that I am trying to keep?
- Does keeping my standards give me a sense of worth?
- How do I judge the worth of those around me?

Then we need to remember who our Heavenly Father really is, and we will rest in His unconditional love and acceptance. Believing who we really are as His children will satisfy our need for significance and worth. We will experience freedom when we reject the treadmill and trust the Holy Spirit to live through us.

God desires for us to cease striving and to rest in His unconditional acceptance.

© COPYRIGHT 1998, 2001, 2005, 2007 SCOPE MINISTRIES INTERNATIONAL INC.

The Guilt Trip

Emotional guilt is "the feeling of wrongdoing that comes when one's behavior conflicts with his belief system."

Guilt is recognized as one of the most painful and destructive emotions. Guilt and fear, as well as other "out of control" emotions, are not part of God's character and are a result of sin. Guilt is so universal and so deeply ingrained in human behavior that most of us accept it as a basic and normal emotion in our everyday experience. We have become so conditioned to it that we believe guilt is the Biblical method that the Holy Spirit uses to convict us of sin.

Guilt is a violation of a specific standard or failure to achieve a specific standard.

True Biblical guilt is defined as, "a contradiction between one's behavior and God's character, as revealed in Scripture." We have all failed to achieve God's righteous character. Realizing our guilt–based upon God's Word–produces Godly sorrow which leads us to deal with the cause of our guilt (sin).

God desires to free His children from the bondage of guilt that comes from our failure to achieve either God's standard of righteousness or our self-imposed rules and regulations.

Guilt is recognized by the symptoms it produces.

- Self-condemnation: the constant blaming of oneself which can lead to depression.
- Self-punishment: some form of punishment inflicted upon oneself, usually to pay for some wrongdoing.
- Depression: the end result of guilt that hasn't been resolved.
- Sense of Disapproval: the result of expectations of self or others that have not been met.
- Physical Symptoms: can include headaches, fatigue, and insomnia.
- Rationalization: an attempt to counteract guilt feelings by justifying one's actions.
- Compensation: another attempt to counteract guilt feelings by doing things considered to be good in an attempt to soothe the conscience.
- Anger: a feeling of hostility toward those who seem to stir up guilt feelings.
- "Goody Two-Shoes": exemplary behavior which is often an attempt to conceal or deal with internal feelings of guilt.
- Fear and Dread: two closely related emotions, often associated with unresolved guilt feelings.

Unresolved guilt creates an unhealthy dependence on our feelings.

This will hinder us from hearing and responding to the voice of the Holy Spirit. The feeling of guilt can easily become our final authority for what is right or

© COPYRIGHT 1998, 2001, 2005, 2007 SCOPE MINISTRIES INTERNATIONAL INC.

wrong. When this happens, we think that what feels good is good and what feels bad is bad, regardless of what the Bible has to say. A Christian worker justified her affair based on her feelings, saying, "You cannot convince me that what feels so good is wrong."

Feelings of guilt can cause us to focus on the symptom, rather than the cause. Guilt is so painful that we focus on getting rid of the guilt, rather than dealing with the root problem.

When we are motivated by guilt, we engage in activity designed to alleviate or remove the feeling of guilt. King David, in an effort to cover up the guilt of his adultery, arranged Bathsheba's husband's murder (2 Samuel 11).

Feelings of guilt can lead to worldly sorrow. This sorrow is best characterized by the guilt created by getting caught, rather than any sorrow for the wrong done. Many people, including Christians, will do wrong as long as they feel that they won't get caught.

God's solution for our guilt is the cross.

Our guilt before God could not be overlooked or ignored, but somehow it had to be removed. It could be removed only by Jesus willingly accepting our guilt and paying our debt – the wages of sin is death (Romans 6:23). Christ's death on the cross has provided us with total and complete forgiveness. As believers in Christ, we are declared "not guilty" by God. Christ took the guilt and punishment for all our sins and gave us His righteousness.

God has mercifully dealt with the fact of our guilt through Christ's death on the cross. We must view our sin in light of the Cross or we experience unresolved guilt. This unresolved guilt robs us of enjoying experientially the forgiveness and grace that God gives to us. Guilt causes us to withdraw from God and others.

Confession allows us to enjoy God's forgiveness and grace.

There is much confusion and misunderstanding about confessing our sins. The word "confess" does not mean "ask for forgiveness." It means to "agree with God." We are not to ask for what we have already been given, total forgiveness. Rather, we are to acknowledge our sin and thank Him that we have been forgiven. We are also to agree with God concerning the truth about our new identity in Christ because, when we sin, we are living in contradiction to who we really are.

> If we say that we have no sin, we are deceiving ourselves, and the truth is not in us. If we confess [agree with God about] our sins, He is faithful and righteous to forgive us our sins and to cleanse us from all unrighteousness.
>
> 1 John 1:8-9 NAS

As believers in Christ, we are declared . . . NOT GUILTY!

© COPYRIGHT 1998, 2001, 2005, 2007 SCOPE MINISTRIES INTERNATIONAL INC.

At the cross Jesus took the penalty of our sin and broke the power of sin. Confession is not something we *do*, but faith that we exercise. Forgiveness is not something we *seek*, but something we possess!

Why is confessing our sin important? The right kind of confession is God's means for us to enjoy the forgiveness that we already have and to be filled with the Spirit. The point to remember is that confession is not something we do to receive forgiveness. Confession is acknowledging by faith what Christ has already accomplished for us.

> Through Him then, let us continually offer up a sacrifice of praise to God, that is, the fruit of lips that give thanks to His name.
> Hebrews 13:15, NAS

The words "give thanks" in this verse are the same words translated "confess" in 1 John 1:9. Confession is an expression of faith and thanksgiving for Christ's payment of our sins.

Whenever we do something that is inconsistent with either God's Word or God's character, the Spirit of God uses the Word of God to reveal to us wrong and sinful choices or behavior. Hebrews 4:12 tells us that the Word of God is alive and powerful, sharper than any two-edged sword, piercing even as far as the joint and marrow, discerning the thoughts and intents of the heart. In response, we acknowledge in faith that God's Word is true, that what we did was wrong, and that what Christ has done is right.

God does not use guilt or fear to motivate us. Instead, He motivates us with His love and grace. The Holy Spirit reveals the truth to our minds and works in us to both will and do for His good pleasure (Philippians 2:13). The more we know and receive God's love for us, the more we desire to do those things that please Him.

Receiving God's Unconditional Love And Acceptance Produces Freedom

Freedom comes from living by faith in the grace of God.

The word "grace" means "that which causes joy, pleasure, gratification, favor or acceptance. A favor done without expectation of return; the absolute freeness of the lovingkindness of God to men finding its only motive in the bounty and benevolence of the Giver; unearned and unmerited favor" (Spiros Zodhiates, *The Complete Word Study Dictionary*). In His grace, God has made us worthy and given us a new identity. This can be experienced only by faith and not through self-effort.

Freedom comes from responding to the Holy Spirit's leading.

God has given us His Holy Spirit, so we can live dependent on His life within us instead of living by external rules (Law or legalism) and standards (John 6:63, Galatians 5:16). By depending on the Holy Spirit, we experience our new identity, we experience His unconditional love, and we know Him as the Father He really is (Ephesians 3:16-18). As we rely on the Holy Spirit, He changes our thoughts and beliefs, and transforms our lives (Romans 12:1-2).

© COPYRIGHT 1998, 2001, 2005, 2007 SCOPE MINISTRIES INTERNATIONAL INC.

┌─ SUMMARY: ──────────────────────────────┐

1. Living by law, legalism, and/or standards puts us on the "Performance Treadmill" and produces a cycle of "Trying Harder" and "Giving Up."

2. Living by the Law is trying to earn salvation by keeping God's commands. This self-effort produces religion, not relationship.

3. Legalism is attempting to earn acceptance or blessing from God by obeying the Law. This self-effort produces self-righteousness, not love.

4. Standards are any objective measure or ideal that must be met in order to accept ourselves or others. This self-effort produces bondage, not freedom.

5. Freedom from the self-effort of the "Performance Treadmill" comes from receiving God's unconditional acceptance of us and resting in the power of the Holy Spirit to work in us.

└──┘

© COPYRIGHT 1998, 2001, 2005, 2007 SCOPE MINISTRIES INTERNATIONAL INC.

A Life Transformed, con't.

The summer before my last year at the university, through a small group Bible study, I began to learn about my identity in Christ, and I learned to see myself in a new way. I realized that God doesn't look at what I do but that He cares about who I am. I discovered that I had a wrong understanding of who God is. When we talked about legalism and standards, things really began to change in my life.

I realized that I had believed that I could make myself good enough for God by doing all the things I thought I was supposed to do. God showed me that Christian activities and disciplines are never a replacement for having faith in Him to complete me. I had taken tools designed to help me know God and used them as standards to measure my acceptability to Him. At that moment, I visualized myself as the tree that is used to illustrate man's three-part nature. I saw fruit all over the tree, but it was attached artificially with glue instead of growing naturally from the branches. God showed me that I needed to let go of the fake fruit in my life and to concentrate on my spirit, the roots of my life.

I began to see that I needed a big change in my life. I needed to believe that God accepts me, and that His responsibility is to make me stand as I follow Him in faith. When I returned to school in the fall, I relinquished some of my commitments. I knew that I had not accepted them from God but because of my own attempt to be accepted by Him.

God immediately poured out His grace to me through my fiancé. When I told him that I was relinquishing some of my commitments, he believed that God had spoken to me. He accepted my decision and affirmed that it was the right choice. That was a tangible affirmation to me that God does love me and is involved in my life because a person who knew me very well saw God working in me.

I was amazed by the freedom I felt. Suddenly I had time to pursue knowing God instead of trying to persuade Him to like me. I began to know the length, breadth, height, and depth of Christ's love. My quiet times used to be a duty, but now they are a joy. Instead of being self-conscious of how much and how well I'm doing it, I'm God-conscious. Now I don't have to work hard enough to be worthy to come into God's presence. I have the freedom just to come.

I'm free to grow and explore who He has made me to be. I have learned that God has made me unique and that how I find God may not be the same as how other people around me find Him. For example, I love to read books, and God gives me glimpses of Himself through the characters as I read.

My life did not change instantly. Even now, I sometimes hear a voice in the back of my mind telling me that I am guilty and that I still don't measure up, but now I know the truth. I can answer the voice with the certainty that God is working in me. As I listen to His Holy Spirit, He guides me into the places and situations He has planned for me. I don't need to constantly seek ways to measure my worth. God has relieved me of a huge burden and replaced it with His joy.

Julianna - Teacher

© COPYRIGHT 1998, 2001, 2005, 2007 SCOPE MINISTRIES INTERNATIONAL INC.

The Performance Treadmill and Guilt - Day One

Goal: To understand the purpose of God's Law and to recognize how I might be misusing it in my life.

1. Complete the following statements:

   God would be more pleased with me if . . .

   I would be a good/better Christian if I could . . .

   I feel God expects me to . . .

   God is disappointed with me when I . . .

   Your answers to these questions may reveal that you are still trying to be "good enough" to go to Heaven or to be loved and accepted by God.

   The Law (of the Old Testament) is an objective external standard that expresses the expectations of a righteous and holy God. Jesus summarized the Law with two commands: "Love the Lord your God" and "Love your neighbor as yourself." The Law reveals what this should look like in human behavior.

2. What do each of the following verses reveal concerning the purpose of God's Law?

   Now we recognize *and* know that the Law is good if any one uses it lawfully [for the purpose for which it was designed], Knowing *and* understanding this: that the Law is not enacted for the righteous (the upright and just, who are in right standing with God), but for the lawless and unruly, for the ungodly and sinful . . .   1 Timothy 1:8-9a Amplified

   What then was the purpose of the Law? It was added [later on, after the promise, to disclose and expose to men their guilt] because of transgressions *and* [to make men more conscious of the sinfulness] of sin.. . .   Galatians 3:19 Amplified

   So that the Law served [to us Jews] as our trainer [our guardian, our guide to Christ, to lead us] until Christ [came], that we might be justified (declared righteous, put in right standing with God) by *and* through faith.   Galatians 3:24 Amplified

© COPYRIGHT 1998, 2001, 2005, 2007 SCOPE MINISTRIES INTERNATIONAL INC.

> If you seek to be justified *and* declared righteous *and* to be given a right standing with God through the Law, you are brought to nothing *and* so separated (severed) from Christ. You have fallen away from grace (from God's gracious favor and unmerited blessing).
>
> Galatians 5:4 Amplified

The Law is not the Gospel. The Law was intended to be a "thermometer, not a thermostat." It reveals our standing in relationship to God's standards, but it does not make us capable of gaining or achieving those standards. The main purpose of the Law is to reveal to us God's holiness and our need of Him.

3. Read Romans 7:5-8.

   What is aroused by the Law?

   How are we released from the Law?

   What does the Law show you?

   The Gospel is the good news about God's grace in response to man's sin (failure to love God and others). The word "grace" means, "that which causes joy, pleasure, gratification, favor, acceptance. A favor done without expectation of return; the absolute freeness of the loving kindness of God to men finding its only motive in the bounty and benevolence of the Giver; unearned and unmerited favor." (Spiros Zodhiates, *The Complete Word Study Dictionary*)

   > For it is by free grace (God's unmerited favor) that you are saved (delivered from judgment *and* made partakers of Christ's salvation) through [your] faith. And this [salvation] is not of yourselves [of your own doing, it came not through your own striving], but it is the gift of God; not because of works [not the fulfillment of the Law's demands], lest any man should boast. [It is not the result of what anyone can possibly do, so no one can pride himself in it or take glory to himself].
   >
   > Ephesians 2:8-9 Amplified

4. Spend a few minutes expressing gratitude to God for the free gift of salvation by personalizing and praying the verse above.

8.16

© COPYRIGHT 1998, 2001, 2005, 2007 SCOPE MINISTRIES INTERNATIONAL INC.

The Performance Treadmill and Guilt - Day Two

Goal: To evaluate how I'm trying to meet my needs for acceptance and approval and to receive God's acceptance and approval of me.

If you are already convinced that you are saved by grace and not through keeping the Law, can you still be living on the "performance treadmill?" You are if you are trying to gain approval and acceptance from God, others, or self through keeping the Law or standards.

1. To discover if this is true, look at question 1 of Day One. What do your answers reveal?

2. How are you trying or what are you trying to do to gain God's acceptance and approval?

3. In what areas do you feel unaccepted by God? Do you feel unaccepted because you have failed to keep God's commands or because you have believed a lie about yourself or God?

© COPYRIGHT 1998, 2001, 2005, 2007 SCOPE MINISTRIES INTERNATIONAL INC.

4. What do the following verses tell you about your acceptance and approval by God?

> Yet now has [Christ, the Messiah,] reconciled [you to God] in the body of His flesh through death, in order to present you holy and faultless and irreproachable in His [the Father's] presence.
> Colossians 1:22 Amplified

> Therefore, [there is] now no condemnation (no adjudging guilty of wrong) for those who are in Christ Jesus.
> Romans 8:1 Amplified

> Even as [in His love] He chose us - [actually picked us out for Himself as His own], in Christ before the foundation of the world; that we should be holy (consecrated and set apart for Him) and blameless in His sight, *even* above reproach, before Him in love.
> Ephesians 1:4 Amplified

> Wherefore, accept one another, just as Christ also accepted us to the glory of God.
> Romans 15:7 NAS

5. God's approval and acceptance of us is not based on our performance but on who we are: His Spirit-born children. Choose to accept by faith what God says in His Word and to receive God's approval and acceptance of you. Write Him a thank-you note.

© COPYRIGHT 1998, 2001, 2005, 2007 SCOPE MINISTRIES INTERNATIONAL INC.

The Performance Treadmill and Guilt - Day Three

Goal: To recognize any standards I am living by and learn what it means to walk by the Spirit.

Many times, we feel that we have to "stick to the rules" or "maintain certain standards" in order to make sure we live a Godly life and are accepted by others. We may fear that we will lose control of our life if we cease trying to achieve our standards. However, the truth is that living by self-imposed rules has absolutely no value in "restraining sensual indulgences" (the flesh). In fact, according to Romans 7, rules actually arouse sin!

> But sin, finding opportunity in the commandment [to express itself], got a hold on me *and* aroused *and* stimulated all kinds of forbidden desires (lust, covetousness). For without the Law sin is dead [the sense of it is inactive and a lifeless thing].
> Romans 7:8 Amplified

> For sin, seizing the opportunity *and* getting a hold on me [by taking its incentive] from the commandment, beguiled *and* entrapped *and* cheated me, and using it [as a weapon], killed me.
> Romans 7:11 Amplified

1. As you grew up, what were some of the family rules or standards (spoken or unspoken) that you were expected to live up to?

2. What are some of your church's standards that you feel you need to meet in order to be considered a "good Christian?"

© COPYRIGHT 1998, 2001, 2005, 2007 SCOPE MINISTRIES INTERNATIONAL INC.

3. List a standard you use to judge whether others are acceptable or worthy. (Hint: What are your pet peeves? When others don't conform, do you become angry?)

4. According to Colossians 2:20-23, living by standards and Laws appears to be beneficial, but actually has no profit (does not make us loving in our actions or attitudes). In your relationships, what are some of the negative consequences of living by the Law or standards?

5. Make a list of your standards that you have used to measure your worth or to gain acceptance. One by one, give your standards to God, acknowledging that living by your standards will never empower you to love God or others. Thank God that they are not His demands on you.

6. Ask God to teach you how to "walk by the Spirit" rather than walking in the "flesh" (living by Laws and standards). Meditate on the following verse and on what it means in your daily life. Write on a 3 x 5 card or sticky note, and put it where you will see it often.

> I have been crucified with Christ; and it is no longer I who live, but Christ lives in me; and the *life* which I now live in the flesh I live by faith in the Son of God, who loved me, and delivered Himself up for me. I do not nullify the grace of God; for if righteousness *comes* through the Law, then Christ died needlessly.   Galatians 2:20-21 NAS

© COPYRIGHT 1998, 2001, 2005, 2007 SCOPE MINISTRIES INTERNATIONAL INC.

The Performance Treadmill and Guilt - Day Four

Goal: To discover the difference between living on the performance treadmill and living and walking in the freedom of the Spirit.

1. Read Galatians 3:2-3. What is your part in living by the Spirit?

       Rather than living by external rules, we are to live and walk by the Spirit, responding in faith to His inner prompting. "Walk" speaks of a continuous process, a moment-by-moment dependence on the Holy Spirit. Our part is to respond to His leading, and God's part is to empower us with His supernatural life.

2. Read the "Old Way of Law vs. New Way of Spirit" chart on pages 8.27-28 Note any old ways of living under the Law that apply to you. Ask God to begin to make the new way of the Spirit your experience.

Jesus invites all who are tired, exhausted, and frustrated from trying to live the "Christian" life by their own efforts to come to Him and rest. The word "rest" means to cease from living the Christian life by self-effort. It is putting our faith in Jesus and allowing Him to live His life through us.

> Come to Me, all you who labor and are heavy-laden *and* overburdened, and I will cause you to rest. [I will ease and relieve and refresh your souls.] Take My yoke upon you and learn of Me, for I am gentle (meek) and humble (lowly) in heart, and you will find rest (relief and ease and refreshment and recreation and blessed quiet) for your souls. For My yoke is wholesome (useful, good—not harsh, hard, sharp, or pressing, but comfortable, gracious, and pleasant), and My burden is light *and* easy to be borne.
>
> Matthew 11:28-30 Amplified

3. List some of your "red flags" (indicators) that tell you that you are not "resting" in Jesus (trusting Him to live through you).

    Examples:
- When I become anxious and stressed about all I have to do.
- When I think that God is disgusted or disappointed with me for some failure in my life (and I feel shame and condemnation).

© COPYRIGHT 1998, 2001, 2005, 2007 SCOPE MINISTRIES INTERNATIONAL INC.

4. For each of the examples you listed above, describe how you could "rest" in Jesus?

   Examples:

   • When I am stressed, cast all my worries on Him. Give Him my list of things to do, as well as my expectations, and trust Him to empower me and direct my day.

   • When I fail, agree with God concerning my sin and thank Him that He has not only forgiven me, but made me acceptable. Choose to renew my mind with the truth about my new identity and trust the Holy Spirit to empower me to do what is right.

5. Look back at your answers on page 1.11, Day One of "Discovering the Root of Our Problems." In what ways are the problem(s) you described a result of living by your own standards or self-effort instead of relying on the Holy Spirit?

6. Personalize Matthew 11:28-30 as your prayer, trusting in Jesus to give you rest from your self-effort and to empower you through His Spirit.

   Example:

   "Jesus, I am tired and weary of trying to do things for You and trying to please others. Thank You Jesus for inviting me to come to You to find rest. I am exhausted from trying to live the Christian life through self-effort. Teach me what it means to rest in You and depend on Your Spirit in my daily life."

© COPYRIGHT 1998, 2001, 2005, 2007 SCOPE MINISTRIES INTERNATIONAL INC.

The Performance Treadmill and Guilt - Day Five

Goal: To recognize and heal emotional guilt.

1. Check below the symptoms of emotional guilt which you recognize in your life. Write one reason why you feel guilty and how you experience this guilt.

❏   Self-condemnation: the constant blaming of oneself. This can lead to depression.

❏   Self-punishment: any form of punishment which is inflicted upon oneself, usually to pay for some wrongdoing.

❏   Depression: The end result of guilt that hasn't been addressed.

❏   Sense of Disapproval: The result of expectations of yourself or others that have not been met.

❏   Physical Symptoms: can include headaches, fatigue, and insomnia.

© COPYRIGHT 1998, 2001, 2005, 2007 SCOPE MINISTRIES INTERNATIONAL INC.

❑   Rationalization: an attempt to justify one's actions to counter guilt feelings.

❑   Compensation: An attempt to soothe the conscience by doing things considered to be good. Another attempt to counter guilt feelings.

❑   Anger: A feeling of hostility toward those who seem to prompt guilt feelings.

❑   "Goody Two-Shoes:" Exemplary behavior which is often another attempt to mask internal guilt feelings.

❑   Fear and Dread: Two closely related emotions which are often associated with unresolved guilt feelings.

2. For each example you wrote above, confess (agree with God; give thanks) concerning His complete forgiveness of you and for giving you the righteousness of Christ.

© COPYRIGHT 1998, 2001, 2005, 2007 SCOPE MINISTRIES INTERNATIONAL INC.

The Performance Treadmill and Guilt - Lesson Eight

Name _____ Date _____

Answer the following questions. To turn in page to small group leader, use identical
perforated page in back of book.

1. How is living on the "Performance Treadmill" evident in your life?

2. What laws or standards have you tried to live up to in order to earn God's approval
   and acceptance? What has been the result of living by these laws or standards?

3. What standards have you tried to live up to in order to gain a sense of self-worth or
   to get approval and acceptance from others?

4. How has living on the "Performance Treadmill" affected the quality of your life?
   Your relationship with God? With others?

5. What is your understanding of how you are to live the Christian life?

6. Mark the graph to indicate how much of this week's assignment you completed.

| None | 50% | 100% |

© COPYRIGHT 1998, 2001, 2005, 2007 SCOPE MINISTRIES INTERNATIONAL INC.

Record Your Prayer Requests:

_____

_____

_____

_____

_____

_____

_____

_____

_____

_____

_____

_____

_____

_____

_____

_____

_____

_____

_____

_____

© COPYRIGHT 1998, 2001, 2005, 2007 SCOPE MINISTRIES INTERNATIONAL INC.

Old Way of Law vs. New Way of Spirit

Old Way of Law

1. External Code
The moral precepts of God are only an external code of conduct. The Law commands obedience but provides no inclination or desire to obey.

2. Commanding
The Law commands obedience but gives no enabling power.

3. Hostility
Because of our hostility to God's Law before becoming a Christian, the Law's commands actually provoke and incite our flesh to sin.

4. Fear
The Law produces a legalistic response to God. We try to obey because we fear punishment for disobedience or we hope to win favor with God.

5. Working
Under the Law, we perform in order to be accepted by God. Because our performance is always imperfect, we never feel completely accepted by Him. We live from a position of weakness, because we work to be accepted, but never achieve it.

New Way of Spirit

1. Internal Desire
The moral precepts of God are written on our hearts. The Spirit prompts us in our thoughts and gives us a desire to obey.

2. Enabling
The Spirit empowers us to obey the law of love.

3. Delight
The Spirit, by removing our hostility, giving us a new spirit and writing the Law on our hearts, causes us to delight in God's Law.

4. Gratitude
The Spirit, by showing us God's grace, produces a response of love and gratitude. We obey, not out of fear or to earn favor, but out of gratitude for favor already given.

5. Relying
The Spirit bears witness with our spirit that we are accepted by God through the merit of Christ. By relying solely on His perfect righteousness, we know we are accepted by Him. We live from a position of strength, because we have been made acceptable.

© COPYRIGHT 1998, 2001, 2005, 2007 SCOPE MINISTRIES INTERNATIONAL INC.

Old Way of Law	New Way of Spirit

6. Principles

Under the Law we live by principles and rely on our knowledge and self-discipline. This is reliance upon the natural cause and effect.

6. Promises

Living by the Spirit is living by the promises of God and relying on the Holy Spirit. Living by the Spirit requires faith in the supernatural.

7. Striving

Living under the Law creates pressure to perform in order to earn God's blessing and acceptance. Because we cannot keep God's Law, we never feel accepted by God.

7. Resting

Living by the Spirit brings freedom to rest in the faithfulness of God who has already blessed us with every spiritual blessing. It is trusting in Christ's perfect life within to live a life pleasing to God.

8. Persecution

Those who live under the Law tend to persecute and judge those around them for not keeping the Law.

8. Blessing

Those who live by the Spirit understand the grace of God and extend it to others. They bless others with God's unconditional love and acceptance.

9. We Are Responsible

Under the old covenant of the Law we were responsible to obey the Law in order to receive God's promised blessing. Failure to keep the Law brings a curse.

9. God Takes Initiative

Under the new covenant God takes the initiative and responsibility for living the Christian life through us. Our part is to live by faith and God's part is to conform us to Christ.

10. Performance Consciousness

Living by the Law creates a performance consciousness, focusing on self. This drains us of spiritual life and robs us of joy and peace.

10. God Consciousness

Living by the Spirit creates a God consciousness, focusing on who He is and what He has done for us. This causes us to love and worship God, resulting in joy and peace in our life.

11. Failure

Living by the Law leads to further sin and failure because we are walking in the flesh.

11. Victory

Walking by the Spirit produces freedom and victory over sin and the fruit of the Spirit is produced in our life.

© COPYRIGHT 1998, 2001, 2005, 2007 SCOPE MINISTRIES INTERNATIONAL INC.

Be Transformed

Part Three

Putting It All Together

A Life Transformed

But we all, with unveiled face beholding as in a mirror the glory of the Lord, are being transformed into the same image from glory to glory, just as from the Lord, the Spirit.

2 Corinthians 3:18 NAS

Lesson 9

I was one of those people who always did my best. I always gave 110% because I wanted everything in my life and everyone else's life to run smoothly. I knew that I could run the world if everyone would do just what I told them.

Despite all my efforts to keep my marriage together, it was falling apart. I was miserable. I had reached the end of my rope and knew that I could not continue the way I was and still survive. Of course, I thought that things would be fine again if my husband Jeff would change.

I turned to God looking for ways to fix Jeff and my marriage, but, instead I found the way to allow God to change me and to mend my relationship with Him. He taught me that my ability to handle the challenges in my life depends upon my relationship with Him and how I view Him.

I had always related to people in my life by performing, and I thought that I had to relate to God as a performer too. I had many fears of being close to God because that meant more things to do and more tasks to complete. When I didn't meet what I imagined were God's expectations, I thought that He was punishing me by allowing my marriage to fail.

I discovered that my identity is based on what God has done for me, not what I have done for Him. I was so relieved to know that God cares for me the same no matter what I was doing or experiencing in my life. He wants to care for me and assume control of my life, but giving up that control to God was very difficult for me because I thought that I knew what was best. I learned that my greatest weakness was my independence from God. God's goals for my life are that I am closer to Him, that I am more like Him, that I depend upon Him, and that I find my worth, value, and identity through Him.

I thought I had mastered these concepts and I was feeling pleased with myself. I was doing the right things, so I expected God to fix my marriage, but Jeff and I reached another crisis point, and my world began to fall apart again. I realized that even as I had applied these principles to my life, I was still trying to stay in control. I had given God all of my options, and I expected Him to pick one. I finally let go.

to be continued...

© COPYRIGHT 1998, 2001, 2005, 2007 SCOPE MINISTRIES INTERNATIONAL INC.

A Life Transformed - Lesson Nine

Through the past eight lessons we have laid a foundation for experiencing a transformed life. We have discovered some of our corrupted beliefs about the Gospel, who we are, Who God is, and the Spirit-filled life. We have also identified some of the obstacles to experiencing the truth of what God has done in our lives. We have recognized that the presenting problem is merely the symptom of a deeper problem: our corrupted beliefs which keep us from relating to God as He really is. This final lesson will help us understand how all of life is connected to our relationship with God.

Life's Problems Are Our Motivation to Seek God

Without life's problems, we probably would never recognize our need to know and relate to God in a personal way. Our problems and even our sins become the environment in which we can experience and appreciate Who God really is. If we do not recognize and acknowledge our failure, we cannot understand God's unconditional love and acceptance. We cannot know experientially God's character, and God's grace has no meaning.

The following chart is a summary of each of the root problems we have identified in the previous lessons and the solution to each of them.

The Problem	The Solution
1. Our belief system is corrupted. Proverbs 14:12; 23:7a	Renewing our minds transforms our lives. John 8:31-32; Romans 12:2
2. Being born separated from God causes us to be dysfunctional as human beings. Not understanding the implications of the Gospel makes us dysfunctional as God's children. Ephesians 2:1-3	Through faith in Jesus Christ we are reconciled to God and receive His Eternal Life. We can experience God's quality of life now. John 5:24; Colossians 1:19-20
3. The memory of our old identity causes us to live in defeat and in bondage to the flesh. Romans 7:17-18	Believing the truth of our new identity and depending on the Holy Spirit gives us victory over the flesh. 2 Corinthians 5:16-17; Colossians 3:9-10
4. Our corrupted view of God robs us of joy and intimacy in our relationship with Him and keeps us from growing in our spiritual lives. John 6:46	Seeing the Father through Jesus and seeing ourselves as His deeply loved children frees us to rest in God's unconditional love. John 1:18, 14:6-9; 1 John 3:1-2

© COPYRIGHT 1998, 2001, 2005, 2007 SCOPE MINISTRIES INTERNATIONAL INC.

5. Living independently of God leads to self-sufficiency and to trying to live the Christian life in our own strength. This does not produce real life. Philippians 3:3-4	Continually coming to Jesus and believing in Him allows us to be filled with His Spirit, which results in a productive life filled with joy and peace. John 7:38; Galatians 5:16; Ephesians 5:18-19
6. Our emotions become our final authority, controlling what we believe and the choices we make.	Expressing emotions to God (REED) and making God's Word the final authority for what we believe. This results in greater intimacy with God and viewing life from God's perspective. Psalm 34:4; 1 Peter 5:7
7. Blocked expectations produce inappropriate expressions of anger. Unresolved anger produces bitterness (which destroys relationships) and eventually depression. 2 Peter 1:9; Hebrews 12:15	Yielding expectations and rights to God, agreeing with God concerning forgiveness, and extending God's forgiveness toward others leads to freedom. Romans 12:1; Colossians 2:13-14, 3:13
8. Motivation by guilt results in a performance-based Christian life. We work hard to try to earn our salvation, spirituality, acceptance, and worth. Our efforts to improve the flesh produces only more failure. Galatians 3:2-3, 10	Receiving God's unconditional love and grace and resting in Christ for our acceptance and worth, and depending on the Holy Spirit to live through us. Galatians 2:19-20; 3:2; Ephesians 2:8-9

Everything we've covered has led us to the core issue of life, which is:

9. Our distorted concept of God leads us to worship people and things, resulting in bondage to fear and all sorts of sins. Romans 1:25-32	Worshipping God for Who He really is results in an abundant and transformed life in the midst of life's problems. John 4:23-24; 2 Corinthians 3:18

Right Worship Leads to a Transformed Life

Ultimately all of life depends upon the answer to the question, "Who is my God?"

As beings created to worship, we will worship something or someone, and we become like the one we worship. Worship simply means "worth - ship." When we worship something or someone, we are believing in its superior value and worth. The dictionary defines "worship" as "giving reverence, honor and devotion; to be full of adoration."

© COPYRIGHT 1998, 2001, 2005, 2007 SCOPE MINISTRIES INTERNATIONAL INC.

We worship that which we view as most important and vital to life. We depend upon what or who we worship. If we believe money or possessions are the source of worth and value and are vital for life, then we are worshipping money. If we believe our family is what is most important and vital to life, then we are worshipping our family. To worship God rightly means that we view Him as the most vital, important, and worthy person in our lives.

Only when we recognize God for Who He really is can we rightly worship Him. Only as we begin to worship God for Who He truly is can we see ourselves as we really are. Right worship of God allows us to experience our new identity in our daily lives and to be a blessing to others.

God reveals Himself in the midst of life's problems.

We can know God only because He chooses to make Himself known. Our needs and problems become the opportunity for God to make Himself known to us experientially. God can be seen and experienced best in the midst of life's problems.

- Obstacles become opportunities to see God overcome;
- In pain and loss, we receive God's comfort;
- Our weakness gives way to His strength;
- Our lack brings God's supply;
- Through our trials we experience Him as our deliverer;
- In our failure we receive His grace;
- In our defeat He becomes our Victory;
- In times of stress and turmoil He gives us peace;
- During times of sorrow He gives us His joy; and
- When we are rejected, He fills our hearts with His unconditional love.

By letting God be Who He is in us, we become outwardly whom God has already made us inwardly in Christ. One of the most important things God wants to do in us is to renew our minds with the TRUTH of Who He is and who He has made us to be.

Through right worship of God we can see ourselves as God sees us, created in His image. He becomes the Source of everything we need for life and Godliness. When we are rightly connected to God, we can then see life from His perspective.

We Are Living, Thinking, Believing, Worshipping Beings

Scripture addresses us on all four levels: as a **living being** (our behavior and emotions); as a **thinking being** (our thoughts and reasoning); as a **believing being** (our beliefs, values, and convictions); and as a **worshipping being** (our spiritual nature and relationship with God). To address our problems from God's perspective, we need to address all four of these areas. At times, we need to deal

A Life Transformed

God can be seen and experienced best in the midst of life's problems.

© COPYRIGHT 1998, 2001, 2005, 2007 SCOPE MINISTRIES INTERNATIONAL INC.

9.5

with our emotions and what they are telling us about what we are thinking and believing. But we also need to identify the root issue in order to expose our wrong perception of God (which is idolatry) and to see God as the loving, trustworthy Father that He is. By acknowledging our wrong beliefs at this level, we can begin to worship God in spirit and in truth. Through right worship of God, we are transformed into His likeness a little at a time.

The funnel chart below is a visual example of the relationship between the four levels of our experience and our view of God. Before we can permanently and effectively address our behavior, emotions, thoughts, and beliefs, we must deal with Who God is to us personally. Some change is possible without addressing this root issue; however, no permanent change is possible without growing in an intimate relationship with our Creator.

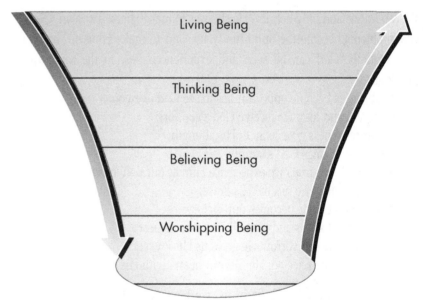

The Living Level

Working down the left side of the funnel chart, we first record what is happening on the "living" level. In other words, how are we responding in our behavior and emotions to the presenting problem?

The Thinking Level

Our behavior and emotions tell us something about what is happening in our thought processes, which is the rational level. Here we record what we are actually thinking about the problem or issue being addressed.

The Believing Level

Our thoughts then reveal what we are really believing in that particular situation. This level reveals our beliefs about ourselves, which control how we respond to life situations. It also reveals the standards by which we are living.

The Worshipping Level

Our beliefs define what we really believe about God, because generally, how we think God views us is what we also believe about ourselves. This reveals how we are really viewing God in this situation.

© COPYRIGHT 1998, 2001, 2005, 2007 SCOPE MINISTRIES INTERNATIONAL INC.

> But we all, with unveiled face beholding as in a mirror the glory of the Lord, are being transformed into the same image from glory to glory, just as from the Lord, the Spirit.

2 Corinthians 3:18 NAS

By working down the left side of the chart, we discover our wrong beliefs about God. Then we can begin putting off the old way of viewing God and putting on the new. To work back up the right side of the funnel, we start at the **worshipping level** and begin to look to the Word to know what is really true about God. We compare the things we believe about God on the left side with the Word, writing the Scripture verses that address the wrong beliefs. First, we need to acknowledge to God the way we have viewed Him, and then choose to reject the lies we have believed about Him. Finally, we thank God for Who He really is and ask Him to make Himself known in this way.

On the **believing level**, we accept the truth about God and proclaim that what is true about us is based on Who God is and Who He has made us to be in our new identity. We reject and renounce the lies we have believed about ourselves and put on the truth of who we are in Christ. As a new creation, we choose to see ourselves as God sees us. Again we thank God for changing us and giving us His nature. Because God is love, we are loved and able to love others. We must understand that we are able *only* because He is able. We give out of what we receive from Him.

On the **thinking level**, we write the thoughts that will result from our new beliefs about God and about who we are in Christ. As Philippians 4:8 tells us, we choose to think about those things that are true, honorable, right, pure, lovely, attractive, excellent, and worthy of praise. We choose to think about our problems and circumstances from God's perspective, rejoicing in the Lord and giving thanks in everything. We set our thoughts on the thoughts from the Spirit instead of on the memory of the old way of life.

On the **living level**, we write the behaviors and emotions that will result from our renewed beliefs and thoughts about God and ourselves. Remember, our feelings are the last to change. We acknowledge any sinful patterns of behavior that have resulted from our believing lies about God and ourselves. We then act on our new beliefs and thoughts. As we make right choices, our feelings will eventually change. We now choose to live by faith rather than by what we perceive with our physical senses. As we talk to God about everything, He will continue to reveal Himself to us, giving us His perspective of life.

Our need to know God is more important than earthly relationships, worldly possessions, and temporal pleasures.

© COPYRIGHT 1998, 2001, 2005, 2007 SCOPE MINISTRIES INTERNATIONAL INC.

Our Purpose Is Not to Avoid Problems, But to Know God

Renewing our minds is a process which involves changing our purpose and goal in life.

Because our purpose is to be the friend and companion of God and to reflect His character, our goal is to know God experientially as He really is. This involves our viewing God as our most vital necessity in life. Our need to know God is more important than our earthly relationships, worldly possessions, and temporal pleasures. Delighting in the Lord and relating to Him in the midst of our personal struggles will result in a transformed life.

The solution to any problem is found in knowing and relating to God.

We can use the tools received from this study to address our problems from God's perspective, and not just our present problems, but also our future ones.

> And this is eternal life, that they may know Thee, the only true God, and Jesus Christ whom Thou has sent.   John 17:3 NAS

> Seeing that His divine power has granted to us everything pertaining to life and Godliness, through the true knowledge of Him Who called us by His own glory and excellence. For by these He has granted to us His precious and magnificent promises, in order that by them you might become partakers of *the* divine nature, having escaped the corruption that is in the world by lust.
>
> 2 Peter 1:3-4 NAS

Our part is to seek to know and relate to God in the midst of life's problems.

Seeking to know God requires being open and honest with God concerning our beliefs and behaviors. This requires the personal involvement of our mind, will, and emotions. Without the involvement of all three, we will not experience a fully personal relationship. To get to know another person, we have to be in each other's company and be open and transparent with one another. God has taken the initiative to make Himself known to us through His Word and His Son. He loved us before the foundation of the world. What matters most is not that we know God, but that He knows us.

- We are tattooed on the palm of His hands. (Isaiah 49:16)

- We are never out of His mind. (Psalm 139:17-18; Psalm 40:5)

- He knows the very number of hairs on our head. (Matthew 10:30)

- He saves all our tears in His bottle. (Psalm 56:8)

- He knows us as a Father, and there is no moment when His eye is off us or His attention distracted from us. Therefore, there is no moment when His care falters. (Luke 12:6-7)

© COPYRIGHT 1998, 2001, 2005, 2007 SCOPE MINISTRIES INTERNATIONAL INC.

It is a tremendous relief to know that God's love for us is totally realistic and is based, at every point, on prior knowledge of the worst about us. There is no discovery that can disillusion Him about us or quench His determination to bless us. When we realize that He sees all the twisted things about us that even others do not see, yet He looks beyond the outer man and sees the new person He has created us to be, there is no room for pride. The knowledge of His unconditional love and acceptance of us creates in us the desire to worship, adore, and love God with all our heart, mind, soul, and strength.

Intimacy With God Results in an Abundant Life

We must address any obstacles to our experiencing intimacy with God.

These nine lessons were designed to help you recognize and address the obstacles that may be limiting your intimacy with God. To experience intimacy with any person, we need a correct view of ourselves and of the other person. This is the primary reason why lessons three, Seeing Ourselves as God Sees us, and four, Getting to Know Your Heavenly Father, are so critical. Consider this question: Do you want a close relationship with someone who you think ...
- Is untrustworthy?
- Does not care about you?
- Merely tolerates your presence?
- Gets mad at you when you fail?
- Loves you only when you perform well?

You can complete this list with any of the false beliefs the Holy Spirit revealed to you about God in lesson four. You must address these false beliefs if you are going to experience God as He truly is. If you have an accurate view of God, you will desire intimacy with Him. Any false belief about God will limit your intimacy with Him, because it will give you a concept of God less than He really is. It is impossible for you to believe He is more loving than He is. He is love personified! Likewise, it is impossible for you to believe He is more good, more holy, more forgiving, or more anything than He is.

Consider this question: Do you want a close relationship with someone if you think . . .
- You are unacceptable?
- You are going to be rejected if the other person really gets to know you?
- You will never meet the other person's standards?
- You will be condemned by the other person?

You can complete this list with any of the false beliefs you identified about yourself from lesson three. (The list, "Creating a Christian Identity" on page 3.28 is especially helpful). Any one of these beliefs will hinder you from developing an intimate relationship with God.

Why is an intimate relationship with God so important? It is only within this relationship that you will experience abundant life—God's quality of life which has been given to us through Christ.

© COPYRIGHT 1998, 2001, 2005, 2007 SCOPE MINISTRIES INTERNATIONAL INC.

The abundant life that Jesus promised you is not contingent on your circumstances. He did not say, "I came that you might have life and have it abundantly if your marriage is fulfilling, your bills are paid, your past is not filled with pain, etc." No one is excluded from Jesus' promise of abundant life. You can experience it, regardless of your circumstances, because you experience it as you experience God in the midst of your circumstances.

Only God can meet all your needs.

God revealed Himself to Moses as "I AM WHO I AM." Think of your current needs, and fill in God's revelation of Himself: "I AM" (whatever you need). Your Abba Father loves you deeply and longs to meet your needs.

Often we do not experience Him as "I AM," because we turn to other sources to meet our needs. God expressed this through Jeremiah when He said,

> For My people have committed two evils: They have forsaken Me, the fountain of living waters, to hew for themselves cisterns, broken cisterns, that can hold no water.   Jeremiah 2:13 NAS

Like the people of Jeremiah's day, we are not turning to God, the only fountain of Living Water, to meet our needs. Rather, we have used our own means to meet our needs. But as Jeremiah wrote, our methods are "broken" and ineffective. Will you choose today to begin seeking your loving Abba Father to meet the needs of your life? He longs to do so, and He is the only one Who truly can.

We Have Only Just Begun

Seeking to know God is a lifelong process.

God desires for us to continue the discovery process. Don't set this workbook aside, but use it as a reference tool when facing future problems. Review and re-ask the personal application questions when encountering a new problem. The "Creating a Christian Identity" lesson (page 3.13) and the list of characteristics describing our Heavenly Father can be wonderful Bible studies. Use the "REED" lesson(page 6.7) to develop more intimate communication with God. The appendix includes some suggestions for long-term assignments which will help you continue to apply what you have learned from this study. There is also a list of resources on pages 9.22 and 9.25 which will direct you to further reading material on the subjects covered.

© COPYRIGHT 1998, 2001, 2005, 2007 SCOPE MINISTRIES INTERNATIONAL INC.

┌─ SUMMARY: ─────────────────────────────────────┐

1. The problems we experience in life are opportunities to know God experientially.

2. Right worship is recognizing and valuing God for Who He really is: the most important and worthy Person in our lives.

3. We were created to know and worship God, and this is what changes us to be more like Him.

4. We need to address our problems in light of how we view and relate to God.

5. Intimacy with God leads to satisfaction and joy in life.

└──┘

A Life Transformed, con't.

In the midst of that crisis, God opened my heart to see Him as He really is and myself as He sees me. I had doubted the everyday involvement of God in my life, but I began to recognize that some things aren't just a coincidence but are the evidence of His involvement with me personally. I finally realized that I can know that God loves me because He made the ultimate sacrifice of His Son, not because my life is free from problems. I experienced His love and care and peace in the darkest days of my life. I know that He is the only reason that I survived the last few years of separation and then the rebuilding of our marriage. In this whole process, He has changed me.

As a performer, I was always very concerned with pleasing people. I'm not nearly as compulsive as I used to be. When I had to choose between my parent's wishes or plans and my husband's plans, my parents always won because I was so worried about what they would think of me. Last Christmas I took a huge step. I chose not to visit my parents because I knew it wasn't best for my family. That spoke volumes to Jeff to show that I was valuing him over my extended family. If this had happened before, I would have felt very guilty for disappointing them. Now I can make decisions that are best for my marriage and family because I do not find my identity in the approval of everyone else.

On Mother's Day, my kids each gave me a card that listed things they thought about me like my favorite song, my favorite movie, etc. One sentence read "my mother loves me best when . . . ," and my son Jordan wrote "my mother loves me best all the time." This reinforced to me that God feels that way about me. He can't get disappointed with me. My actions and choices may affect the quality of my life, but His love for me is not going to change. That's how I feel about God. No matter what I do, He loves me best all the time.

Shari - Nurse

© COPYRIGHT 1998, 2001, 2005, 2007 SCOPE MINISTRIES INTERNATIONAL INC.

© COPYRIGHT 1998, 2001, 2005, 2007 SCOPE MINISTRIES INTERNATIONAL INC.

A Life Transformed - Day One

Goal: To recognize how my response to my problems reveals my view of God.

1. Read over the funnel chart explanation.

2. Funnel a present situation that you are struggling with using the blank funnel provided.

USING THE "FUNNEL CHART"

Ask the Holy Spirit to guide your thoughts. Complete the left side of the funnel chart in regard to the feelings and actions in your life. Begin by thinking of a situation that really bothered you this past week or month.

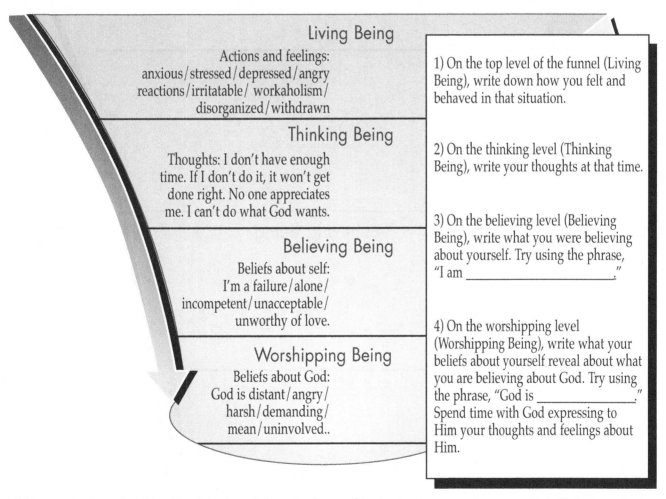

Living Being

Actions and feelings:
anxious/stressed/depressed/angry
reactions/irritatable/ workaholism/
disorganized/withdrawn

1) On the top level of the funnel (Living Being), write down how you felt and behaved in that situation.

Thinking Being

Thoughts: I don't have enough time. If I don't do it, it won't get done right. No one appreciates me. I can't do what God wants.

2) On the thinking level (Thinking Being), write your thoughts at that time.

Believing Being

Beliefs about self:
I'm a failure/alone/
incompetent/unacceptable/
unworthy of love.

3) On the believing level (Believing Being), write what you were believing about yourself. Try using the phrase, "I am _____."

Worshipping Being

Beliefs about God:
God is distant/angry/
harsh/demanding/
mean/uninvolved..

4) On the worshipping level (Worshipping Being), write what your beliefs about yourself reveal about what you are believing about God. Try using the phrase, "God is _____." Spend time with God expressing to Him your thoughts and feelings about Him.

5) Now, go back up the right side of the funnel chart. At the worshipping level, contrast your negative beliefs about God to what is true about Him. Give Scripture references. Stop and reject the lies you have been believing about God, and thank Him for Who He really is. (You may not feel this yet, but it is true nevertheless.) Refer to page 4.22 for truths about God relating to us and pages 4.16-4.17 for characteristics of God.

© COPYRIGHT 1998, 2001, 2005, 2007 SCOPE MINISTRIES INTERNATIONAL INC.

6) On the believing level, write what is true about you in light of God's Word and His character. (See "Creating a Christian Identity" page 3.13.) Acknowledge to God the lies you have been believing about yourself, and replace the lies with the truth.

7) On the thinking level, write what thoughts will result from your new beliefs about God and yourself.

8) On the living level, write what behaviors will result from your new beliefs about God and yourself. Your feelings will eventually follow. Ask the Holy Spirit what step of faith (an action, belief to accept, attitude to be willing to change, etc.) He wants you to take.

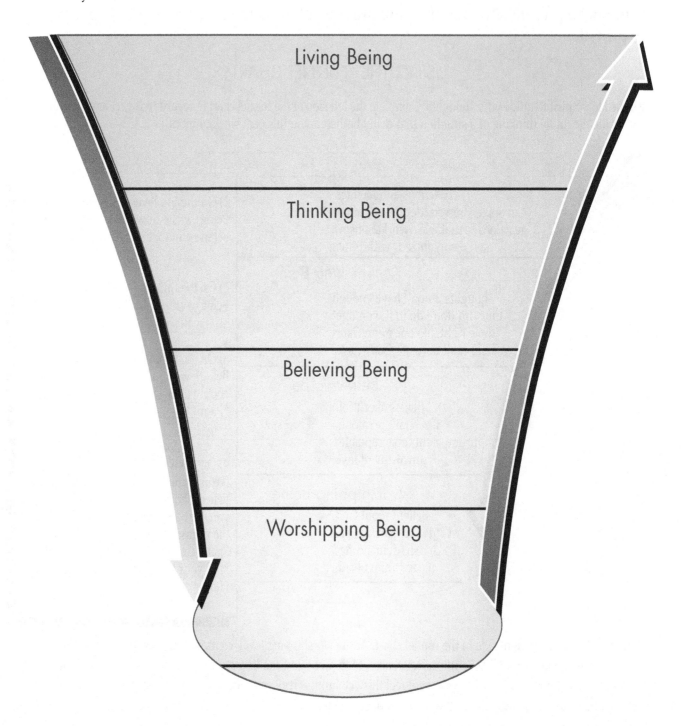

Living Being

Thinking Being

Believing Being

Worshipping Being

© COPYRIGHT 1998, 2001, 2005, 2007 SCOPE MINISTRIES INTERNATIONAL INC.

A Life Transformed - Day Two

Goal: To recognize how God wants to make Himself personally known to you in the midst of life's problems.

1. Look back to "Summary" at the end of each lesson. List the ones about which God has given you a greater understanding.

2. What changes are resulting from your new understanding of these truths?

3. Read over "Problem Solving in Light of Who God Is" on the next page and then list the characteristics of God that He wants to reveal to you through your present problems.

4. Spend time worshipping God for Who He is.

© COPYRIGHT 1998, 2001, 2005, 2007 SCOPE MINISTRIES INTERNATIONAL INC.

PROBLEM SOLVING IN LIGHT OF WHO GOD IS

GOD IS COMPASSIONATE - He cares about all of my problems, and He cares about me. He feels my pain. (2 Corinthians 1:3; 1 Peter 5:7).

GOD IS OMNIPOTENT - He is able to solve my problems. Nothing is too hard for Him, and no problem is too big. Through Him I can do all things (Philippians 4:13).

GOD IS OMNISCIENT - He knows all about my problems, and He knows the solution. He has already planned to work these problems together for my good (Romans 8:28-29).

GOD IS WISE - He allowed this problem in my life because He knows what is best for me, and He also knows the best solution.

GOD IS OMNIPRESENT - As I face problems, He is with me and in me. He never asks me to solve problems by myself. The living God is my Helper (Isaiah 41:10; Matthew 28:20; Hebrews 13:5,6).

GOD IS IMMUTABLE (NEVER CHANGING) - The same God Who saved me (solved my biggest problem) is able to help me in whatever problem I face. The God Who helped David, Daniel, Paul, etc., in their problems is the same God Who is able to help me. I can always count on God being God (Hebrews 13:8).

GOD IS SOVEREIGN - He is in complete control of the situation. He allowed this problem to come into my life. Both my problem and I are in His loving hands.

GOD IS FAITHFUL - As I trust God for the solution to this problem, He will not fail me. His promises cannot fail. I can rely on God in this situation. God is absolutely trustworthy, dependable, and reliable. (2 Corinthians 1:20)

GOD IS TRUE - I can trust God's promises in His Word because God does not and cannot lie! What He says He will do, He will do! (Numbers 23:19; Titus 1:2)

GOD IS ETERNAL - As I view my problems in light of eternity, they become quite insignificant (Deuteronomy 33:27; 2 Corinthians 4:17).

GOD IS GOOD - In the midst of my problems and difficulties, God wants to bless me. He wants to make me more like Jesus (Romans 8:28-29).

GOD IS RIGHTEOUS - In allowing these problems to come into my life, God did what was right. God makes no mistakes!

GOD IS LOVE - God wants to reveal His love to me through these problems. There is no problem, no matter how great, that can separate me from His love (Romans 8:35-39).

GOD IS JUST - God is absolutely just in all that He does, including allowing these problems in my life.

GOD IS IN THE MIDST OF PRESSURES AND PROBLEMS! (Exodus 33:14; Deuteronomy 4:29-31; 31:8; Isaiah 43:10-11).

© COPYRIGHT 1998, 2001, 2005, 2007 SCOPE MINISTRIES INTERNATIONAL INC.

A Life Transformed - Day Three

Goal: To identify areas where you need to grow in understanding and faith.

1. Read over the "Summary" at the end of each lesson. List the key points which you do not fully understand.

2. Spend some time asking God to help you understand them.

© COPYRIGHT 1998, 2001, 2005, 2007 SCOPE MINISTRIES INTERNATIONAL INC.

© COPYRIGHT 1998, 2001, 2005, 2007 SCOPE MINISTRIES INTERNATIONAL INC.

A Life Transformed - Day Four

Goal: To review what God has taught you through these lessons.

1. What did God identify as one of the major root problem(s) in your life?

2. What corrupted beliefs did God reveal to you?

3. How has your perspective of yourself changed?

4. How has your perspective of God changed?

5. How has your perspective of living the Christian life changed?

© COPYRIGHT 1998, 2001, 2005, 2007 SCOPE MINISTRIES INTERNATIONAL INC.

6. What are some lies the enemy uses against you to rob you of joy and peace?

7. What truth have you learned to combat these schemes?

8. What is your part in building an intimate relationship with God?

9. Spend a few minutes thanking God for all that He has taught you and for the changes you see Him making in your life.

© COPYRIGHT 1998, 2001, 2005, 2007 SCOPE MINISTRIES INTERNATIONAL INC.

A Life Transformed - Day Five

Goal: To make a plan for continuing to renew your mind with God's truth.

1. Read through "Additional Helps for the Renewing Process" on the next page. Check the ones that stand out to you as possible future assignments.

2. Of those you checked, with which will you start? Schedule a time to get started.

3. Which of the assignments you checked needs to be an ongoing lifestyle change? Ask the Holy Spirit to motivate, empower, and remind you to implement these changes.

© COPYRIGHT 1998, 2001, 2005, 2007 SCOPE MINISTRIES INTERNATIONAL INC.

Additional Helps for the Renewing Process

What you have learned and applied in these nine lessons is only the beginning of the renewal process. The following are some suggestions to help you continue on in this process.

1. Read the Bible with the single purpose of seeing Who God is. It is helpful to start with a Bible that has not been written in, and with a color highlighter, highlight each verse that reveals something about the character of God. Start in the Gospels and then go to the Psalms (John is an excellent place to start).

2. Keep a personal notebook to record the lies that God reveals to you that need to be put off and the truth that needs to be put on. This will be a good reference tool when encountering future problems.

3. Practice meditating on the Truth and "Truth talk." Meditating simply means "to think about something." Truth-talking is the practice of telling yourself the Truth and praying the Truth back to God. Psalm 23 is a good example of this type of prayer. Start by praying back Scripture, personalizing it in your own words.

4. Develop the habit of meditating on the Truth by writing down a specific helpful Truth on a 3 x 5 card and carrying this with you. Connect meditating on this Truth with another repetitive practice, such as getting a drink, eating a meal, or going to the bathroom. Soon you will have the Truth cemented into your thinking.

5. Take the FatherGod Test in the "FatherCare" booklet. Write on 3x5 index cards the characteristics of God for which your faith is the weakest. As needs or fears arise, practice Truth-talking about God as your Father.

6. Continue to practice putting off the lies you have believed about yourself as instructed in the handout, "Creating a Christian Identity" (page 3.28). Use one of the methods mentioned in #4 and #5.

7. Practice keeping a REED journal (see week six: Controlling Emotions). Be sure to record the date and circumstances that prompted the negative feelings. This will help you recognize if there is a pattern to these negative emotions. Be sure to work all the way through REED to the "evaluate" and "decide" steps; otherwise, all you will accomplish is obtaining a little relief from suppressing your emotions. Record the lies you have believed and the truth from God's perspective.

8. Make worship a lifestyle. Pray Scripture back to God. Sing songs of praise and worship to God. Practice "doing" the Psalms instead of just reading them. Listen to and sing along with praise and worship music. This will help you focus on God instead of yourself and your circumstances. Talk to God about everything, as you would your closest friend.

9. Read Christian books and listen to teaching tapes that will reinforce the truth that you have learned through this workbook. Look over the Suggested Reading list (page 9.25) and check the books that would help reinforce the truths you need to focus on. You cannot hear the truth too much. Remember how long you have listened to the lies.

10. Fellowship with other believers who are seeking to know God and grow in their new identity. It is imperative that you stay connected and involved with people in the Body of Christ who will pray for you and encourage you in your faith. Standing alone against your three-fold enemy is very difficult.

11. Remember, your goal is to know God experientially in the midst of life's problems and to allow God to transform you into Christ-likeness. To "seek first the kingdom of God and His righteousness" begins by receiving God's unconditional love for you. Make it a habit to spend a few minutes several times each day receiving God's love. This is not a time of Bible study or prayer but a time to be still and know that He is God and to receive His love by faith.

12. Share with others what God is teaching you and what He is doing in your life. Giving to others what God has freely given you will reinforce the truth in your own life.

13. Daily practice consciously and verbally yielding your expectations and rights to God. Trust Him to meet your needs in the very best way and at the right time.

14. Practice asking yourself and God two questions: What is God doing in my life? What does He want me to do? Expect God to speak to you through His Word and through His indwelling Spirit. We do not have to live in continual confusion or bondage. When you have trouble discerning the answer to these two questions, talk to someone whom you respect for his walk with God. None of us hears God perfectly all the time. That's why we need to stay connected to the Body.

15. Reread the lessons in this workbook, and work through the specific assignments that address your particular needs.

Remember that this is an ongoing, moment-by-moment, lifelong process.

© COPYRIGHT 1998, 2001, 2005, 2007 SCOPE MINISTRIES INTERNATIONAL INC.

A Life Transformed - Lesson Nine

Name _____ Date _____

Answer the following questions. To turn in page to small group leader, use identical perforated page in back of book.

1. What has been the most significant thing God has revealed to you through this nine-week study?

2. How has this truth begun to change your life?

3. How has God worked in your life during your Discovery Group experience?

4. What is one area of your life in which you would like to experience transformation?

5. Mark the graph to indicate how much of this week's assignment you completed.

None	50%	100%

© COPYRIGHT 1998, 2001, 2005, 2007 SCOPE MINISTRIES INTERNATIONAL INC.

Record Your Prayer Requests:

_____

_____

_____

_____

_____

_____

_____

_____

_____

_____

_____

_____

_____

_____

_____

_____

_____

_____

_____

© COPYRIGHT 1998, 2001, 2005, 2007 SCOPE MINISTRIES INTERNATIONAL INC.

Suggested Reading

Belief Systems/Renewing the Mind:

"A Study of the Mind," booklet - Preston and Anabel Gillham

"Changing Your Thought Patterns," booklet - George Sanchez

"Fiddling with the Feece, Discovering the Will of God," booklet - Jim Craddock

Search for Freedom - Robert McGee

Search for Significance - Robert McGee

Sidetracked in the Wilderness - Michael Wells

"Sufficiency of Scripture," booklet - Jim Craddock

"The Hidden Heresy, The Problem of Syncretism in the Church," booklet - Jim Craddock

The Good News/God's Forgiveness

The Gift of Forgiveness - Charles Stanley

"A Treasured Possession, God's Unconditional Forgiveness," booklet - Jim Craddock

"Forgiven Forever," booklet - Bob George

Seeing Yourself as God Sees You:

Seeing Yourself Through God's Eyes - June Hunt

Lifetime Guarantee - Bill Gillham

Classic Christianity - Bob George

Jesus Loves Me - Herbert L. Roush

Living Free in Christ - Neil Anderson

Knowing God as Father:

"FatherCare," booklet - Jim Craddock

What is the Father Like? - W. Phillip Keller

Your Parents and You - McGee, Springle & Craddock

Let God Love You - Malcolm Smith

The Healing Heart of God - Malcolm Smith

The Father Heart of God - Floyd McClung

The Singing God - Sam Storms

Emotions/Guilt, Anger, Forgiveness:

Healing for Damaged Emotions - David Seamands

Where is God When it Hurts? - Philip Yancey

Freedom of Forgiveness - David Augsburger

"Anger, Fear in Disguise," booklet - Bob George

Forgiveness - Malcolm Smith

Search for Peace - Robert McGee

"Agony & Ecstasy, God's Answer to Man's Anxiety," booklet - Jim Craddock

"Finding Meaning in a World of Madness, A Many Colored Miracle," booklet - Jim Craddock

"Becoming a Candidate for a Miracle, Discovering the Catalyst for a Transformed Life" previously entitled "Touched by the Spirit," booklet - Jim Craddock

Performance Treadmill/Spirit-filled Life:

"Touched By the Spirit," booklet -Jim Craddock

Growing in Grace - Bob George

Grace Walk - Steve McVey

"Living on the Cutting Edge of a Transformed Life," booklet - Jim Craddock

The Promise -Tony Evans

The Secret to the Christian Life - Gene Edwards

Transforming Grace - Jerry Bridges

Tired of Trying to Measure Up - Jeff VanVonderen

Grace Works - Dudley Hall

This workbook and the above resources are available through the Scope Resource Center:

700 NE 63rd Street, Oklahoma City, OK 73105-6410 405.843.7778. www.scopeministries.org

(These books and Scope's Teens Transformed workbook, are made available as a service by Scope Ministries International. These are resources to be used in conjunction with the Biblical personal guidance ministry or in the Biblical training program. The inclusion of these books does not imply that Scope is in agreement with all of the contents of these books).

© COPYRIGHT 1998, 2001, 2005, 2007 SCOPE MINISTRIES INTERNATIONAL INC.

Nature of Man

Appendix A – Lesson 3

Terms in Brief

These terms are defined as Scope understands and uses them:

1. Old Nature (old Man)

The old race of fallen man that has been damned because of sins through Adam. The identity with which every descendant of Adam is born. (Romans 5)

2. New Nature (new man)

The regenerated spirit of the believer. The human spirit made alive by, indwelt by, and united with the Holy Spirit. The new man is Christ's life within regenerate man.

3. Flesh (self-life)

A condition and tendency within man to operate in his own strength and/or for reasons centered in himself. In the non-Christian it is the natural method of functioning that is, by means of body and soul only. In the Christian it is the selfish inclination to function as though he were body and soul only.

The flesh may be described as "My claim to my right to myself."

4. Sin

The deception that fulfillment (needs being met), meaning, and purpose in life may be experienced apart from God. In the Christian it is that unholy principle which indwells him, but is separate from the new man because the new man is the very life of Christ within the believer and sin cannot be part of Christ Himself.

5. Sins

Acts contrary to the will of God. Actions in man which "fall short" of revealing God's glory. "Sins" are what result when "sin" is obeyed.

© COPYRIGHT 1998, 2001, 2005, 2007 SCOPE MINISTRIES INTERNATIONAL INC.

About Scope Ministries International

Scope Ministries International is a ministry of deeply committed Christians who desire to help God's people discover and experience their full potential in Christ. Scope has been the laboratory since 1925 in which Biblical truth has been developed into transferable concepts which have proven to be incredibly effective in dealing with life events and human problems. Out of this crucible of human experience, Scope has developed a strategic model that is touching thousands of lives in this country and abroad.

Scope's goal has been to serve the Body of Christ by ministering to and equipping Christians to be effective in meeting the needs of hurting people. Scope ministers to the emotional, relational and spiritual needs of people by using God's Word and depending on the Holy Spirit. Every concept has been applied to real life situations.

Scope is unique in that it focuses on solutions rather than therapies, on causes rather than symptoms, on a person's potential rather than their problems, on transforming a person rather than just informing a person. Whether through marital, individual, or crisis counseling, literally thousands of people who have sought help from Scope have experienced changed lives.

For many years, our main ministry was through one-on-one ministry. To meet an ever increasing demand for Scope's services, a new approach to ministry, called Discovery Groups, was developed. The Discovery Group strategy is to involve everyone who comes to Scope in an intensive small group study where our concepts are applied to personal needs and problems. The success of the Discovery Group approach has allowed Scope to increase greatly the number of people being helped.

Unfortunately, while our contemporary society produces a mass of human hurt and need, it has nothing with which to address man's basic problems. The only real answer is to train an army of godly men and women to handle the challenge. Because the only army available today is the Church, the strategy of Scope is to train and equip lay people and church leaders to lead Discovery Groups and to do Biblical personal guidance.

We are Scope Ministries International, compelled by God's call to demonstrate the sufficiency of Christ and His Word. We share the life of Christ worldwide through comprehensive research, thorough training, and effective Biblical personal guidance. We are your servants!

Spiritual Guidance Training Opportunities

Scope Ministries International equips people to do effective Biblical personal guidance and discipleship. We have invested thousands of hours in research, observation, and practical experience to develop a model of ministry called Pneumanetics. This thirteen week course is our first level of training and is offered days and evenings at Scope and through correspondence. Pneumanetics is a prerequisite for all other classes at Scope.

© COPYRIGHT 1998, 2001, 2005, 2007 SCOPE MINISTRIES INTERNATIONAL INC.

Testimonies from Pneumanetics Class Members:

"I have grown since I started this class, and I've become so much more familiar with the Word in fourteen weeks, more than in three and a half years of seminary training."

"Pneumanetics has shown me the truth about God and myself. I have learned in this class what I should have learned when I was saved. I now show others the truth . . . I show them Jesus and His nature and really, really tell them about the Holy Spirit."

"I have been really blessed. I thought I knew some things. I found out that I only knew them intellectually, but God has been moving them to my heart. My relationship with God has improved dramatically along with my marriage and my relationship with my children."

Classes in Biblical personal guidance and Biblical personal guidance related issues are conducted throughout the year at Scope. The training year is divided into three semesters: fall, spring, and summer. The classes are offered to the public to serve as a resource to equip Christians for dealing with their own life issues and for ministry to others. The principles taught give a Biblical perspective on the root causes of and solutions to life's problems.

Other Classes Offered:

- **Pneumanetics for Young Adults** - this class is suggested for high school students
- **Character and Skills of a Counselor** - a two semester study necessary for the ministering process
- **Old Testament Survey** - emphasizes the application of Scripture to life issues
- **New Testament Survey** - emphasizes the application of Scripture to life issues
- **Bible Study Method**s - enables student to accurately interpret Scripture and apply it to life situations.
- **Small Group Facilitating** - prepares student to lead the *Be Transformed* Discovery group.
- **Evangelism and Discipleship** - applies it to the personal guidance process
- **Managing Your Money** - teaches what Scripture says about money and gives practical tools
- **Marriage Guidance** - teaches basics of Biblical marriage
- **Grace** - teaches Biblical concept of grace and how it applies to all areas of life
- **Christians and Suffering** - studies Biblical passages and examples of suffering

Scope's Two-Year Training program

Scope's two-year training program is an opportunity for Christians to be more equipped in their Biblical personal guidance ministry. This program is required of all Scope personal guidance ministers. It is also open to lay people and Christian workers who desire to be equipped in Biblical personal guidance principles and skills.

The program requires eighteen hours per week of class attendance, staff and supervisor meetings, and Biblical personal guidance practicum. It provides a complete curriculum of courses in Biblical personal guidance and theology, along with personalized supervision and practicum in actual ongoing Biblical personal guidance cases. The program requirements are vigorous, involving eight to ten hours of personal study per week, in addition to the eighteen hours spent at the Scope office.

© COPYRIGHT 1998, 2001, 2005, 2007 SCOPE MINISTRIES INTERNATIONAL INC.

Biblical research is an ongoing part of the training process. Completion of a related research paper is required in order to graduate. This research is presented to a Scope staff review board. Graduates of the training program receive a certificate of completion.

Scope's training year is divided into three semesters: fall, spring, and summer. The program can be entered at the beginning of any semester. Application to the program is required.

Short-Term Internship:

The short-term internship program is usually available during the summer. It is a training opportunity for Christians considering a ministry in Biblical personal guidance. It also serves as a Biblical personal guidance training opportunity for those already involved in discipleship ministry.

Some of the questions that will be addressed are the following:

- Does Scripture really address the problems we face in life today?
- Just how do I change habits?
- If am a new creation, why am I still sinning?
- How do I deal with emotions from a Biblical perspective?
- Does the Bible have anything to say about the hurts in my life?
- How can I have a meaningful relationship with God and others?

The internship program requires thirty-five hours per week attendance and provides a curriculum covering the basic principles and skills of Biblical personal guidance. Class attendance, personalized supervision, interaction with experienced Biblical personal guidance ministers, personal guidance observations, independent study, and staff meetings are included in the weekly schedule. There is a fee for the internship.

For more information about these and other opportunities with Scope or for class schedules, please contact:

Scope Ministries International
700 NE 63rd Street
Oklahoma City, OK 73105-6410
USA
405.843.7778
training@scopeministries.org
www.scopeministries.org

© COPYRIGHT 1998, 2001, 2005, 2007 SCOPE MINISTRIES INTERNATIONAL INC.

Discovery Group Guidelines

1. Time

Every effort will be made to start and end on time. Do your best to be on time.

2. Confidentiality

We all need to feel free to express ourselves openly without the fear of being discussed later, even by other group members; therefore nothing said in this group leaves this group. When you discuss your group experiences with a friend or spouse, share only what you gained or learned. Do not share anyone's experiences but your own. Do not share any names, descriptions or occupations of group members, etc., with people outside the group. During the week, do not discuss any other group members, even among yourselves.

3. Communication with each other

- Don't try to "fix" anyone else
- Use "I" statements, not "you" statements
- Follow Ephesians 4:29; "Do not let any unwholesome talk come out of your mouths, but only what is helpful for building others up according to their needs, that it may benefit those who listen."

4. Participation

This will make your group time more meaningful for you and for everyone else as you share your thoughts, experiences and feelings. We will all benefit from one another, so don't deprive others of your input. However, in the spirit of James 5:16 ("therefore, confess your sins to one another, and pray for one another, so that you may be healed."), share only your own sins or weaknesses, not those of others.

5. Attendance

Each member's attendance is very important. Your absence affects the dynamics of the group, therefore, give the group meeting a high priority. If you cannot attend, please call and inform your group leader prior to the meeting.

6. Homework

The daily assignments are intended to help you interact with God each day concerning your individual needs and problems. Change and healing are possible only when we allow God to be involved in our daily lives. Each assignment will usually require about 20-30 minutes.

©COPYRIGHT 1998, 2001, 2005, 2007 SCOPE MINISTRIES INTERNATIONAL INC.

Discovery Group Covenant

To encourage a high level of trust, love, and openness in my discovery group, I,
_____, covenant with my group's other members to do the following:

- I will make attendance at each group session a priority for the next agreed number of weeks. During these weeks, I will choose this group first when making decisions about my priorities and my time.

- I will commit my time each week to complete the appropriate assignments before the group session.

- I will keep confidential all information group members share. I will not share matters from the group with any outside person or mention the information as a prayer concern. I understand that breaking the confidentiality of the group could result in being asked to leave the group.

- I will support the other group members in their desire to grow emotionally and spiritually by encouraging them to evaluate honestly their beliefs and behavior.

- I will be honest about my own feelings and emotions as I participate in the group.

- I will be patient with other group members as we allow God to work in each of our lives. I will not try to give advice or to pressure other group members to do what I think best.

- I will inform my group leader of any physical or emotional problems that might arise and prohibit my participation in the group.

Signed: _____ Date: _____

_____   _____

_____   _____

_____   _____

_____   _____

© COPYRIGHT 1998, 2001, 2005, 2007 SCOPE MINISTRIES INTERNATIONAL INC.

© COPYRIGHT 1998, 2001, 2005, 2007 SCOPE MINISTRIES INTERNATIONAL INC.

© COPYRIGHT 1998, 2001, 2005, 2007 SCOPE MINISTRIES INTERNATIONAL INC.

10.8

© COPYRIGHT 1998, 2001, 2005, 2007 SCOPE MINISTRIES INTERNATIONAL INC.

We Would Like to Hear From You!

We would be very encouraged to hear how God's Spirit has used this material to change your life. Please use this page to write us a note. Mail your testimony to the address below:

700 NE 63rd Street• Oklahoma City, OK • 73105-6410 • USA or email us at info@scopeministries.org.

_____

_____

_____

_____

_____

_____

_____

_____

_____

_____

_____

_____

_____

_____

_____

_____

_____

_____

_____

_____

© COPYRIGHT 1998, 2001, 2005, 2007 SCOPE MINISTRIES INTERNATIONAL INC.

Discovering the Root of Our Problems - Lesson One

Name _____ Date _____

Answer the following questions. To turn in page to small group leader, use identical
  perforated page in back of book.

1. Briefly describe from DAY ONE the problem with which you are presently struggling.

2. What are some of your "beliefs" that relate to your area of struggle?

3. How are these beliefs affecting you (emotionally, relationally, behaviorally)?

4. What is God showing you from this week's lesson?

5. How often do you turn to God's Word for answers to your problems?
   ___never   ___seldom   ___often   ___ very often ___ always

6. What questions do you have concerning this week's assignment?

7. Mark the graph to indicate how much of this week's assignment you completed.

None	50%	100%

© COPYRIGHT 1998, 2001, 2005, 2007 SCOPE MINISTRIES INTERNATIONAL INC.

Record Your Prayer Requests:

_____

_____

_____

_____

_____

_____

_____

_____

_____

_____

_____

_____

_____

_____

_____

_____

_____

_____

_____

© COPYRIGHT 1998, 2001, 2005, 2007 SCOPE MINISTRIES INTERNATIONAL INC.

Understanding the Good News - Lesson Two

Name_____Date_____

Answer the following questions. To turn in page to small group leader, use identical perforated page in back of book.

1. What has your understanding of salvation been before this lesson?

2. What new understanding of the "good news" did you gain from this lesson?

3. When did you personally believe the "good news" and receive eternal life?

4. Is there anything you have done that you believe God has not forgiven? If so, what?

5. How confident are you of God's presence in your daily life?

6. What wrong beliefs did you recognize from this week's lesson?

7. Mark the graph to indicate how much of this week's assignment you completed.

None	50%	100%

© COPYRIGHT 1998, 2001, 2005, 2007 SCOPE MINISTRIES INTERNATIONAL INC.

Record Your Prayer Requests:

© COPYRIGHT1998, 2001, 2005, 2007 SCOPE MINISTRIES INTERNATIONAL INC.

Seeing Ourselves As God Sees Us - Lesson Three

Name _____ Date _____

Answer the following questions. To turn in page to small group leader, use identical perforated page in back of book.

1. According to what you have learned about the nature of man, what changed in you at salvation?

2. How does understanding that you have a new nature give you confidence concerning your salvation and spiritual growth?

3. What wrong beliefs about yourself do you need to put off?

4. How would believing your new identity and relying on the Holy Spirit in your daily life affect the way you respond to your present problems?

5. What questions do you have concerning the nature of man and your new identity?

6. Mark the graph to indicate how much of this week's assignment you completed.

None	50%	100%

© COPYRIGHT 1998, 2001, 2005, 2007 SCOPE MINISTRIES INTERNATIONAL INC.

Record Your Prayer Requests:

_____

_____

_____

_____

_____

_____

_____

_____

_____

_____

_____

_____

_____

_____

_____

_____

_____

_____

© COPYRIGHT1998, 2001, 2005, 2007 SCOPE MINISTRIES INTERNATIONAL INC.

Getting to Know Our Heavenly Father - Lesson Four

Name _____ Date _____

Answer the following questions. To turn in page to small group leader, use identical perforated page in back of book.

1. What corrupted beliefs about God as Father did you recognize through this lesson?

2. How would knowing and relating to God as your Father affect your life (emotionally, relationally, behaviorally)?

3. How would relating to God as an unconditionally loving and perfect Father affect your life?

4. What from this week's assignment was most meaningful to you?

5. What characteristic(s) of God need strengthening in your life?

6. Mark the graph to indicate how much of this week's assignment you completed.

None	50%	100%

© COPYRIGHT 1998, 2001, 2005, 2007 SCOPE MINISTRIES INTERNATIONAL INC.

Record Your Prayer Requests:

© COPYRIGHT 1998, 2001, 2005, 2007 SCOPE MINISTRIES INTERNATIONAL INC.

Living By the Spirit - Lesson Five

Name _____Date _____

Answer the following questions. To turn in page to small group leader, use identical perforated page in back of book.

1. What encouraged you most about this week's study on the Holy Spirit?

2. List any fears or concerns you have about surrendering control of your life to the Holy Spirit.

3. What do you feel would keep God from filling you with His Spirit?

4. How would living by the Spirit affect your life and your current struggles?

5. Mark the graph to indicate how much of this week's assignment you completed.

None	50%	100%

© COPYRIGHT 1998, 2001, 2005, 2007 SCOPE MINISTRIES INTERNATIONAL INC.

Record Your Prayer Requests:

© COPYRIGHT 1998, 2001, 2005, 2007 SCOPE MINISTRIES INTERNATIONAL INC.

Controlling Emotions - Lesson Six

Name _____ Date _____

Answer the following questions. To turn in page to small group leader, use identical perforated page in back of book.

1. What negative emotion did you experience most this past week? What kind of thoughts usually produced this emotion?

2. What did these thoughts tell you about what you were believing?

3. What new insight or perspective did God give you when you expressed your feelings honestly to Him?

4. How will practicing REED improve your relationship with God and your quality of life?

5. Mark the graph to indicate how much of this week's assignment you completed.

None	50%	100%

© COPYRIGHT 1998, 2001, 2005, 2007 SCOPE MINISTRIES INTERNATIONAL INC.

Record Your Prayer Requests:

© COPYRIGHT 1998, 2001, 2005, 2007 SCOPE MINISTRIES INTERNATIONAL INC.

Expectations, Anger, and Bitterness - Lesson Seven

Name _____ Date _____

Answer the following questions. To turn in page to small group leader, use identical perforated page in back of book.

1. About what have you been the most angry?

2. What expectations or rights are you holding onto that are contributing to this anger?

3. How are unforgiveness and bitterness affecting your life and relationships?

4. Have you forgiven those who have hurt you? If not, what do you think are the obstacles to forgiving them?

5. Whom did God lead you to forgive through this assignment?

6. Mark the graph to indicate how much of this week's assignment you completed.

None	50%	100%

© COPYRIGHT 1998, 2001, 2005, 2007 SCOPE MINISTRIES INTERNATIONAL INC.

Record Your Prayer Requests:

© COPYRIGHT 1998, 2001, 2005, 2007 SCOPE MINISTRIES INTERNATIONAL INC.

The Performance Treadmill and Guilt - Lesson Eight

Name _____ Date _____

Answer the following questions. To turn in page to small group leader, use identical perforated page in back of book.

1. How is living on the "Performance Treadmill" evident in your life?

2. What laws or standards have you tried to live up to in order to earn God's approval and acceptance? What has been the result of living by these laws or standards?

3. What standards have you tried to live up to in order to gain a sense of self-worth or to get approval and acceptance from others?

4. How has living on the "Performance Treadmill" affected the quality of your life? Your relationship with God? With others?

5. What is your understanding of how you are to live the Christian life?

6. Mark the graph to indicate how much of this week's assignment you completed.

None	50%	100%

© COPYRIGHT 1998, 2001, 2005, 2007 SCOPE MINISTRIES INTERNATIONAL INC.

Record Your Prayer Requests:

© COPYRIGHT 1998, 2001, 2005, 2007 SCOPE MINISTRIES INTERNATIONAL INC.

A Life Transformed - Lesson Nine

Name _____ Date _____

Answer the following questions. To turn in page to small group leader, use identical perforated page in back of book.

1. What has been the most significant thing God has revealed to you through this nine-week study?

2. How has this truth begun to change your life?

3. How has God worked in your life during your Discovery Group experience?

4. What is one area of your life in which you would like to experience transformation?

5. Mark the graph to indicate how much of this week's assignment you completed.

| None | 50% | 100% |

© COPYRIGHT 1998, 2001, 2005, 2007 SCOPE MINISTRIES INTERNATIONAL INC.

Record Your Prayer Requests:

© COPYRIGHT 1998, 2001, 2005, 2007 SCOPE MINISTRIES INTERNATIONAL INC.

The next page is representative of some "flash cards" that are available at SMI.

These cards are composed of heavy laminated card stock.

The cards are available at: Scope Ministries International

www.scopeministries.org

or at the Resource Center

405-843-7778

Scope Ministries International

700 NE 63rd St.

Oklahoma City, OK 73105

TRANSFORMING
LIVES
TRANSFORMING
LIVES
TRANSFORMING
LIVES
TRANSFORMING
LIVES
TRANSFORMING
LIVES
TRANSFORMING
LIVES
TRANSFORMING
LIVES

The more we know God
as He really is,
the more we love Him.

The more we love Him,
the more we
become like Him.

The more we become
like Him, the more
we desire to know Him.

SCOPE
MINISTRIES INTERNATIONAL

700 NE 63rd Street • Oklahoma City, OK 73105-6487 • 405.843.7778 • www.scopeministries.org

The Truth About Me Is
Always What God Says!
Not What I Think Or Feel;
Not What Others Say,
Think Or Do.

The Truest Thing About Me
Is What God Says!

SCOPE
MINISTRIES INTERNATIONAL

700 NE 63rd Street
Oklahoma City, OK 73105-6487
405.843.7778 • www.scopeministries.org

SCOPE
MINISTRIES INTERNATIONAL

700 NE 63rd Street
Oklahoma City, OK 73105-6487
405.843.7778
www.scopeministries.org

This insert is for your personal use.

Tear insert out of booklet
and separate

RECOGNIZE Your Emotions!
  • Ask God to show you what emotions
    you are feeling.

EXPRESS Your Emotions To God!
  • He already knows them.
  • I'm so mad I could...

EVALUATE Your Emotions In Light of God's Word!
  • Are my emotions in charge?
  • What do they reflect about my beliefs?

DECIDE To Replace Your Thinking and Behavior
With God's Truth!

SCOPE MINISTRIES INTERNATIONAL
700 NE 63rd Street • Oklahoma City, OK 73105-6487
405.843.7778 • www.scopeministries.org

MY HEAVENLY FATHER IS...

Compassionate - He cares about me and all my problems . . . . 2 Cor 1:3; 1 Peter 5:7

Powerful - He is strong and His strength becomes my strength . . . . Ps 93:1; 2 Cor 12:9,10; Eph 6:10

Ever Present - He is with me and in me. He will never leave me or forsake me . . . Heb 13:5,6; Matt 28:20

Loving - He loves me for who I am, not for what I do . . . . John 3:16; Rom 5:8; 1 John 4:9,10

Approving - His approval of me is based on who I am in Him and not on what I do . . John 6:27; Col 3:3

Listening - He listens to His children and takes time to be involved with me . . . . Ps 55:17

Awesome - He is awesome in His ability to love and protect me . . . . Ex 15:11; Ps 99:3

Victorious -He is victorious over all things and makes me victorious . . . . Zeph 3:17; Rom 8:37

Honorable - My Father is distinguished and upright. I am proud to call Him my Father . . . . Phil 2:9

Good - My Father is good in every sense and gives to me out of His goodness . . . . Ps 34:8; Ps 106:1

Just - My Father is impartial. He will be just with me no matter what. . . . . Deut 32:4; Rom 2:11

Forgiving - He has forgiven me totally for all my sins, past, present and future . . . Ps 103:10,12; Heb 10:17

Protective - My Father protects me as His precious child . . . . Ps 91; Ps 118:6-9; 2 Thess 3:3

Sufficient - He is enough for every need, in every situation . . . . 2 Cor 9:8; 2 Cor 12:9,10; Eph 3:20

Kind - He is considerate and always encouraging to me . . . . Ps 103:13; Rom 2:4; Eph 1:5

Faithful - His absolute faithfulness to me will never lag or end . . . . Num 23:19; Ps 89:1,2,5; Lam 3:23

God Says That In Christ I Am...

a new creation . . . . 2 Cor 5:17; Eph 4:22-24

adequate in Christ . . . . 2 Corinthians 3:5-6

totally forgiven . . . . Colossians 2:13-14

of great value. Matthew10:30-31;
and worth   1 Peter 1:18,19

God's child . . . . John 1:12; 1 John 3:1-2

God's co-worker . . . . 1 Cor 3:9,11; 2 Cor 6:1

a saint. . . . . Ephesians 1:1; Col 1:2,4

God's masterpiece! . . . . Ephesians 2:10

Jesus' friend. John 15:15

one spirit with Him . . . . 1 Corinthians 6:17

perfect and complete. . . . . . . Col 2:10; Heb 10:14

free from condemnation. . . . . Romans 8:1

holy and blameless . . . . Eph 1:4; Col 1:22

completely accepted. . . . . Romans 15:7

partaker of His divine nature . . . . 2 Peter 1:4

empowered with His strength . Eph 1:19; Phil 4:13

unconditionally loved. . . . . John 15:9, 16:27

dead to sin. . . . . Romans 6:11, 8:2

being transformed. . . . . Romans 12:1-2

joint heir with Christ . . . . Romans 8:17

reconciled to God . . . . . . Romans 5:1; 1 Cor 6:11

never alone or forsaken. . . . . Hebrews 13:5b

indwelt by God's Spirit. . . . . 1 Cor 3:16, 6:19

no longer under the law . . . . . Gal 2:19-21, 3:12,13

precious in His sight . . . . Isaiah 43:4

eternally saved . . . . Eph 2:8; 1 John 5:11-13

safe and secure. . . . . Psalm 32:7, 91; Isaiah 43:1-3

chosen by God. . . . . 1 Peter 2:9

absolutely righteous . . . . Romans 8:10; 2 Cor 5:21

uniquely gifted by God . Romans 12:4-8; 1 Cor 12

a victorious . . . . 1 John 4:4; Rom 8:37;
overcomer   2 Cor 2:14

blessed with every. . . . . Eph 1:3, Rom 8:32;
spiritual blessing   1 Cor 3:21-23

Emotions Are:

MESSENGERS

Emotions are
messengers
of internal beliefs
about God, self and
others. Emotions
remind us of our
need to relate to
God and see life
from His perspective.

MESSY

When they seem
more true than
God's Word.
Emotions are messy
when they become
the final authority
in our life,
controlling our
beliefs and behavior.

MANAGEABLE

The REED process
is continuous and
life-long. For our
emotions to be
manageable we
must relate to God
and allow Him to
renew our minds
with Truth.

Cast All Your Cares Upon Him, For He Cares For You. 1 Peter 5:7

■ **Biblical Personal Guidance**

■ **Biblical Training/ Seminars**

■ **North American Affairs**

■ **International Outreach**

■ **Prison Outreach**

■ **Teens Program**

■ **Be Transformed Materials and Programs**

For information concerning ministries, outreach, programs and resources contact

Scope Ministries International
405.843.7778
www.scopeministries.org

Romans 12:2
Do not conform any longer
to the pattern of this world,
but be transformed by the
renewing of your mind

Made in the USA
Coppell, TX
07 September 2024

36914301R00155